Mastering Slavery

Advance Praise for the Book

"Fleischner offers intricate, multilayered readings of nineteenth-century women's writings about the institution of slavery. In treatments of autobiographical accounts by former slaves, Fleischner traces narrative paths of great personal loss and mourning for family, for home, for memory, and shows how these intriguing texts manifest their authors' negotiations with identity and family, race and gender. *Mastering Slavery* opens further the many difficult questions that women's texts about slavery raise concerning the relations of gender and race to social networks of power."

—Minrose C. Gwin,
author of *Black and White Women of the Old South:*
The Peculiar Sisterhood in American Literature
Professor of English, University of New Mexico

"*Mastering Slavery* casts new light on the psychological dynamics of the slave narrative. Especially welcome is the way Jennifer Fleischner restores such writers as Elizabeth Keckley, Kate Drumgoold, and Julia A. J. Foote to their rightful place alongside Harriet Jacobs as founding mothers of a literary/historical/psychological tradition that reaches down to the present time."

—James Olney
Voorhies Professor of English
Louisiana State University

"Though Nathan Huggins, Nell Painter, Gerald Early, and Deborah McDowell have called for psychological readings of the slavery experience, Jennifer Fleischner is the first literary critic to fully engage with the literature of the peculiar institution in this way. In her readings of Lydia Maria Child and Harriet Beecher Stowe, Harriet Jacobs and her little-known brother John, Elizabeth Keckley, Julia Foote, and Kate Drumgoold, Fleischner shows a remarkable literary and psychological sensitivity that makes her novel interpretations compelling and at times moving. *Mastering Slavery* is an accomplishment of the first order."

—Werner Sollors
Henry B. and Anne M. Cabot Professor of English Literature
and Professor of Afro-American Studies
Harvard University

Mastering Slavery

Memory, Family, and Identity in Women's Slave Narratives

Jennifer Fleischner

New York University Press

NEW YORK AND LONDON

NEW YORK UNIVERSITY PRESS
New York and London

Chapter 2 is a reworking and expansion of my essay, "Mothers and Sisters: The Family Romance of Antislavery Women Writers," which appeared in *Feminist Nightmares: Women at Odds. Feminism and the Problem of Sisterhood,* ed. Susan Ostrov Weisser and Jennifer Fleischner (NYU Press, 1994).

A version of chapter 6 was published as "Memory, Sickness, and Slavery: One Slave Girl's Story," *American Imago* 51:4 (Winter 1994).

Chapter 3 is an expanded version of my essay "Remembering the Family: Rereading the Slave Narratives of Harriet Jacobs and John S. Jacobs" in *Recasting Intellectual History: African American Cultural Studies,* edited by Walter Jackson (Oxford University Press, 1996).

Library of Congress Cataloging-in-Publication Data
Fleischner, Jennifer.
Mastering slavery : memory, family, and identity in women's
slave narratives / Jennifer Fleischner.
p. cm. —(Literature and psychoanalysis; 8)
Includes bibliographical references and index.
ISBN 0-8147-2630-5 (cl. : alk. paper). — ISBN 0-8147-2653-4
(pbk. : alk. paper)
1. Women slaves—Southern States—Biography—History and
criticism. I. Title.
E444.F577 1996
305.5′67′0975—dc20 96-4519
CIP

New York University Press books are printed on acid-free paper, and their binding materials are chosen for strength and durability.

Manufactured in the United States of America

10 9 8 7 6 5 4 3 2 1

To the Memory of My Grandparents,
Henry Fleischner and Irma Milker Fleischner
1896–1961   1899–1989

And in exactly the same way that the South imagines that it "knows" the Negro, the North imagines that it has set him free. Both camps are deluded. Human freedom is a complex, difficult—and private—thing. If we can liken life, for a moment, to a furnace, then freedom is the fire which burns away illusion.

—James Baldwin, "Nobody Knows My Name: A Letter from the South," 1959

CONTENTS

ACKNOWLEDGMENTS

I am indebted to many people for their support and guidance during the years it took me to research and to write this book. My former teachers, Karl Kroeber, Ann Douglas, and Jonathan Arac, helped me to launch my project when it was just a proposal; without their steady encouragement I would not have been able to begin. I am especially grateful to Professor Kroeber, who has been unfailingly generous with his wisdom and support throughout the years; I thank him for nudging me toward completion. I am also grateful to Werner Sollors, Jeffrey Berman, Berel Lang, Jean Fagan Yellin, William L. Andrews, Renee Tursi, Randall Craig, Eric Haralson, Melissa Knox, Richard Hardack, and Hilary Beattie, all of whom took the time to read and criticize portions of the evolving manuscript. Jewell Parker Rhodes, a reader for *Feminist Studies,* offered invaluable suggestions. And I want to thank Dagmar Herzog, Edward Wheatley, Mary Jaeger, Christopher Bongie, Michael Staub, and Mary Mackay, scholars and friends met during a year at Harvard; they continue to inspire and to sustain me. Above all, I am deeply indebted to Wolfgang Mann, whose thoughtful comments on several drafts of the manuscript benefited my thinking and writing immeasurably. Without him, this book would have been far more difficult to write. Needless to say, its limitations are entirely my own.

I am also grateful to the Mellon Faculty Fellowship Program at Harvard University for giving me the opportunity to devote myself to my book for a year. Richard M. Hunt and Jay Maclean deserve special mention for making the fellowship program so successful. I am especially obliged to K. Anthony Appiah and

Henry Louis Gates, Jr., for welcoming my participation in the Afro-American Studies Department. The Society of Fellows for the Humanities at Columbia University graciously gave me a forum to present my research. A Nuala McGann Drescher Award from the United University Professors enabled me to finish my book. In addition, I am thankful to my many colleagues at the University at Albany, particularly Warren Ginsberg and (again) Jeff Berman, for supporting my work over the years. Niko Pfund and his colleagues at New York University Press have also been unvaryingly enthusiastic and helpful.

Several others remain to be acknowledged. I owe lasting thanks to Dr. Shirley Herscovitch Schaye, whose wise and abiding influence is behind every page; I am eternally grateful to her. Finally, I want to express my gratitude to my parents, Ruth and Irwin Fleischner, from whom I learned to love books and the study of the past.

> I do not think one can assess a writer's motives without knowing something of his early development. His subject will be determined by the age he lives in . . . but before he ever begins to write he will have acquired an emotional attitude from which he will never completely escape.
> —George Orwell, "Why I Write," 1946

Slave narratives are necessarily about escapes from childhood; the remarkable ex-slaves who became autobiographers could not have written about their pasts had they not sprung themselves free from them. Yet slaves are not born, but made—and (taking "enslavement" in its widest possible sense) psychological emancipation will also be a protracted journey. One does not readily forget, though one may travel far from, the lessons of identity learned in childhood. What slave narrators say about their reasons for writing confirms George Orwell's claim: no writer—and certainly no slave autobiographer—can write except as a fugitive from childhood, "never completely escaped."

One post-Reconstruction slave narrator, Lucy A. Delaney, speaks of "the unaccountable longing of the aged to look backward and review" their youth, even when memory can bring only unhappiness (vii). Another 1890s narrator, Kate Drumgoold, confides that her "mind is so full of" thoughts about her life as a slave girl, which ended nearly four decades earlier (3). Elizabeth Keckley, who bought her own freedom in 1855 and became Mrs.

Lincoln's White House seamstress and confidante, defends her desire, in 1867, to return South for a postbellum reunion with the family who had owned her. She explains, "the past is dear to everyone, for to the past belongs that golden period, the days of childhood. . . . To surrender it," she continues, using a metaphor that hints at the recent Southern defeat, "is to surrender the greatest part of my existence" (241).

The recognition that individual identity is constituted by personal memories beginning in childhood emerges in these women's remarks as a reason for writing, behind the more immediate and overtly political goals of abolitionism or racial uplift. But cultural ideology, individual psychology, and strategies of representation are intimately entwined. Harriet Jacobs, whose 1861 narrative *Incidents in the Life of a Slave Girl* is considered the classic antebellum woman's narrative, views her master's seemingly isolated assaults against her personal memory as part of a systematic attack against the collective memory of her family and, by logical extension, the history of slaves. Her master, whom she calls Dr. Flint, "wish[es] the past could be forgotten, and that we might never think of it" (145). Abusers require a conspiracy of silence, both to enforce their rule and to protect their name. Against Dr. Flint, Jacobs struggles for her own memory against silence and repression, knowing that this struggle is not hers alone. Writing about her early separation from her daughter, a consequence of Dr. Flint's relentlessly menacing threats, Jacobs despairs that her daughter will grow up "without a mother's love to shelter her from the storms of life; almost without memory of a mother!" (139). In her association of "love," "shelter," and "memory," Jacobs brings together the physical and psychological functions of the maternal (or paternal) presence in a young child's life; the mother who holds her child also holds her child's memories. Accordingly, Jacobs recalls how, during the two years they live together in Boston after Jacobs's escape, she longs to

2

tell her daughter "something about her [daughter's] father" (a white man). But fearing her daughter's rejection, because of her "great sin" against the culturally sanctioned ideals of feminine virtue and motherhood, she keeps silent (188).

The autobiographical impulse, according to George Gusdorf, is the "desire to endure in . . . memory" (31). The *deepest* intention of autobiography, Gusdorf continues, "is the final chance to win back what has been lost" (39). Embedded in the slave narrators' insistence that the stories they tell about their slavery pasts are *true* is their complete understanding that the violent theft of *their* memories—of their own selves and of themselves by others—lay at the sick heart of slavery. When by way of their narratives they cross over the threshold of visibility into cultural memory, they effectively steal themselves back (as the Negro spiritual urged, "Steal Away"), but they nonetheless carry the internalized burdens of their individual experiences of slavery for years.

My project in this book is to examine the deployment of psychologically coded strategies of remembering and representing in slave narratives by ex-slave women, from the Civil War through post-Reconstruction. I analyze the particular intra- and interpsychic struggles of the individual narrators to emphasize the individualized effects of slavery on each autobiographer. One of my primary assumptions is that each slave narrator I discuss used her narrative as a form of symbolic action with reference to a real world. As such, the narratives cannot be abstracted from their specific historical and cultural contexts. Social taboos, cultural currents and conventions, political structures, personal prohibitions, literary forms, and popular taste all have a hand in shaping narrative. Slave narratives dramatize their individual narrators' ongoing internal and external efforts to construct a sense of self and a relation to an audience out of the confluence of ideological, social, psychological, and literary conditions: the absolute dualism of "black" slavery and "white" freedom; racist beliefs that naturalized the enslavement of blacks by enshrining notions of the moral and physical difference between the races; the disruption of the slave family and its embeddedness within the dominant white family; the sexual exploitation and other soul-murdering physical and psychological assaults against the slave's identity; the significance of literacy for slaves; and the claims of the slave narrative as a form of social protest.

Growing up a slave meant having to come to terms with the conflicting currents of identity and identification that arose out of the profoundly intimate relations that frequently bridged the worlds of slaveholder and slave, and the radical social, economic, and political gulfs segregating "black" from "white." Becoming a slave *narrator* meant trying to give expression, shape, and significance to those conflicts, as they made themselves felt as internal pressures, within the inevitably prescriptive limits of literary language and narrative form. It also meant repeating the encounters between the marginalized black self and the dominant white world, in both senses of repeating—retelling the past and reenacting it in the present—in order to transform the terms, structure, and outcomes of their interactions.

Although the encounters and experiences these narrators depict have affinities, they are not identical. The narrators respond to and recall the specific traumas of their enslavements in a variety of ways; and they rely upon widely differing devices for dealing with the cultural anxieties that inform their individual narrative struggles for self-conception.

I begin in chapter 1 by discussing some of the theoretical positions I draw upon and the methodological strategies I apply in my work. Psychoanalytic theory, insofar as it enables an approach to antebellum U.S. slavery that emphasizes its function as a system designed to oppress, demoralize, and terrorize its black captives through regularly practiced abuse, including obvious child abuse, offers a mode of entry into the slave narrator's mind that is flexible enough to account for historical specificities and individual differences. Moreover, from its founding, psychoanalysis as a method of treatment for psychological distress has regarded narrative as liberating, and silence and repression as enslaving; at the same time, in response to the problems of representation and the obvious gaps between telling and psychological relief, it has contributed to our understanding of the complicated ways in which narrators, through mechanisms of defense, compromise, and adaptation, remain partially bound to their psychological enslavements, even in the process of narration. Thus, it provides an exacting tool for analyzing narrative self-representations in which the narrating selves speak from a position of distrust of their audience. Given the nature of internalized prohibitions against self-assertion and self-expression—a likely legacy of actual enslavement—coupled with the external constraints against black candor in a white world, the unspoken, the masked, the ruptured, and the contradictory are palpable presences in slave narratives.

My approach also assumes that women's slave narratives evolved in part out of the ex-slave women's engagement with the codes and conventions of white-authored antislavery fiction— especially the works of white women, whose developing feminism was patterned upon abolitionism. These antislavery texts, derived from sentimental forms, helped to popularize certain images of black women that were fundamental in shaping Northern attitudes in the debates over slavery. The tragic quadroon, the suffering slave mother, and the helpless slave girl were among the most successful and appealing of these images, most obviously because they served to empower white women to activity on behalf of their powerless "sisters," thereby fostering a conception of a white, female self that was not similarly debased. Chapter 2 compares the ways in which Lydia Maria Child and Harriet Beecher

Stowe imaginatively deal with their anxieties about propagating the ideal of an interracial sisterhood within the context of cultural beliefs about racial difference and deeply ingrained social taboos against interracial sexual relations. Out of this conflict emerges the two authors' radically differing fantasies about female sexuality and aggression. Also, the ways in which these various levels of tension are manifested in these representations of relations between black slave and white free women provide insight into the effects of slavery and racism on the self-perception of Northern as well as Southern women (and men), white as well as nonwhite.

Child was Harriet Jacobs's editor for *Incidents in the Life of a Slave Girl,* and Stowe, who knew Jacobs's story, wanted to use it in her own work. In writing her autobiography, Jacobs both inhabits and renovates the interrelated abolitionist images of the helpless slave girl and suffering slave mother, the supplicants in chains beseeching the help of their more powerful, white sisters. Following the demands of cultural and literary convention, she seems to measure herself against an internalized version of the dominant ideal of the virtuous mother, embodied in her memories of her mother, and reinforced by her maternal grandmother. Yet, Jacobs's account yields a far more amplified and complicated notion of familial dynamics and identity than her emphasis on motherhood and sisterhood indicates. Overlooked in this reading is Jacobs's strong identification with her outraged and enraged father, who lives on in her mind after his death as a powerful internal imago; it is this paternal identification that is energized and nurtured in Jacobs's close bond with her rebellious younger brother, John S. Jacobs. In chapter 3, I interpret John's short slave narrative, "A True Tale of Slavery," which was serialized in a London journal a month after the publication of Harriet's narrative, in textual counterpoint to *Incidents in the Life of a Slave Girl* in order to enlarge the scope of our reading of this canonical woman's text. *Incidents* does far more than expose the impact of sexual exploitation upon its female victims, as it is conventionally understood to do; more deeply, it reveals the ways in which sexual exploitation impinged upon the entire Jacobs family, interfering drastically with their affective and sexual relations. Ultimately, it is Jacobs's ability to integrate her father's memory into her conception of self that enables her to run from slavery.

In chapter 4, I analyze the drama of identity of the black self in a white world in Elizabeth Keckley's *Behind the Scenes; or, Thirty Years a Slave, and Four Years in the White House* (1868). In moving from Jacobs to Keckley, we move from a slave narrator enmeshed within the abolitionist project to a narrator whose rhetorical position is suddenly that of a free person in a postslavery world. But the presumption of economic and political success that underwrites Keckley's narrative identity is marked by striking suppressions or repressions, ruptures, substitutions, splittings, and inversions. It is in these moments that Keckley's narrative suggests the hidden presence of a cluster of more primary scenes, associated with feelings of sorrow, rage, and longing for her (by now) dead black slave family; these scenes exist "behind the scenes" of the liberated (white) world, represented in the White House, in which—as a mulatta woman—she necessarily serves. Keckley tries to manage her anxiety-producing confrontations with her own "otherness" in her dealings with the family in the White House by utilizing the figure of Mrs. Lincoln as Other, placing her in the imaginary role of social and economic outcast. This strategy constitutes a dramatic inversion of the positioning of the mulatta / black woman as outcast "Other" by white anti-slavery women writers; as such, Keckley's narrative can be read as resisting the images of black slave women that were codified by Child and Stowe and integrated into Jacobs's self-perception. Most importantly, perhaps, Keckley forces her predominately white audience into a confrontation with a nonwhite woman's self-conscious aggression.

Socially and politically forbidden aggression is a central theme in chapter 5. There, I examine two narratives that seem fraught with the tensions of being an ex-slave (Kate Drumgoold) or the child of former slaves (Julia A. J. Foote) in a post-Reconstruction America, when the idea of liberation—narrative or otherwise—must have seemed like a receding illusion in the ugly light of white supremacism. These narratives by Drumgoold and Foote are written long after slavery's end, but they are profoundly shaped by their narrators' conscious and unconscious links to slavery. In their ways of remembering their oppressive pasts, charged with intensifying anxieties about the culturally validated racism of the present, the narrators seem driven to strategies of narrative extremes of passivity and aggression—Drumgoold, as invalid narrator, and Foote, as muscular narrator. In this chapter, I also take up some of the issues involved in the African American adaptation of the God of their masters to their own strategic purposes.

In chapter 5, I return directly to the complex interrelation of black and white women as a relation between self and other. The narratives of Foote and especially Drumgoold shed light on the origins and nature of this interaction in the relationships they depict between the serving or slave girl and her mistress on the one hand, and the serving or slave girl and her own mother on the other. Psychoanalytic theory suggests that the model for the relation between self and other evolves in the early interactions between the child and, usually, the mother. Slavery complicated this dyad frequently by separating the child from her mother, thereby forcing the child to turn to a surrogate mother for love and protection. Older female slaves often substituted as maternal figures, but one striking feature of women's slave narratives is their shared account of the ways in which the slave girl turns to her mistress in search of maternal care, self-esteem, and a sense of self. The contradictory psychological positions that result from this racially divided maternal splitting contribute to the shape of the complicated questions of identity and identification that concern all of the narrators who appear in this book. Therefore, I end with a brief epilogue, in which I revisit *Incidents in the Life of a Slave Girl* to reexamine Jacobs's autobiographical account in light of this complicated "motherhood."

In focusing on slave narratives, I have confined myself to tracing the impact of the entangled relations of master and slave on the sense of identity of individual slave narrators—to explore the ways in which, out of these social, psychological, and biological crossings, they created mixed, dynamic narrative selves. But the repercussions of the "crossings" of slavery, as Nell Irvin Painter would remind us, "belong not to one race or the other, but reside squarely in southern history" (94).[1] That Northern and Southern whites alike found these more than cultural crossings threatening to their self-conception is suggested by their fantasies about "mongrels," "mutations," and "miscegenation"—a term coined in 1863, the year of the Emancipation Proclamation, by David Goodman Croly (father of the *The New Republic's* founder, Herbert Croly).[2]

It is not surprising, given the role that the idea of "blackness" played in the white Victorian unconscious, that what slave narratives reveal about slavery's legacy of mixed identities might have been—and might remain—difficult to hear. But then, the narrators themselves knew to be careful about their revelations. "Manage your own secrets," Mattie Jackson, seizing the power of silence, advised other would-be autobiographers in 1866, "and divulge them by the silent language of your own pen" (29).[3]

CHAPTER 1

Introduction

The Critical Legacy

In my interpretation of the narratives as psychologically revealing autobiographies, I go against the current of much recent work. Indeed, two generations of scholars have pointedly rejected psychological approaches to slavery, at least partially in strong reaction against Stanley Elkins's *Slavery: A Problem in American Institutional and Intellectual Life* (1959). As Nell Irvin Painter observes in an essay arguing for the study of "slavery's psychological costs" in light of theories of trauma and child abuse, "to speak of black people in psychological terms can be problematical, for this history has a history" ("Soul Murder and Slavery," 130).

Briefly, Elkins depicted the slave as the psychological casualty of a closed and repressive system that he compared to the Nazi system of concentration camps; slavery, Elkins argued, infantilized the slaves, producing adults who were childlike, docile, loyal, deceitful, and irresponsible. "Absolute power for [the master]," Elkins wrote, "meant absolute dependency for the slave—the dependency not of the developing child but of the perpetual child" (130). Historians fired back in full force to dispute Elkins's claims about the "Sambo personality"; and the debate with Elkins spawned important studies on the slave community, the slave family, slave culture, and, eventually, slave women.[1]

By documenting the significance of slave family and culture in the lives of slaves, historians sought to refute the central premise of Elkins's thesis: that the slave personality was determined solely by the slave's relationship with an absolute master. Meanwhile, they were revolutionizing the historiography of slavery by establishing the use of slave narratives, speeches, interviews, and letters as authentic historical documents—source material Elkins did not use. Historians also turned to slave songs, spirituals, sayings, and folktales to provide insight into the slave community.

Another arm of the "slavery debate" dealt with Elkins's use of psychology. Taking their cue from Elkins, historians disputed his claims about the so-called slave personality by offering alternative "personality types" and views about the roles slaves played or did not play. Thus, questions of the appropriateness of psychological approaches to slavery turned upon an understanding of psychology as primarily a social and political phenomenon.

However, a distinction must be made between Elkins's psychological approach and my own psychoanalytic one. Elkins's application of a theoretical model involving role playing, personality types, and interpersonal relations is basically nonpsychoanalytic, in that it analyzes personality primarily as the product of ongoing interpersonal interactions. In contrast, psychoanalytic theory understands character as being motivated by individual intra- and interpsychic conflicts that are considered the expression of the entangled interplay of innate and acquired needs. In the broadest terms, where Elkins speaks of "absolute" external forces that have been imposed on the helpless slave, psychoanalysts would speak of imposingly powerful inner needs in a dynamic encounter with the external world.

Thus, the methodological problems for historical interpretation caused by Elkins's failure to consider slave testimony also makes his work objectionable from a psychoanalytically oriented point of view, for it eliminates precisely that evidence—narrated memories of childhood experiences—which psychoanalytic theory is best suited to interpret. Accordingly, also missing in both Elkins's idea of the "absolute master" who creates a "slave personality" and its critical reception is the essential psychoanalytic insight that slavery, rather than transforming adults into docile children (or rebels, or whatever), structured the physical and psychological development of enslaved children who grew up into enslaved, fugitive, and freed adults.[2]

Finally—and crucially—the question of the usefulness of psychoanalytic strategies for interpreting individual slave narratives was not actually engaged by the debates over Elkins's work. Indeed, identifying personality types (which are, of necessity, relatively coarse-grained) is of limited usefulness when it comes to telling textured stories about particular human beings. Psychoanalytic theory, of course, utilizes general principles and rubrics; but as an interpretive practice it is thoroughly committed to the historically specific nature of individual experience.

Literary critics have had their own reservations about psychological approaches to slavery through slave narratives. One pillar of critical belief has been that the narratives are not amenable to psychological analysis because the limiting demands of the genre and the market prohibited their individuation, one from another. By this logic, the psychoanalytic question of how individual memory operates at the stress points of autobiographical identity—the intersections of mind, body, experience, and language—is irrelevant to a study of slave narratives.

One of the more persuasive proponents of this view has been critic James Olney, who takes up the problem of memory in slave narratives in order to discount its autobiographical significance.[3] Olney interestingly argues that because of the very restricted intention and premise of the narratives (to describe slavery "as it *is*") they are practically devoid of the kind of autobiographical, symbolic memory that assigns significance to the events of the past—discovering in them, and then creating out of them, a pattern that brings the life and the reader "in and through narration" into the present (149). For Olney, slave narratives are "most often a non-memorial description fitted to a pre-formed mold": thus, exists the repetitiveness that occurs *across* slave narratives (of theme, content, form, and style) (151).

Olney's insightful arguments against reading autobiographical memory in slave narratives have found wide-ranging indirect support. As Toni Morrison has pointed out, the constrained conditions of the narratives' production—mostly edited, published, and read by whites—inhibited self-revelation and self-expression. Indeed, Morrison has said that she wrote *Beloved* to create / remember the interior life of the slave that, in her view, slave narrators of necessity deliberately suppressed—the story they did not "pass on" ("The Site of Memory," 303; *Beloved*, 274–75). And as Ruth Shays, the daughter of slaves, told an interviewer not long ago: "When it comes to the old times, you can' go to books and courthouses because most of our foreparents had sense enough not to spill their in-gut to whitefolks, or blackfolks, either, if they didn' know them" (Gwaltney, 31).

The important recognition of the mask of narrative has given critics a powerful metaphor for the slave's resistance to slavery. Moreover, it has usefully focused readings on the larger political motivations of the narrators and the ideological significance of the genre. Indeed, an important goal for these narrators *was* the creation of a collective identity through which to gain social, political, and economic recognition. Reading narratives as primarily cultural and ideological constructs, critics have also been able to erect a helpful typology for interpreting slave narratives.

But there are limitations to the premise that these narratives are shaped by and reflect nothing but cultural and ideological currents. For how, then, can we account for the differentiated memories the narrators actually do depict, and the idiosyncrasies of theme, content, and style? How can we explain the autobiographical commitment that the narrators insist they bring to their work? Indeed, the ruptures, suppressions, and repetitions that have dissuaded critics from treating the narratives as open texts are the very points at which the narrators tip their hands. In these moments, the narratives seem to remember what has been forgotten or deliberately suppressed.

In the 1980s, a range of scholars systematically began formulating theories of the slave narrative as an African American literary form. Henry Louis Gates, Jr., contextualized and crystallized the concerns of rhetoric-based studies of the slave narrative when he asserted: "The slave narrative represents the attempts of the blacks to *write themselves into being*" (Davis and Gates, eds., *The Slave's Narrative,* xxiii).[4] Elaborating on this statement in later works, Gates helped usher in a central line of thinking about African American literature as an oppositional tradition, devised to refute racist allegations that "its authors did not and *could not* create 'literature.' "[5]

Gates understands the narratives to have emerged within the context of Enlightenment values, specifically the belief that the mark of humanity is reason, of which the visible sign is written language, for this belief was deployed to justify the enslavement of black Africans who, unable to write and read Western languages, could be relegated to the category of subhuman. Gates cites Immanuel Kant's influential conflation of color and intelligence, presented in *Observations on the Feeling of the Beautiful and the Sublime* (1764), in which, commenting upon an obviously shrewd and intelligent remark made by a "Negro carpenter," Kant reasons, "it might be that there was something in this which perhaps deserved to be considered; but in short, this fellow was quite black from head to foot, a clear proof that what he said was stupid" (cited in *Figures in Black,* 19).

Gates's critique suggests the ways in which signs (in a text), through the operation of politics, acquire ontological import; and therefore, the hundreds of narratives written by ex-slaves in the United States (the earliest of which was published in 1760) *by their very existence* posit the selfhood of human beings of African descent who undercut the racist view of the inferior "nature" of the Negro. This helps to explain why questions of "authenticity" and "truth-telling" are self-consciously addressed in the narratives, for example, in subtitles, such as "Written by Himself" or "Written by Herself," and why the narratives were published with their textual frames of authenticating documents (letters, papers, and introductions by white editors or friends) meant to prove the black slave's literary authority.

The argument that slaves wrote themselves "into being" has other crucial resonances as well. For instance, literacy becomes the key to the slave's resistance to slavery; consequently, in this interpretive tradition, scenes of reading and writing figure prominently. The *Narrative of the Life of Frederick Douglass, An American Slave, Written by Himself* (1845), the representative text for this view, exemplifies the explicit connection between literacy and freedom. In numerous scenes, Douglass reinforces the lesson he learned when his master forbade his wife to continue giving the young slave boy reading lessons: that the "white man's power to enslave the black" lay in keeping him illiterate (37). After this eye-opening discovery, Douglass, with great determination and single-mindedness, forges his "pathway from slavery to freedom" through the written word (38).

Critical emphasis on the relation between literacy and power illuminates other aspects of the confrontations between master and slave. In the antebellum years, proslavery ideologues set up an elaborate system of rules (about dress, mobility, or education) and documents (traveling passes, free papers) meant to enable whites to tell the difference between enslaved and free black—and sometimes white—people (thereby, of course, contradicting their own arguments about the "naturally inferior Negro"). In this discursive system, being able to master texts could be literally liberating: to use the famous example of Douglass, he escapes, traveling North by train, using a borrowed sailor's protection, a certificate that both described the person holding it and asserted that he was a free American sailor. (An early thwarted plan to escape with fellow slaves involved traveling passes forged by Douglass.)

Interest in the slave narratives as subversive deployments of what had been the master's language has also spurred critics to examine the particular rhetorical devices employed in the narratives. Gates's *The Signifying Monkey: A Theory of Afro-American Literary Criticism* (1988) set a direction for study of the relation between the African oral tradition, the African American vernacular, and the African American literary tradition. As Gates argues, through the use of the trope of "signifying," a rhetorical device emphasizing a subversive use of repetition and revision, African American writers have been able to "inscribe their voices in the written word"—into the Western literary tradition—and to reverse the power relations in that tradition (130). In this view, slave narratives are the site of the emergence of an African American tradition of signification, in which self-expression is aligned with subversion of the culturally dominant discourse.

Feminist critics, similarly building upon the idea that the narratives are sites of resistance, subversion, and self-creation, high-light questions of sexual difference and gender identity. In-tensely concerned with language and power, these critics have suggested that overemphasis on the functional and figurative implications of literacy has tended to occlude important themes and strategies in slave autobiographies by women.[6]

Probably the galvanizing moment in the study of women's slave narratives came when Jean Fagan Yellin authenticated Har-riet Jacobs's authorship of *Incidents in the Life of a Slave Girl: Written by Herself* (1861). Yellin's 1987 edition of Jacobs pre-sented indisputably the narrator who would become the repre-sentative female slave voice in the African American literary tradition; *Incidents* was canonized, raised alongside Douglass's narrative. The outline of female identity, as perceived in Jacobs's narrative, took the contours of a life shaped by resistance to sexual exploitation, the problematics of enslaved motherhood, and the necessity of negotiating relationships with black and white women.[7]

With *Incidents* as a focus, critical attention reoriented ques-tions of language and power around matters of sexuality and sexual abuse, womanhood, motherhood, and inter- and intrara-cial sisterhood. Several studies explored the ways in which slave women narrators deploy and transform nineteenth-century fe-male stereotypes (the virtuous [white] woman, the sexually rapa-cious black woman [Jezebel], the Mammy-figure [Aunt Je-mima]); and they examined slave narrator's strategic use of popular narrative forms (sentimental fiction, gothic novel, *Bil-dungsroman*) to dramatize their struggle for self-definition within the racial, sexual, and economic hierarchies of U.S. culture. These studies also analyzed the ways in which archetypal slave narrative figures—the outraged slave mother, the lecherous mas-ter, the victimized slave girl, the jealous mistress—functioned to further the interrelated causes of feminism and abolitionism.

Hortense J. Spillers locates *Incidents* within an analysis of slavery's impact on "the symbolics of female gender" ("Mama's Baby, Papa's Maybe," 80). Brutally leaving its marks on the female body, slavery is the ground for the "originating metaphors of captivity and mutiliation" and the "grammar of description" of the African descendant as Other that still imbue the "dominant symbolic activity" of American culture (68, 70). Moreover, as Spillers argues, slavery's disruption of the African family, beginning with the kidnappings in Africa and continuing with the Middle Passage, threw the "customary lexis of sexuality [for the slave woman], including 'reproduction,' 'motherhood,' 'pleasure,' and 'desire' . . . into unrelieved crisis" (76). Slave narratives, Spillers suggests, participate in the reconfiguration of the American "cultural text" in terms of the different "representational potentialities" for African Americans (80).

A Compulsion to Repeat

Any study of slave narratives must rely on some assumptions about the vexed concept of the "self" which stands at the center of autobiography. Where does the sense of "self" come from? How is it constituted? Where does it end? How can it be expressed, described, named? Historians and literary critics who study slave narratives seem generally to assume a correlation between the historical life and the narrated life, and between the slave as narrator and the slave as protagonist. However, there has also been a counter tendency, suggested by poststructuralism, to interpret the narrated self as invention and form, rather than as having reference to a real self in the past. But how these linguistic self-constructions come to be, and how they relate to the self, whose past experiences and present memories are the subjects at hand, is not clear.

In *Touching the World: Reference in Autobiography*, John Paul Eakin elaborates on the implications of the idea that autobiography is the special form of narrative that takes as its referent one's own life. As Eakin argues, "poststructuralist criticism on autobiography characteristically—and mistakenly—assumes that an autobiographer's allegiance to referential truth necessarily entails a series of traditional beliefs about an integrated, unified, fully-constituted self and mimetic theories of language and literary form" (30). Instead, he believes, the making of autobiography involves not so much an attempt to reflect the world as to transform it—and so also, oneself in the world; it is evidence of "a simultaneous acceptance of and refusal of the constraints of the real" (46). Accordingly, to write an autobiography is to act on the desire to repeat one's past in order to "supplement" it, because the past is and was "never acceptable" (46, 51).

Eakin's suggestive commentary posits a view of desire in the writing of autobiography that is analogous to Freud's key notion of the "compulsion to repeat." This is Freud's phrase for what he saw as the unconscious process of delayed, disguised, and repeated expressions of early powerful encounters, experiences, and impressions that seemed, at the time, unacceptable or overwhelming and so were gradually repressed.[8] Psychoanalytic thinking since Freud has ranged widely from his early formulations, but it still anchors itself in some notion of repression and the idea that, over the course of a life, each individual symbolically restages earlier powerful experiences out of a complex tangle of motivations: to test, verify, and correct reality; and to master or give vent to underlying feelings of rage, fear, frustration, and pressures for revenge.[9] In this way, the psychoanalytic model of the vicissitudes of remembering is consonant with what Eakin describes as the autobiographical project to "supplement" a "never acceptable" past. It would seem that basic psychoanalytic notions about memory, repression, the mechanisms of defense and adaptation, and psychological development might well be

useful tools for interpreting the rhetorical positions and disposi-
tions of individual autobiographical narrators.

To say that the psychoanalytic model of memory and the
autobiographical project are homologous is of course not to
claim that they are identical. Freud's idea of compulsive repetition is surely stronger than Eakin's view of the desire to repeat,
in the sense that the force of "compulsion" for Freud is a "daemonic" force, unconscious and instinctual, that manifests itself
in a variety of phenomena—physical symptoms, character-traits,
inhibitions and phobias, restrictions on thought and feeling,
structures of fantasy and defense, and the like; whereas Eakin
means *self-conscious linguistic* repetition, in which the deliberate
use of language is implicated fundamentally in the constitution
of the self. But we need not read these two positions as mutually
exclusive, nor even as essentially opposed. Certainly, psychoanalysis as a technique is premised on the belief in personal narrative
as *potentially* constitutive of the self, insofar as narrative self-
consciousness is thought to be the means by which the narrating
self, under the lifting of repression, becomes freed from the
compulsions to repeat the past, in all senses of "repeat." My use
of concepts and tools drawn from psychoanalysis rests on the
presumption that there is a continuum between unconscious
and self-conscious narrative positions, along which all narrators
move with varying degrees of freedom and constraint, de-
pending on both internal and external conditions and their
individual relation to them. Social conventions; cultural values;
personal capacities, beliefs, and prohibitions; and narrative models will converge upon the narrating self in complicated, shifting
ways.

African American slave narrators were compelled to put their
grievances against the portion of the dominant white world in
which they had been enslaved (the South) before the authority
of those ruling whites into whose dominion they had fled (the

Consequently, they had to marshal in their narratives
.. strategies of compromise, adaptation, resistance, and defense that they had learned as survival tactics for growing up as
subordinated, oppressed, and abused members of hierarchical
slavery households. Obviously, there is a vast material difference
between actually being enslaved in the South and feeling constrained as a slave narrator in the North. But the *psychological*
tasks of living seem to remain fairly consistent, despite differing
circumstances and fluctuating pressures. In this way, the psychological goals of the ex-slaves' narrating present emerge out of
those of their lived past: that is, they sought to maintain self-
esteem, gain emotional gratification, attain a sense of self-con-
trol, and assert the self as a meaning-making agent in a world of
(more powerful) others.

Accordingly, the language slave narrators use to describe their
present carries haunting echoes of the powerlessness and servitude of their slavery past. So, for example, at the end of her
narrative, Harriet Jacobs speaks of how,

God so orders circumstances as to keep me with my friend Mrs. Bruce [her
white, Northern employer]. Love, duty, gratitude, also bind me to her side.
It is a privilege to serve her who pities my oppressed people, and who
has bestowed the inestimable boon of freedom on me and my children.
(201) [10]

The Self as Other

Yet another assumption underlying my application of psychoanalytic theory is that racial and gender identities contribute to the
shape of narrative self-conception. They are constituent elements in the many-layered confrontations between self and other
out of which the sense of self unfolds within a culture. Black
women's slave narratives are inflected by the conflicted sense of
self that inevitably was born out of their narrators' encounters

with others in a world in which powerful beliefs about the inferior "nature" of blacks and the inferior "nature" of women pre-
vailed.

Focusing on questions of race, the Antillean psychiatrist Franz
Fanon, whose work with colonial subjects led him to rethink
psychoanalysis, has described the plight of the black self in a
white world as a continual confrontation with his or her own
"otherness" in the presence of a normalized culture of whiteness.
According to Fanon, the problems of being the denigrated Other
play a crucial role in the early stages of development in the
psychodynamic interplay of self, body, and culture. In *Black Skin,
White Masks* Fanon notes the way Antillean children, when asked
to write about their summer vacations, describe themselves "like
real little Parisians" running through fields and coming home
" 'with rosy cheeks' " (162). That is, these children do "not altogether apprehend the fact of . . . being . . . Negro[es]"; instead,
they perceive one another "in white terms" (162–63). Feeling
"abnormal on the slightest contact with the white world," the
black child responds by "identification—that is, the young Negro adopts a white man's attitude" (147). In striving to achieve
the state of "normalcy" that is circumscribed by whiteness, the
black self in a white world is at war with his or her own image.[11]
These sorts of tensions would have been heightened by racial
slavery, a condition so bleak that the desire to disidentify with
the enslaved black self would have been reinforced, while at the
same time the sanctions against identification with the free white
world—the larger community with which any slave (or, for that
matter, free black) community was unavoidably enmeshed—
would have been stronger than under colonialism.[12]

Fanon's analysis also provides a way to understand how "blackness" functions in the dominant culture's normalization of
"whiteness." As Fanon notes: "the real Other for the white man
is and will continue to be the black man. And conversely" (161).

etween me and the other world," Du Bois begins *The Souls of Black Folk* [213].)[13] However, a shortcoming of Fanon's analysis is that while he usefully talks about the black male self (in relation to white men and women) he has nothing to say about the woman of color. Indeed, he coolly remarks, "I know nothing about her" (180).

Fanon's accounts of the discrepancy between "black skin" and "white masks" and the ways in which "blackness" is deployed in white culture suggest that we might read the encounters between black and white selves under Southern slavery as being psychologically charged sites for both blacks and whites; accordingly, from these encounters has sprung a history of deliberate suppression (of an external Other) and repression (of the Other within the self) from which the United States has never recovered. Moreover, the erasure of black female selves in Fanon's analysis points a way to understanding the particular significance of the "compulsion to repeat" as it may have functioned in the slave narratives of black women.

Slave women's narratives reveal the psychoanalytic dramas of conflicted identifications that create complex patterns of rupture not unlike those Fanon observes. They manifest their narrators' negotiation of rhetorical positions within the context of culturally reinforced fear of black rage and prohibitions against women's activism and public expression. So, for example, Harriet Jacobs narratively suppresses (and perhaps represses) her identification with her rage-filled father at the same time as she tangles with her conflicting needs to identity and to disidentify with the idealized image of her virtuous dead mother. Her struggles are complicated further by her psychological and physical dependence on white "maternal" figures, from her Southern mistresses to her Northern patrons, perhaps including her editor, Lydia Maria Child. In these relations, Jacobs must contend with ambivalence: she expresses a state of mind in which gratitude and affection vie with envy, resentment and, occasionally, hatred.

Another slave narrator, Louisa Picquet, bought as a concubine by a man with whom she has three children, confronts similarly conflicted feelings toward her owner:

> I begin then to pray that he might die, so that I might get religion; and then I promised the Lord one night, faithful in prayer, if he would just take him out of the way, I'd get religion and be true to Him as long as I lived. ... Then, when I saw that he was sufferin' so, I begin to get sorry, and begin to pray that he might get religion first before he died. I felt sorry to see him die in his sins. I prayed for him to have religion when I did not have it myself. (22)[14]

Disavowing aggression and the self-division and confrontation with ambivalence that follow seem to be intrinsic in the female slave narrator's confrontation with the white world. The use of religious language intensifies the struggle with ambivalence, conveying anger and guilt in the terms of the dominant culture. Kate Drumgoold's account probably provides the most dramatic examples of this process. In her narrative, Drumgoold seemingly deflects resentment against white authority when she speaks lovingly of her long-dead idealized "white mother"—her mistress— whom she wishes to be like ("help my feeble life to be formed like her's"); at the same time, she must portray her own (also deceased) mother—a former slave—as someone whose example she rejects ("[my mother] was not a Christian, and the heaviest burden I have carried was praying for one that ... should have been a leader of her dear ones to the Lamb of God") (16, 19).

As voices in a developing tradition, these narrators—as "black," "female," and "slave"—emerged into narrative being in transgression of the multiple cultural prohibitions against public personhood for slaves, women, and blacks. Thus, black female slave narrators represented one form of the "return of the re-

ed" in antebellum and postbellum American culture, that
⟨e awakened memory of hitherto bound forces that had been
hidden within the cultural psyche. It was a form of return they
acknowledged themselves. As Anna Julia Cooper, who was born a
slave in 1858, wrote in 1892:

> In the clash and clatter of our American conflict, it has been said that the
> South remains Silent. Like the Sphinx she inspires vociferous disputation,
> but herself takes little part in the noisy controversy. One muffled strain in
> the Silent South, a jarring chord and a vague and uncomprehended
> cadenza has been and still is the Negro. And of that muffled chord, the
> one mute and voiceless note has been the sadly expectant Black
> Woman. (i) [15]

Memory, Abuse, and Narrative

There has been much recent debate about the impact of early
abuse on memory. It is not my intention, nor is it necessary, to
engage that debate here; but a few comments on the implications of abuse for memory may be useful. For the survivors of
slavery, the difficulties of being a witness to memory are not
simply a matter of cultural and market restrictions, nor, more
fundamentally a problem of language and representation, but
also of how completely "memory [of reality] and fantasy are
intertwined" (Shengold, 16).[16] According to psychiatrist and psychoanalyst Leonard Shengold, in *Soul Murder: The Effects of Childhood Abuse and Deprivation,* overwhelming abuse essentially im-
pairs the ability to distinguish between external events and
internal fantasies, a kind of annihilating brainwashing to ensure
the victim's obedience. We should recall how Harriet Jacobs's
tormentor, her master, Dr. Flint, wished that "the past could be
forgotten, and that we might never think of it"; and how for
Jacobs, *thinking of it* proved to be her best chance for escape
(145). Then, too, even the "mask of obedience" can lay down

toxic roots in the soul, breeding self-doubt, killing self-esteem. In Harriet's brother's narrative, "A True Tale of Slavery," John S. Jacobs recalls growing "sick of myself in acting the deceitful part of a slave, and pretending love and friendship [to my master] where I had none" (109).

The slave narrator's insistence on the truth of what he or she testifies to ("A True Tale of Slavery") speaks to the erasure of memory—or the illusion of forgetfulness—that reinforces tyrannical abuse. Harriet Jacobs's opening line is "Reader, be assured this narrative is no fiction" (1). Southern slavery, a system of labor that utilized abuse and deprivation, was an assault on each slave's memory, a crucial basis of each person's sense of self and reality. So it may be that slave narrative conventions—among them, the subtitle, "Written by Himself," or "Herself"; the authenticating documents and narrative frame; the prefatory notice that what follows is true—are erected against the internal crumbling caused by repeated blows against the self. Orlando Patterson has emphasized slavery as a "relation of domination" whose constituent elements as he sees them—violence, natal alienation, and dishonoring of the slave—underline the slave's lack of autonomous social and psychological being. James Olney has argued that slave narrators, unlike other autobiographers, before they can claim that the events they describe are factual and true must make a "prior claim": "I exist." Although these critics have the "social death" of the slave in mind, it is easy to imagine how this would overflow into everything concerning the self.

Remember, Harriet Jacobs was barely fifteen when her master, thirty-five years her senior, "began to whisper foul words in [her] ear" (27).[17] In the young adolescent's mind, anger is checked by shame, outrage by self-doubt. And the urge to protest must contend with the likelihood of audience rejection or disbelief. "Surely," Jacobs addresses her readers, "if you credited one half the truths that are told you concerning the helpless millions suffering in this cruel bondage, you at the north would not help to tighten the yoke" by obeying the 1850 Fugitive Slave Act (28). At another point she ponders the limitations of her reader's capacity for empathy: *"O reader, can you imagine . . . ? No, you cannot, unless you have been a slave"* (173).

We have not been slaves; but if we try to imagine the enormous task that confronted women's slave narrators, we must do so with the understanding that slavery was experienced by different slaves in different ways.

Family, Slavery, and Psychoanalysis

Any attempt to understand the psychological underpinnings of narratives of profound and prolonged suffering must first come to terms with the fact of the narrators' creative achievement—a supreme expression of will and hope. Not surprisingly, the best-known of the mid-century slave narrators came of age during an era of intensifying Northern assaults against slavery, when antislavery activism was evolving, Northern slaves were already emancipated, and debates over the status of the Western territories agitated the nation. Though crushed, the slave revolts which occurred during the narrators' childhoods, led by Denmark Vesey, in 1822, and Nat Turner, in 1831, terrified Southern slaveholders. Tensions about slavery were in the air, to be breathed in by all, including slave children who, like most of those who became narrators, lived in close quarters with their white masters and mistresses. Generally light-skinned, household slaves (not field hands), they embodied the tangled web of family, race, and class identifications that slavery produced. For the slave children who would escape or buy their way out of slavery, the *possibility* of gaining "freedom" had to have been a part of their mental world: "freedom" existed for their people as a fact elsewhere, but—

perhaps, more importantly—it dwelled in their imaginations as an evocative symbol, the North: "We often planned together how we would get to the north," Jacobs writes about the childhood dream she shared with her younger brother (42).

Jacobs's use of "we" hints at another powerful source of the narrator / protagonist's underlying hope, and that is, some sense of a positive relation to others. As the narratives show, the concept of "family," however configured, was a crucial counterforce to the soul-murdering abuse and deprivation under slavery. Events that are considered traumatic because, in part, they are exceptional and come as a shock, were for the slave the norm. Physical, sexual, and emotional abuse as well as family loss were common occurrences, and accounts about particular instances and the pain and anxiety they caused fill the pages of their narratives. Indeed, anticipatory anxiety about separation and disruption permeates the narratives: for instance, Jacobs describes how, when just arrived in New York and working for the first Mrs. Bruce, she felt "oppressed" by "a constant feeling of insecurity" (168).

Psychoanalytic theory treats "family" as the site of one's most intense feelings and one's locus of origin; these narratives are invaluable avenues to understanding the complex structure of "family" that emerged under slavery and the complications for identity and identification that were, for the slave, one all-important result. This is the pivotal point for my understanding of the slave's sense of self, and one to which I continually return.

Slavery's disruption of the nuclear slave family created familial groups that were generally in flux, as family members died, were sold, or ran away and others in the slave community (sometimes related, sometimes not) became surrogates for those who were lost. Husbands and wives who were separated and never expected to see one another again sometimes remarried, occasionally with complicated and confusing results.[18] Slave narratives attest to the ongoing and profound longing felt by the narrators for lost parents, siblings, spouses, and children; they dramatize how, when children themselves, faced with such losses, the narrators reproduced a family from among the adults and children around them in their urgent need for a "facilitating environment" (as Winnicott puts it) — for survival, protection, and development.[19]

The reconstitution of "family," however, also takes place in the mind. We know that dead parents may remain "alive" in the inner worlds of their offspring, sometimes resembling less what they may have actually been than what their children need (wish or fear) them to be. So, for example, in the seminal scene in which Harriet Jacobs keeps a vigil at her parents' graves before running away, she enacts an inward visitation in which their mythic voices speak to her, reminding her of her fears on the one hand, urging her toward her wish on the other. Frederick Douglass, in *My Bondage and My Freedom,* the 1855 revision of his 1845 narrative, repeats his earlier admission that word of his mother's death when he was eight or nine elicited no strong emotions from him. But in 1855 he adds: "I had to learn the value of my mother long after her death, and by witnessing the devotion of other mothers to their children. . . . [S]lavery . . . converted the mother that bore me, into a myth; it shrouded my father in mystery, and left me without intelligible beginning in the world" (157). Douglass's search for his "intelligible beginning," spurred by a sense of rootlessness, bespeaks an urge to reconcile himself to long-severed familial attachments that remain vital within.

Douglass's intervolved memories and fantasies of a slave mother and master father underline another important aspect of "family" on the plantation—the degree to which it involved a web of feeling between masters and slaves. While slave women worked all day in the fields, their children played with the children of the mistress, and were often looked after by her. "I stayed with my ma every night," one slave woman told an interviewer; "but my mistress raised me" (Sterling, 6). When Elizabeth Keckley, in a letter written to her mother in 1838, writes, "Give my love to the family, both black and white," she uses what was a common formulation for household relations in the South. And Kate Drumgoold who calls her mistress her "white mother" has had, she tells us, "two darling mothers" (56).

Yet, however necessary "family" was for the psychological and physical well-being of slave narrators as children, it was a tainted wellspring for nourishing the self. That "family" was a common metaphor of master-slave relations owes much to its usefulness to proslavery ideologues, for whom it served as a justification for slavery. Calling the plantation household a "family" served rhetorically to sentimentalize and naturalize slavery as a structure of relations based on domination and dependence.

It is probably the fate of all autobiographers who speak from outside the dominant group to position themselves as a representative voice for their own less powerful people, since this is their culturally sanctioned role. Women slave narrators, like other African American autobiographers, clearly acknowledge gender and racial identifications as potential if not always actual sources of strength; at the same time, like other autobiographers, they seek to present themselves as idiosyncratic, self-creating individuals.

Finally, however, they are not just "like other autobiographers." For slave narrators had to testify to their painful life stories under the thumb of restrictions against telling the truth. They knew they could not say all, and they did not. But the unsaid tells, and the multiple prohibitions against self-assertion and self-expression that were the instruments and consequence of slavery were invariably strained in the very process of living and writing. If in some respects these narratives bear the marks of a compulsion to repeat without recourse, they also manifest the narrators' deliberate, astonishing assertions of will to recreate themselves in literature as no slaveowner would have permitted them to do.

CHAPTER 2

The Family Romances of Lydia Maria Child and Harriet Beecher Stowe

When I was quite a little girl I remember imagining that gypsies had changed me from some other cradle and put me in a place where I did not belong.
—Lydia Maria Child to Lucy Osgood, 1847

Please see to it that I am buried in some ground belonging to the *colored people*. . . . for epitaph inscribe on [my stone] the following: "Buried in this place, at her own request, among her brethren and sisters of dark complexion. . . ." —Lydia Maria Child to Wendell Phillips, 1860

One of the tasks facing antebellum antislavery women writers in the U.S.—both black and white—was to enlist the sympathies of white women on behalf of enslaved African American women. This was complicated, and critical, in a culture structured in part by the absolute dualism between "black" slavery and "white" freedom and by racialist notions of biological difference. Nor was a belief in inherent racial differences limited to racist proslavery ideologues, who naturalized the enslavement of Africans by enshrining notions of the moral and physical superiority of whites over blacks. Identity as being partially a condition of biological inheritance was the premise of many antislavery writers, most notably during the 1840s and 1850s. Harriet Beecher Stowe, for instance, whose spectacularly popular *Uncle Tom's Cabin, or, Life among the Lowly*—which ran in weekly installments in Dr. Gamaliel Bailey's Washington antislavery paper *The National Era* from June 5, 1851, until April 1, 1852, and was published as a book in March 1852—launched a powerful assault on the institution of slavery, yet also promoted racialism and colonization (the idea of sending freed slaves back to Africa).[1] Stowe's belief that Africans were innately gentler, more affectionate, and forgiving than Anglo-Saxons—that is, more naturally Christian—was consistent with what George M. Frederickson has called her era's "romantic racialism."[2] It is this view that lies behind the paternalism in Stowe's abolitionism. She describes the differences that make it necessary for the culturally superior white race to uplift the lowly of African descent: "The Saxon, born of ages of cultivation, command, education, physical and moral eminence; the Afric, born of ages of oppression, submission, ignorance, toil, and vice!" (267). The combination of abolitionist sympathies, religious fervor, and racialist splitting was by no means uncommon, and colonization was one mechanism for dealing with the tensions among them.

But biology also provided grounds for an argument for sameness. For despite laws against "amalgamation," frequent interracial sexual relations (most often between white masters and slave women) produced children whose biological inheritance (contrasted with their *legal* inheritance of a slave status from their slave mothers) was mixed, making it possible to assert racial crossings. In an 1831 tract, Mrs. W. Maria Stewart, considered to be the earliest black feminist, cites racial mixing as one reason "our souls are fired with the same love of liberty and independence with which your [white American men's] souls are fired. We will tell you that too much of your blood flows in our veins, and too much of your color in our skins, for us not to possess your spirits" (19–20). Stewart inverts racialist justifications for social and political inequality into a threat against those white men who have most benefited from such rationalizations. The institution justified primarily by notions of racial difference created a population whose very being undermined its own most vital assumption.[3]

This total subversion of the racial premise of slavery was fairly obvious to behold, as Stewart points out: the slave population was becoming visibly "whiter." Thus, the interlocking motifs of visibility and invisibility, recurring symbols for the ambiguity and dissimulation which inhere in the African African experience (think, for example, of Richard Wright's *The Man Who Lived Underground* or Ralph Ellison's *Invisible Man*), would become important tropes in tales of escapes from slavery.[4] Harriet Jacobs notes that her beloved Uncle Joseph (Benjamin in the narrative), who successfully fled when she was a girl, was helped along by the "disguise" of his white skin. William Craft escapes with his mulatta wife, Ellen, by posing as slave to her in the role of "invalid master." Louisa Picquet describes her pleasure in the mutual, secret recognition of passing for white that she shares with a fellow-fugitive, whom she accidentally encounters on a Northern street. They derive both enjoyment and a sense of power from their visible (to them) invisibility.

Of course, beneath the changing face of slavery was a history of interracial sexual relations. Thus arguments over the fate of slavery became charged with underlying anxieties about sexuality and sexual relations. Abolitionists' depictions of the licentious master were countered by proslavery images of the sexually frustrated female abolitionist with an "insatiable relish" for observing Southern sin.[5] "It is a common observation" writes James Henry Hammond in his "Letter to an English Abolitionist" (1845), that there is no subject on which ladies of eminent virtue so much delight to dwell [as on the sexual intercourse between master and slave], and on which in especial learned old maids, like Miss Martineau, linger with such an insatiable relish. . . . The constant recurrence of the female abolitionists to this topic, and their bitterness in regard to it, cannot fail to suggest to even the most charitable mind, that "Such rage without betrays the fires within." (Hammond; reprinted in Faust, 181)

Reflecting the intensifying anxieties created by the antebellum racial and sexual confusion, proslavery ideologues looked to history, science, and theology to buttress the shaky edifice of their ideology of racial slavery. Nat Turner's 1831 rebellion provoked a number of such anxiety-managing responses. Thomas Roderick Dew—a Virginia slaveholder, political law professor, and social commentator—contended that wherever and whenever in the world's nations "a commingling of the races ensued, it has been found that the civilized man has sunk down to the level of barbarism, and there has ended a mighty work of civilization!" (47). By the 1840s, such ethnologists as V. Josiah Nott were using cranial measurements, census data, and the eighteenth-century naturalist theories of Buffon to support their claims that the "Caucasian and Negro races" were two distinct species and that the "mulatto," like the mule, was a hybrid and degenerate type bred from a crossing of the "two parent stocks." In his pamphlet, "Two Lectures on the Natural History of the Caucasian and Negro Races," published in 1844, Nott singled out mulatta women as being "particularly delicate, and subject to a variety of chronic diseases. . . . bad breeders and bad nurses—many do not conceive—most are subject to abortions" (230). Aligning his science with slavery law, he observed that "the hybrid derives its size and internal structure principally from the mother" (230). When David Goodman Croly coined the term "miscegenation" in 1863, he may have been registering a heightened level of anxiety about interracial sexual relations, in anticipation of the transformation of a whole population of ex-slaves into American citizens.[6]

White advocates of equal rights for African Americans articulated their positions within the context of the rhetoric of fundamental racial differences and white fear of and fantasies about interracial sexual relations. "Now I protest against that counterfeit logic which concludes that, because I do not want a black woman for a *slave* I must necessarily want her for a *wife*," declared Abraham Lincoln, in a speech on the Dred Scott decision of 1857. "I need not have her for either, I can just leave her alone" (120). It is within this climate of belief in the biological danger of black people—what Lincoln terms the "natural disgust" of most white people toward the idea of amalgamation—and its seemingly corollary fixation with or phobic erasure of black women, that antislavery women writers attempt to utilize the rhetoric of interracial sisterhood to agitate against slavery and to feed their growing feminist agenda.[7]

The Suffering Quadroon

Given the lure of romantic racialism and what Ann Douglas has called the feminization of Victorian American culture, it is perhaps inevitable that white antislavery women writers would shape the figure of the suffering mulatta slave woman according to the contours of sentimental genres. Nathaniel Hawthorne—who claimed for himself the rhetorical position of the disinterested observer, while he defensively dismissed the "scribbling women"—complained that American life did not provide sufficient material for the imagination, making romance, which gave a "latitude" to the mind, the appropriate form for an American fiction. In contrast, antislavery feminists such as Harriet Beecher Stowe and Lydia Maria Child considered precisely the *realities* of Southern slavery to be a compelling subject for romance. These women saw romance as a proper form for explicitly political writing, and therefore the tragic stories of slave women as the moral focus for an attack on slavery. For instance, at the end of her 1842 edition of "The Quadroons," Child, an abolitionist and feminist who would edit Harriet Jacobs's *Incidents in the Life of a Slave Girl,* asks, "Reader, do you complain I have written fiction? Believe me, scenes like this are no infrequent occurrence at the South. The world does not afford such materials for tragic romance, as the history of the Quadroons" (*Liberty Bell,* 141).[8]

Child's conflation of history and romance, characteristic of the then relatively new genre of historical fiction, helps to legitimate Northern women's authority as historians of the South, though they are not eyewitnesses, by situating slavery's wrongs in the history of men's wrongs against womankind, for which the quadroons become a synecdoche. As romantic heroines, the quadroons are used to exhibit the moral suffering of feminine virtue betrayed; they also serve to symbolize the pain of enduring the physical and psychological torments (imprisonment, beatings, threats, rape) that potentially threaten all women. As descendants of numerous earlier sentimental heroines, the quadroons are not unlike Pamela, who, despite her servitude, has the "soul of a princess." The quadroon's mixed blood is not unrelated to her "soul": it functions as a symbol of a natural claim to racial superiority over other enslaved women; meanwhile, it is her "highly cultivated" (as Child puts it) mind and manner that, reinforcing nature, prove the ease with which she might be assimilated to the cultural norms of Northern society.[9] But unlike Pamela, the quadroon's fate is racially overdetermined: no amount of virtue can lead to her socially and legally sanctioned marriage to the master of the house.

Indeed, these tragic heroines who "are fated to suffer social ostracism or slavery for the sins of her white father or male relatives" are more than "merely white ingenues in blackface"

(Elfenbein, 2, 5). As shaped through available tropes and forms, the slave woman of mixed racial heritage becomes a symbol in white antislavery writing, enabling negotiation between sameness and difference, an intermediary area of potential intersubjectivity between self and other. That is, imagining the history of the quadroons in terms of tragic romance was a way for white antislavery women writers to manage cultural anxieties emanating from the dissonance between two contradictory principles of belief: the principle of racial difference and the principle of universal womanhood (gender identification). This contradiction was energized at the point at which the facts of slavery most directly came into conflict with the cultural insistence on female virtue and the cult of motherhood.

Accordingly, one project of the woman's antislavery romance was to manage the fear of difference and to neutralize the threat to the integrity of white womanhood implied by total sameness. This could be done by idealizing difference and transforming it into a mode of identification. In other words, the paradigm of feminine suffering, as it established an empathetic bond between white female readers and their enslaved "counterparts," and also affirmed the slave woman's claims to feminine virtue, was a way to sustain a relation between white and black women that accommodated the paradox of two predominating antebellum myths: racialism and the cult of womanhood. In particular, narrative reinforcement of the slave woman's *mute* suffering helped to allay cultural anxieties about the propriety of overidentification. As Franny Nudelman has argued, the narrative codes of sentimental forms employed by white women writers necessitated the separation of the slave woman from her audience (whose sexual degradation excluded her from the domestic culture of her readers), and relied upon the fact that she was the typically spoken-about object, not speaking subject, of sentimental discourse. Indeed, the tradition in which they wrote, though it required empathy and an identification with sexual vulnerability, was maintained by distance. Sentimental forms emphasized difference by stressing the slave woman's subordination and vulnerability in contrast to her sympathizing "sister's." This was iconographically represented in numerous depictions of the kneeling female slave, arms upraised in supplication, beneath the legend, "Am I Not a Woman and a Sister?"[10]

Consequently, the tradition of women's antislavery writing may be seen as an enactment of a conflicted alternation between empathy (based on a culturally subversive sense of symmetry between white and black women) and pity (based on a culturally endorsed idea of asymmetry between white and black women). Thus, Child can write, intimating both aspects of the relation, "*They are our sisters* and to us as women, they have a right to look for sympathy with their sorrows, and effort and prayer for their rescue" (Clifford, 134). Or she can claim, as she did during the Civil War, "The fact is I identify myself so completely with the slaves, that I am kept in alternating states of anxiety and wrath concerning [their fate]"; and yet, a year later, confide to a friend, "I *want* to do other things, but *always* there is kneeling before me that everlasting slave, with his hands clasped in supplication."[11]

The efficacy of romance to enact fantasies of identification and difference in order to satisfy basic impulses as well as to maintain the integrity of a self-image has its analogue in the "family romances" described by Freud, in which the invention of a new family for the self serves to alleviate the internal pressures thought to spring from oedipal wishes and fears.[12] That is, family romances come into being in order to deal with forbidden sexual wishes and anxiety- and guilt-ridden feelings of sexual rivalry. In antislavery romances, the circularity of fantasy and reality suggests the volatile presence of "the return of the repressed": romance becomes gothic when the trope of antislavery family romances merges with the reality of familial relations, when fantasies of incestuous, miscegenetic affairs are embodied in the actual bodies of quadroons.

Calling upon the *metaphor* of family relations (mothers, daughters, sisters) in order to familiarize enslaved African American women to their Northern audiences, sentimental narrators tend to turn away from the implications for identity of *actual* familial relations; at the same time, their invocation of family relations, and their disclosure of the primal scenes of interracial sexual relations, seem to charge their works with the sorts of anxieties that in fact activate the family romance.[13] In this way, narrating the horrors of slavery as a family romance may perhaps have served as a way to give shape and expression to forbidden desires and aggressive feelings. Antislavery romances could provide Northern white women narrators and their readers with fantasies of dark, outcast others, who live in a dark other world, and through whom they could experience a vicarious drama of purity and danger, while disavowing ownership of the feelings it arouses.[14] By allowing identification and disidentification between (light) self and (dark) other, these narratives could also be an outlet for Northern moral outrage that involved not only an intense sense of guilt for the slave's suffering, but, conversely, the disavowal of any identification with Southern white oppression of black people.

Child's Quadroon Sisters

Child's tale "The Quadroons" demonstrates a narrative's successful management of the anxieties of familial (sexual) relations between black and white, successful in that it suggests identification but maintains difference. The narrator uses conventional descriptions to establish the inherent difference between her "pretty rivals"—Rosalie, the quadroon daughter of a wealthy merchant (whom the white antihero, Edward, truly loves), and

41

Charlotte, the white heiress of a popular and wealthy man (whom Edward marries out of political ambition). The narrator relies upon romantic codes of dark and fair, a logic of opposition familiar to readers of Sir Walter Scott (to whom Child refers in her 1833 preface to *Appeal in Favor of the Class of Americans Called Africans*). In this way, she uses the reader's mastery over the signs of the romance form as a mechanism for mastery over the emotional unruliness of sexual rivalry and betrayal. The opposition between heroines is naturalized and idealized, rendered timeless and unchanging: the quadroon's "raven hair," "graceful as an antelope, and beautiful as the evening star," "her complexion as rich and glowing as an autumnal leaf" is contrasted with her rival's "blush-rose-buds" (62, 65). But both share a burden of pain: the mutual betrayal by Edward who, marrying where he does not love, abandons his "heaven-sanctioned" wife (Rosalie) and their daughter, Xarifa, and lives a life of chilly pretense with his legally recognized bride.

Significantly, and broadening Child's political purposes, attention to the women's personal rivalry is deflected into a more socially and politically conscious critique of the arbitrary and unjust "edicts of society," thus emphasizing the women's mutual vulnerability to "man's perfidy." This is a tale of "sisterhood": "I promised thee a sister tale, / Of man's perfidious cruelty," reads the epigraph, quoted from Coleridge. "Come then and hear what cruel wrong / Befell the dark Ladie." Inviting the reader's sympathy for a "sister tale" for "the dark Ladie," Child constructs a reader who is white, and whose story, though it differs in degree from her "sister's," does not necessarily differ in kind (62, 61). In fact, Rosalie is said to "pit[y] his fair young bride" (69); and when Xarifa is left an orphan, it is Charlotte who allows Edward's benevolent domestic arrangements for his daughter to continue uninterrupted—Charlotte who years before had accidentally spotted Xarifa, seen her resemblance to Edward, and discovered the truth.

Thus, reinforcing identification, this sister tale is also a mother's tale, in which maternal feelings might override sisterly conflict. But for the slave woman, virtuous motherhood also becomes conflated with the dark sister's powerlessness to protect her child. Rosalie is like the moon that gazes upon Edward, a "mild, but sorrowful . . . Madonna [who] seems to gaze on her worshipping children, bowed down with consciousness of sin" (67). Earlier, as she contemplates her beautiful daughter, whose fate she fears will follow her own, there is "in the tenderness of the mother's eye . . . an in-dwelling sadness" (64). In these images of the suffering quadroon mother, passivity is intrinsic to the dark woman's transcendent consciousness. The depiction of intraracial sisterhood between mother and daughter affords no outlet for feelings, or field for action: shadowing Rosalie's "tenderness" is an "in-dwelling sadness"—a feeling internalized and immobilized in the secret and silent subjectivity (the "eye") of a socially outcast, already dying woman.[15]

What is in the "eye" of the other, as seen by the narrating self, is a repeated image. Elsewhere, describing Xarifa, Child writes of the "melting, mezzotinto outline" in Xarifa's dark eye that "remains the last vestige of African ancestry, and that gives that plaintive expression, so often observed, and so appropriate to that docile and injured race" (63). The white eye's aesthetic appreciation of the "mezzotinto outline" in the dark eye suggests the displacement of black by white as an aspect of historical and cultural development. In a way characteristic of romantic racialism, the narrator exoticizes Xarifa's African lineage as an ancient, dying trace just visible in its evolution toward whiteness.[16] Thus, paradoxically, the transitional figure of the quadroon figuratively and functionally splits off black from white even further (as opposed to reconciling them): on the "other side" of Xarifa (from Charlotte or from the narrator) is the "excellent old negress" whom the guilty father hires to "take charge of the cottage" and care for the soon-to-be motherless Xarifa (71). It is this slave woman's absolute difference that is implicit in her pervasive blackness and total silence. Indeed, it is her radical "otherness" and potential autonomy that threaten the narrative regulation of sameness, sustained in the figure of the maternal quadroon.

Rosalie is an ethereal Madonna, who figuratively watches over her white male child / husband, yet she is in fact a slave. This "old negress," in contrast, is the embodiment of nature itself; she nurses Xarifa and is in fact legally free. In other words, Rosalie is contained by the white symbolic order, a mother within the white patriarchal law; the "old negress" (mentioned in the story just this once) hints at the narrative awareness of a primary maternal realm, prior to language, potentially disruptive, potentially beyond control. Only in Xarifa, in the end, are these "two mothers" brought "face-to-face," but then they are used to show the dangers to self-integration such a juncture creates. Xarifa appears as a "raving maniac" in a double image that is evocative of internal conflicts between desire and self-denial, outwardly directed rage and self-hatred: "That pure temple was desecrated . . . and that beautiful head fractured against the wall in the frenzy of despair" (76).

That Xarifa ends up being mad is the outcome of a sequence of events which, in some respects, raises hopes that her fate will not duplicate her mother's, but because of her father's failure to act sends her hurtling back into slavery, crushing her even more violently. Edward dies when Xarifa is fifteen, virtually leaving her to fall in love with her white tutor, George Elliot, the only son of an English widow. It is an attachment, Child tells us, that her father had hoped for, thinking that the "English freedom from

44

prejudice should lead [George] to offer legal protection to his graceful and winning child" (72). But because Edward dies without a will, Xarifa is soon seized by the heirs of her mother's former master, put up for auction, and purchased by a "wealthy profligate," who clearly designs to make her his mistress (74). Xarifa plans to escape with her lover, but is betrayed by a fellow slave, and when George is shot dead, she loses all will and desire. It is then that her new master lays his hands upon her; and then that she becomes a "raving maniac" beating her head against a wall (76).

The value endorsed by "The Quadroons"—where the quadroon's desire to protect her rival's feelings ensures that she will never tell, and the white woman's "inexpressive" eye and "reluctance" to interfere with her husband's seemingly benevolent care of his quadroon daughter effectively mutes her as well—is of a sisterhood of empathetic suffering (65, 70, 72). However, the final image of Xarifa implies a counternarrative to the "tragic romance" of suffering women, embodied in suffering dark women, that "The Quadroons" puts forth. That *all* women are (at least potential) victims of men is the *culturally acceptable* basis of identification between the story's central women, according as it does with the idea of female passivity. But the obvious aggression in Xarifa's self-mutilation suggests another possibility for sisterly identifications.

In Child's ironically titled "Slavery's Pleasant Homes: A Faithful Sketch," a variant of the "tragic romance"—published in *The Liberty Bell* one year after "The Quadroons's" initial appearance—a covert, because unacceptable, basis for identification between black and white women explicitly emerges. This story contains a scene of violence that, although it is quickly contained (repressed), nonetheless opens up the possibilities of a secret alliance based not on passivity and recognition of mutual suffering, but rather on the capacity for aggression against one another and, finally, against men.

"Slavery's Pleasant Homes" is an emotionally volatile tale in which the family romance, charged by incestuous relations and intense sibling rivalry, is repeatedly disrupted by outbursts of uncontrolled aggression. One of the story's motifs of instability is the ambiguous "color" marking of the dark heroine, Rosa. She is encoded in every way as a tragic quadroon, yet never explicitly labeled as such. Indeed, her status as something of a racial cipher contributes to a suggestive confusion in her racial positioning relative to other characters, the narrator, and the audience. Then, too, that she is desired equally by three differently racially marked men—white, mulatto, and quadroon—alludes to the illicit sexual history behind the racial, and therefore, narrative ambiguity that hovers above her throughout the tale. The narrator's careful description of Rosa's body and blush associates fluctuating skin color with intemperate (drunken) sexual desire: "Rosa, a young girl, elegantly formed, and beautiful as a dark velvet carnation. The blush, so easily excited, shone through the transparent brown of her smooth cheek, like claret through a bottle in the sunshine" (148).

Racial slippage is one element in the narrative impulse toward disintegration. The other is the narrative obsession with splitting and doubling. This story is about sibling rivalries gone amok, without the controlling presence of maternal or paternal authorities, self-enclosed and simmering, a family of brothers and sisters that acts out the unconscious fantasies said to underlie the family romance.[17] Marion, Frederic Dalcho's bride, is Rosa's foster-sister (they were both nursed by Rosa's mother) and her mistress. This connection merely highlights their opposition; the foster-sisters' attitudes toward one another, and the narrator's attitude toward each of them, switches frequently between aggression and benevolence, the latter perhaps a defense against a more primary aggression and the fear of retaliation.[18] Marion's pleasure in her possession is indicated by the fact that she "loved to decorate her with jewels" (149). Saying, "You shall wear my jewels whenever you ask for them," Marion gives permission to Rosa to desire, but draws clear limitations around this with her ownership. Yet, if Rosa is Marion's doll, so Marion is the narrator's, who calls her a "pretty waxen plaything" (148).

Narrative anxiety (indicated by splitting and reactive shifts) intensifies when sisterhood gives way to sexual rivalry. Frederic's quadroon brother and slave, George, falls in love with Rosa and when Marion asks her husband to allow them to marry, Frederic's interest in Rosa warms. Soon, one night, Marion awakes to find her husband missing. Hearing voices in Rosa's room, "the painful truth flashed upon her. Poor young wife, what a bitter hour was that!" (152). Allied by sisterhood, reinforced by their mutual betrayal, Marion and Rosa are inevitably (for the romance form) pitted against one another as rivals. Their only remaining en- counters highlight the tensions of identification and separation by being represented in modes suggestive of the presence of the unconscious—during a violent outburst and during a dream. In such states, barriers against unconscious impulses are dropped. Until the betrayal, narrative splitting between Rosa and Marion had served to manage passion by keeping it separated from the woman with the means to enact it (that is, the passionate slave woman is imagined as passive; the fragile, impassive white woman is allowed an outlet for rage, at least socially downward, if not up against her husband). But this defense against de- structive impulses collapses when Marion, provoked perhaps by Rosa's reactive, exaggerated obedience (to assuage, for one thing, her sense of guilt), gives Rosa a blow. Thus Marion's clear but relatively benign expressions of domination early in the story are no longer contained, and open out into physical assault:

47

In the morning, Rosa came to dress her, as usual, but avoided looking in her face, and kept her eyes fixed on the ground. As she *knelt* to tie the satin shoe, Marion spoke angrily of her awkwardness, and gave her a blow. It was the first time she had ever struck her; for they really loved each other. The beautiful slave looked up with an expression of surprise, which was answered by a strange, wild stare. Rosa fell at her feet, and sobbed out, "Oh, mistress, I am not to blame. Indeed, indeed, I am very wretched." Marion's fierce glance melted into tears. "Poor child," said she, "I ought not to have struck you; but, oh, Rosa, I am wretched, too." The foster-sisters embraced each other, and wept long and bitterly; but neither sought any further to learn the other's secrets. (152–53)

Marion violates cultural injunctions against female force in two stages: verbal abuse escalates to physical abuse.[19] Her aggressive outburst is contained (repressed) rapidly, though, by a quick reversion to maternal concern ("Poor child"), then to identification as a sister who also suffers. Calling the two "foster-sisters," Child seems to assert reparation and the restoration of the familiar. But, as "foster-sisters" also implies, their relation has developed as a history of displacements: Marion's displacement of Rosa at her mother's breast finds an answer in Rosa's displacement of Marion in bed. It is hinted, too, that Marion is self-alienated in her moment of violence, and alienated from narrator and reader as well. Narrative empathy ("Poor young wife!") and narrative alignment with Marion's perspective (Rosa's eyes are directed downward) are withdrawn in the moment when Rosa "looked up with an expression of surprise," and Marion mutely "answers" with "a strange, wild stare." Rosa initiates the look, positioning the now "mute" Marion as the other, a shift reinforced by the description of Marion's stare ("wild," "strange") in terms conventionally applied to the other. Thus the "strange, wild stare" that looks back at her foster-sister's look, is an expression of the double, the uncanny experience of unconsciously recognizing oneself in the form of another. The return of an early form of rage that has been rejected as unacceptable and, over time, repressed, the double's presence suggests that what Rosa sees ("with an expression of surprise") is the return of her own anger that has been split off and projected onto the other.[20] So, by inversion, Marion's blow is a symbolic enactment of Rosa's aggressive impulses against a white foster-sister kneeling at *her* feet.

If this is so, then the narrator's insistence on the slave girl's excessive passivity is founded partially on fear of the slave girl's anger and aggression against white women. But, alternatively, her insistence that "they really loved each other," in combination with her displacement of the fantasy of *being* beaten onto the childlike other, suggests that this scene is also the compressed expression of the white woman's guilt-ridden rage against the other.[21] That this concentration of rage is not so easily buried is conveyed in Rosa's haunting of Marion's dreams after Rosa's death (brought on by Frederic's sadistic flogging of Rosa when she is pregnant, the result of his raping her). "The memory of her foster-sister mingled darkly with all her dreams. Was that a shriek she heard? It was fearfully shrill in the night-silence! Half sleeping and half waking, she called wildly, 'Rosa! Rosa!' " (157). Rousing herself, Marion learns that her husband has been just discovered dead, "a dagger through his heart," murdered, it turns out, by his half-brother George in vengeful fury (157). In the world of the dream, the internal (unconscious) world and external reality intermingle, and the prohibitions (internalized as conscience, or a value, such as self-denial) against the rage and aggressive impulses of both women find their final discharge in Frederic's murder.

The fetishization of suffering and the defenses meant to bind feminine aggression (idealization and splitting) are the very markers of the forces they are meant to contain. For indeed, by another inversion, the narrator's insistence on the slave girl's passivity is a way to ease the anxieties raised by Marion's role in, and the narrator's powerful fascination with, the violence that surrounds Rosa. The rage against the other—who stands for the repressed elements of the self—is internalized aggression that is felt to have no other acceptable outlet.

Child's biographer, Deborah Pickford Clifford, believes that Child might have identified with the quadroons in her stories, since she felt betrayed and frustrated by her impractical husband, David, whose fruitless political ambitions and unrealistic business schemes were not only the cause of numerous separations, but because they invariably failed, put the burden of earning a living completely on her. In light of "Slavery's Pleasant Homes," this is a suggestive comment. For if dreams are also wishes (as Freud claimed), then Marion, who dreams her husband's death (she hears him shriek), awakens to find her dream come true. When she thinks of Rosa in the trauma of awakening, Marion may be seeking disavowal of her own thoughts by conjuring up the image of her split-off, projected negative self. Horror occurs when real events correspond to unacceptable fantasies, for that is when repressed thoughts seem to have caused real events; casting off forbidden wishes as if they were another's is the self's bid for decontamination.

Child's use of the tragic romance, with its emphasis on passivity, purity, and pain as positive values, seems meant to deal with an array of feelings that in part emerge out of anger and frustrated desire. Yet it also suggests an effort to repress the fantasies of sexual threat and uncontrollable rage that are triggered by the terrors of a totalizing identification or an unrelieved difference. Such are the primary childhood anxieties caused by fears of engulfing merger with the maternal object or fears of loss of the object. Interestingly, motherlessness, as represented in "Slavery's Pleasant Homes" and at the end of "The Quadroons," not only exposes the daughters to sexual dangers, but also pro-

vides a space—with the mothers out of the way—for the enactment of the daughters' own impulses and desires.

Thus, insofar as Child resists structuring the relations between
her dark and fair protagonists and antagonists in terms of domination and dependence sentimentalized in the relation of
mother to child, she points to the possibilities of equality between her white audience and enslaved women. By temporarily
inverting Rosa's and Marion's positions, she demystifies the benevolent iconographic image of the dark supplicant and her
white patroness; she gives literary life to fantasies of a real sisterhood, fraught with tensions of rivalry, competition, hatred, and
revenge. In this way, Child's goal (as she wrote in 1834), to
"familiarize the public mind with the idea that colored people
are *human beings*—elevated or degraded by the same circumstances that elevate or degrade other men," is inseparable from
the idea that *women* are human beings, as well. As she says in
Appeal in Favor of That Class of Americans Called Africans (1833):
"Some authentic records of female cruelty would seem perfectly
incredible, were it not an established law of our nature that
tyranny becomes a habit, and scenes of suffering, often repeated,
render the heart callous" (28).[22]

Child's dramatizations of the life of the tragic quadroon are a
felt presence in later antislavery depictions by former slaves and
sympathizers of slavery's perversion of familial relations. The
mulatto slave narrator William Wells Brown interpolates "The
Quadroons" into both versions of his novel about the quadroon
slave woman, Clotel (in the 1853 edition), or Clotelle (in the
1864 revision). And—as I hope to show in my analysis of Harriet
Jacobs's *Incidents*—Child's fantasies of a female aggression suppressed beneath the cultural ideals of virtuous womanhood and
selfless motherhood are profoundly resonant with Jacobs's experiences and self-representation.

Stowe's Quadroon Mothers

Although there is a great deal one could say about Stowe's fervent and panoramic *Uncle Tom's Cabin,* my purpose here is simply to examine the ways in which Stowe's construction of an interracial bond between women differs from Child's, and the implications of that difference. My central argument is that in *Uncle Tom's Cabin,* Stowe reproduces a relation of domination between white and black women in her deployment of the figure of the quadroon and of the ideal of motherhood.

There is a chapter called "The Quadroon's Story" in Stowe's *Uncle Tom's Cabin,* told by the desperate slave mother, Cassy, who escapes from Simon Legree after a long history of abuse and accidentally recovers her daughter, whom she joins in freedom. Stowe's story of the quadroon's and her daughter's escape and freedom, though set off by the "feminine" self-sacrifice of Uncle Tom, points to a radically different vision from Child's and, therefore, underlying set of needs. By the time Stowe wrote *Uncle Tom's Cabin,* slave narratives—stories of escape—had been a staple feature of antislavery literature for over ten years, and she read them with admiration. Stowe herself was on the periphery of abolitionist activity when her sense of moral outrage was ignited by the Fugitive Slave Act in the Compromise of 1850, which required Northerners to capture and return runaways to slavery. Thus, her appropriations of Child's themes (like Brown's and Jacobs's appropriations of both Child and Stowe) are structured by the plot of escape and the anxieties of the fugitive.[23]

Stowe, like Child, would wish to emphasize slavery's irredeemable darkness; Uncle Tom's martyrdom—his "victory"—speaks to the immensity of the *sin* of slavery.[24] Perhaps, here is Stowe's religious reworking of the sadomasochism in Child's tales (in "A Child Is Being Beaten," Freud cites *Uncle Tom's Cabin* as providing a model for many of his patients' beating-fantasies). Indeed,

Stowe described the seed of her novel as a mental vision during a church service of a weeping slave being whipped to death by a cruel overseer.

But Stowe's particular use of the figure of the quadroon slave woman seems motivated by a sense of relations between black and white women different from Child's—one that *requires* the successful escapes of the slave women. Stowe herself said that in writing *Uncle Tom's Cabin* she felt like a mother entering a burning building to rescue her child. In this penetrating comparison (it conveys the narrative's urgent tone), Stowe, the mother of seven, echoes the feelings of slave mothers (including those she depicts) whose instincts to protect their children provoke them to desperate acts.[25] But the slave as her child is also at the heart of this image of rescue. Perhaps it is not surprising that Stowe should imagine herself thus, as savior mother; she had been unable to save a beloved toddler son from the Cincinnati cholera epidemic of 1849. In contrast, Child, who was childless and, though married, practically husbandless, might well have been moved to envision her relation to the slave woman in terms of sexual rivalry and betrayal.

Stowe's Maternal Vision

It is motherhood as the quintessence of female suffering that underwrites Stowe's narrative position in *Uncle Tom's Cabin,* and forges the link she endeavors to create between white Northern reader and black slave woman. A hyper-involved narrator/preacher, Stowe exhorts the white "mothers of America" to turn their motherly eyes toward the "daughters of an injured race," and act upon their sympathetic identification with the sufferings of slave mothers (472). Stowe's argument is that slavery dismembers families, slave and free, and it remains for America's mothers to put an end to the institution that disrupts motherhood and destroys homes. A wish-fulfilling fantasy, the quadroon mother Eliza's "desperate leap" to safety across the icy Ohio River, bearing her son in her arms, "impossible to anything but madness and despair," conveys the power of a mother's love to rescue her children (72). Maternal affection structures the narrator's relation to her reader, whom she guides, like a watchful mother leading her children, through scene after scene of pathos and pain, educating the reader in, quite simply, how to feel. Stowe instructs her reader in the process of identification, most notably, for example, in the Quaker Ruth Stedman's response to Eliza and her son, who have found sustenance and safe haven in the ample warmth of Rachel Halliday's kitchen. Ruth explains why she can empathize immediately with Eliza: "If I didn't love John and the baby, I should not know how to feel for her" (153). Implicit in Stowe's method is the idea of witnessing; empathetic understanding entails such identifications based on a recognition of shared emotional experiences.

Throughout the novel, the watchful mother that the narrative evokes is—psychoanalytically speaking—the good preoedipal mother, associated with ample food, warmth, comfort, security, order, continuity, and bodily and emotional presence. Rachel's kitchen is "large, roomy, neatly painted . . . , its yellow floor glossy and smooth, and with out a particle of dust; a neat, well-blacked cooking-stove; rows of shining tin, suggestive of unmentionable good things to the appetite" (148). Seated by Eliza's side in her rocking chair, Rachel promises eternal connection and, by metonymy, a lap (chair) in which to sit: "for twenty years or more, nothing but loving words, and gentle moralities, and motherly loving kindness, had come from that chair;—headaches and heartaches innumerable had been cured there,—difficulties spiritual and temporal solved there,—all by one good, loving woman, God bless her!" (148–50). As George Harris, Eliza's runaway husband, recognizes after he arrives, Rachel's house is a "home," a domestic heaven, radiating outward from a mother in her kitchen serving up communion with griddle-cakes: "Rachel never looked so truly and benignly happy as at the head of her table. There was so much motherliness and fullheartedness even in the way she passed a plate of cakes or poured a cup of coffee, that it seemed to put a spirit into the food and drink she offered" (156). Goodness is repeatedly associated in the preoedipal terms of a body that supplies the other's (the child's) needs, identical at this early stage with its pleasures, as with the little mother "Eva, who carried a large satchel, which she had been filling with apples, nuts, candy, ribbons, laces, and toys of every description, during her whole homeward journey" to distribute among her family's slaves (182).

The novel strengthens its argument that the (preoedipal) mother might heal the deformation of humanity that slavery causes in the negative example of Marie St. Clare. Marie's cruelty to her slaves is related to her primary failing as a mother, suggested in her self-involvement, instability, hypocrisy, coldness, selfishness, and artificiality, all negations of motherhood, illustrated in one brief image: there she "stood, gorgeously dressed, on the veranda, on Sunday morning, clasping a diamond bracelet on her slender wrist" (198). Querulous, self-centered, and casually cruel, Marie stands ready for attendance at her "fashionable church," clasping not a child to her heart, but a hard-chiseled stone to her pulse. Marie, the antithesis of a mother, loves no one but herself, and so is utterly lacking in the power of sympathy: "I don't feel a particle of sympathy for such cases [Prue, the distraught, grieving slave mother who was whipped to death]. If they'd behave themselves it would not happen" (253).

But the narrative bifurcation between "good" mother and "bad" mother has a purpose beyond drawing an obvious contrast. Indeed, it works to check the aggressive impulses of the narrative's own mothering against her "children"—the slaves over whom she bends with concern. That "true womanhood" not entail passion, erotic or destructive, is essential to the narrative's defensive posture.[26] However, the quadroon Cassy complicates this picture. Of Cassy, Simon Legree's property, it is said that "despair hardened womanhood within her, and waked the fires of fiercer passions, [and] she had become in a measure his mistress, and he alternately tyrannized over her and dreaded her" (428). Cassy exemplifies a woman active in her outrage against those who violate her, one whose feminine influence over "her man" is, as Ann Douglas puts it in her introduction to the novel, "a kind of voodoo version of the *Godey's* model" of "moral suasion" and "mild precept" (17–18).

However, the tendency of the narrative is to keep feminine activity reserved for the maternal protection of others; so much so that the motherhood that destroys (even in the name of love), as when Cassy murders her infant son, necessarily subverts the splitting that sustains the narrative's overt maternal vision. Inherent in motherhood (parenthood) are both narcissism and domination, and especially powerful is the infant's mother, a fact culturally obscured by sentimentalizations of mother and babe. Having lost two older children to slavery, Cassy determines, "I would never again let a child live to grow up!" (392). Though, perhaps, inviting ambivalent responses, the violence in Cassy's past is radically divorced from the narrator's maternal attitude: Cassy's "wild, passionate utterances" are presented as an interpolated tale, told by Cassy herself to Tom. More to the point, this chapter constitutes Cassy's confession to Tom, a necessary beginning in her moral conversion. That Cassy's storyline culminates with her recovery of her daughter at least implies that had she not killed her son, he too might have been recovered from slavery. The danger in this vision of maternal rage against a son who could not be saved is dissolved by the recovery of the mother-daughter bond in the more wholesome air of freedom.

Yet, despite the complicated disavowal of overbearing passion in the mother-child bond, the maternal imago idealized by the narrative is also that of a mother who will not let her "child grow up." The maternal affection expressed toward the slave girl depends upon the slave's infantilization—specifically, upon her powerlessness in relation to the white mother.

When she [Eliza] awoke [in Rachel's house], she found herself snugly tucked up on the bed, with a blanket over her, and little Ruth rubbing her hands with camphor. She opened her eyes in a state of dreamy, delicious languor, such as one has who has long been bearing a heavy load, and now feels it gone, and would rest. The tension of the nerves, which had never ceased a moment since the first hour of her flight, had given way, and a strange feeling of security and rest came upon her; and, as she lay, with her large, dark eyes open, she followed, as in a quiet dream, the motions of those about her. She saw the door open into the other room; saw the supper-table, with its snowy cloth; heard the dreamy murmur of the singing tea-kettle; saw Ruth tripping backward and forward with plates of cake and saucers. . . . She saw the ample, motherly form of Rachel, as she ever and anon came to the bedside, and smoothed and arranged something about the bedclothes, and gave a tuck here and there, by way of expressing her good will; and was conscious of a kind of sunshine beaming down upon her from her large, clear, brown eyes . . . there were low murmurs of talk, gentle tinkling of teaspoons, and musical clatter of cups and saucers, and all mingled in a delightful dream of rest. (154–55)

Swaddled in the bed, watching passively the movements of those over her, registering dreamily sensations of sight, smell, sound, and touch in a series of appearances and disappearances not causally or temporally related, Eliza is that preoedipal mother's infant, before murmurs, tinkling, and clatter rearrange themselves as sounds distinguishable from one another and oneself, a level of consciousness, reinforced by the vagueness ("something about the bedclothes") and uninflected ("She saw . . . saw . . . saw. . . . She saw. . . .") quality of her comprehension. And when she awakes from a dream of "a beautiful country," in which she sees her "son playing" and hears her "husband's footsteps," and finds her weeping husband beside her, his double appearance, first in her dream, then out of her dream, suggests the child's sense of omnipotence in her own thoughts, an illusion derived from a feeling of merger with the mother. The good-enough mother who anticipates her child's wishes and produces them fosters this illusion of omnipotence, then disperses it. After the Quaker mothers produce the husband, the narrator intones, "It was no dream" (155).[27] By keeping the agency entirely outside of Eliza, the maternal domination of Eliza seems to disenfranchise her from equality with the white mothers—a subordinate position implicitly reinforced in the chapter "The Freeman's Defence," when George exclaims, "O, Eliza, if these people only knew what a blessing it is for a man to feel that his wife and child belong to *him!*"[28]

Invitations to readerly identification with the suffering quadroon mothers are ultimately rearranged as relations structured by white maternal domination. Thus, the narrative maternalism that characterizes *Uncle Tom's Cabin,* fixed in the preoedipal, depends on the image of the dependent, passive slave whose identity (racial and spiritual) is conceived of as moving toward symbiosis with the all-powerful, all-absorbing white mother. So Tom (a model for feminine virtue in self-sacrifice) is imagined as "now entirely merged with the Divine," and passing into a state of "cheerfulness . . . alertness . . . and quietness which no insult or injury could ruffle" (419). So comes "Death, the consoler," as Longfellow promised in his popular long poem of feminine toil, travail, patience, and faith—*Evangeline* (1847)—over whose heroine's fate antebellum readers wept rapturously, an experience Stowe invites them to recall and renew in the life and death of Evangeline St. Clare.[29] Stowe's "Divine" maternal figure, insusceptible to the kind of destabilizing oedipal rivalries at work in Child's two stories, suppresses difference, or more precisely, difference from *her.* The incorporation of the (m)other by the Mother also characterizes the narrative representation of its own composition. In "Concluding Remarks," Stowe explains that her narrative incorporates the stories of those on whose behalf she speaks: "The separate incidents that compose the narrative are, to a very great extent, authentic, occurring, many of them, either under her own observation or that of her personal friends" (467).[30]

In Stowe's family romance, mothers are best; and matrilineage is a way to preserve racial segregation. As George says, explaining his desire to return to Africa, "My sympathies are not for my father's race, but for my mother's. To him I was no more than a fine dog or horse; to my poor heart-broken mother I was a *child.*" This clear-cut division, in conjunction with Stowe's narrative splitting between "good" mother and "bad" mother, helps to maintain the narrative separation between black and white, despite the ambiguous presence of the figure of the quadroon.

Conclusion

As linguistic outlets for the negotiation of sameness and difference, these antislavery narratives evidence some of the conflicts inherent in the effort to create an interracial sisterhood within the context of romantic racialism. As such, they alert us to the strategies of self-representation deployed in slave narratives by African American women whose lives these white authors—literarily, politically, and socially—touched.

Child's radical difference from Stowe, her ability to imagine an interracial sisterhood that can tolerate a fantasy of inverted earthly power relations, offers an alternative view to Stowe's millenarian maternalism. Child's strange tales penetrate more acceptable ideas about womanhood and sisterhood to the level of antisisterly rage and potential for violence that absolute racialism—predictably racist—makes inevitable. Stowe's narrative, though it certainly challenges conventional nineteenth-century prescriptions for the proper conduct of women in public *in the name of its author,* does not extend that same rhetorical position of defiance to its slave women characters.

And, unlike Stowe, whose use of the figure of the quadroon functionally and figuratively reinforces racial separation, Child toys with the idea and implications of racial ambiguity. This is a strain that runs through Child's works, including her first antislavery story, "The St. Domingo Orphans" (1830), based on her research into the Santo Domingo slave uprising of 1791–1804. In this tale, the orphaned daughters of slaveholders are forced to sign a paper calling themselves mulattoes, for whom they have already been mistaken because (as Child says) of their exposure to the West Indian sun. The paper also states that their parents had sold them as slaves.

Thus, displacement and substitution—two mechanisms at work in the construction of the family romance—rearrange identity to the child's satisfaction. The two excerpts from Child's letters that are juxtaposed at the head of this chapter have their place here.[31]

> When I was quite a little girl I remember imagining that gypsies had changed me from some other cradle and put me in a place where I did not belong.
> —Lydia Maria Child to Lucy Osgood, 1847

> Please see to it that I am buried in some ground belonging to the *colored people*. . . . for epitaph inscribe on [my stone] the following: "Buried in this place, at her own request, among her brethren and sisters of dark complexion. . . ." —Lydia Maria Child to Wendell Phillips, 1860

"*We* Could Have Told Them a Different Story!": Harriet Jacobs, John S. Jacobs, and the Rupture of Memory

Harriet Jacobs's *Incidents in the Life of a Slave Girl* (1861) rightly has been read as a powerful expression of the often entwined nineteenth-century reform causes of abolitionism and feminism. Jacobs's stated intention was to rouse the sympathies of the "women of the North" on behalf of their sisters, the "two millions of women at the South," suffering the sexual degradations that made slavery "far more terrible for women" than for men (*Incidents*, 1, 77). If the "incidents" of Jacobs's narrative represent her experiences in slavery, her account's structure, themes, and style reflect the time she spent in Rochester and Boston among anti-slavery and women's rights activists, whose developing feminism was modeled on abolitionist arguments.

Presenting her narrative as being by, for, and about women, Jacobs encouraged her readers to read her history through the women she depicts; and this is what most critics have done.[1] A great deal has been written about Jacobs's pseudonymous Linda

Brent's relationships with her first mistress, her maternal grand-mother, her daughter, her jealous Southern mistress, the slave women who help hide her, and her Northern employer.[2] Also, there has been discussion of the symbolic significance of Jacobs's mother, who died when Brent / Jacobs was six: Jacobs's sense of womanhood and her critique of slavery hinge on her image of her mother as representing the embodiment of female virtue in a slave—a slave, Brent / Jacobs notes, who had no master to persecute her.

In contrast, important male relatives—particularly Jacobs's father Elijah and brother John S. Jacobs—have been largely neglected in the critical literature (more has been written about her relationships with white men), with the result that our under-standing of Brent / Jacobs, as narrator, character, and historical figure, has been strangely restricted.[3] The limitations that follow from this critical omission are especially striking in the case of Harriet's brother. Two years younger, John was his sister's early confidant and model of resistance, and he figures as an im-portant presence and support throughout the narrative. But what makes John S. Jacobs's relative invisibility all the more intriguing is the existence of his short narrative of slavery, "A True Tale of Slavery," which was published in a London journal one month after his sister's book came out in Boston. Cited frequently by Jean Fagan Yellin in the detailed footnotes to her 1987 edition of *Incidents*, John Jacobs's narrative has not been unknown, but forgotten. It has not, in other words, been seized upon as an obvious text to read alongside *Incidents*.[4]

Why this is so, and why there has been no sustained explora-tion of these male figures in connection to Brent / Jacobs's auto-biography, are interrelated questions that I will be addressing toward the end of this chapter. My basic contention, however, is that we cannot understand Brent / Jacobs if (to borrow from Woolf) we think back only through her mothers. Her psychological and political narrative engagement with women in her life is, without question, profound. But her story also demonstrates how much her narrated desires, fears, and actions are bound up with the Jacobs men as well.

The narrative makes this point almost immediately: the first two dramatized sections of *Incidents* contain memorable scenes in which the central figures are Brent / Jacobs's father, her brother (called William in the narrative), and her teenaged uncle Joseph (Benjamin), whom she loved "like a brother" and would name her son after (6).[5] The opening anecdote of the narrative (in chapter 2), in which William / John responds to his mistress's command instead of his father's, introduces the generic theme of slavery's corrosive effect upon the authority of the slave father. But more than this, it characterizes and individuates the father, Elijah, a slave whose traits of independence and defiant anger will prove themselves in his two children's rebellions against their masters. In similar two-pronged fashion—that is, treating the slave's hatred of slavery as both an exemplary motif and a dominant family trait (in *this* family)—chapter 4, entitled "The Slave Who Dared to Feel Like a Man," recounts Benjamin / Joseph's perilous struggle to escape: his initial attempt, his recapture, imprisonment, and then his successful flight. In this episode, Brent / Jacobs depicts how she and her maternal grandmother (Aunt Martha / Molly Horniblow) evince conflicted feelings about Benjamin / Joseph's determination to run ("Go and break your mother's heart" Brent / Jacobs impulsively hurls at him, "repenting" immediately), and how Uncle Philip / Mark Ramsey (Aunt Martha / Molly's son) gives the fugitive crucial help. This becomes a pattern for the later episodes of her brother's rebelliousness and imprisonment, and of Brent / Jacobs's own protracted flight, involving her period of isolation in the prisonlike "loophole of retreat," and her grandmother's initial disapproval. As Brent / Jacobs structures her memories, the grandmother is used to articulate the ideal of the slave mother who "stand[s] by [her] own children, and suffer[s] with them till death," a value against which she basically revolts—following her father's outraged desire and the examples of her brother and young uncle—when she takes flight (21, 114, 91). Reading these episodes within the framework of overall narrative themes and motifs underlines the degree to which Brent / Jacobs's escape to freedom evolves primarily out of her identification and association with the men in her family and not the women who, though they may support her, cannot show her the way.[6]

In this chapter, I plan to read Harriet Jacobs's slave narrative against John S. Jacobs's in order to amplify and complicate our understanding of the affective family dynamics, both intra- and interracial, that contribute to Harriet's narrative sense of self. I use these two narratives not only to analyze the ruptures, deliberate suppressions, and unconscious repressions in individual memory that the traumas of slavery imposed upon its victims. I am also interested in reconnecting, if possible, the broken links in what Mary McCarthy once called the "chain of recollection—the collective memory of a family," breaks that slavery ruthlessly caused (5). In the case of the Jacobs family, the "chain of recollection" was cut by loss and secrecy—the death of parents and other family disruptions, and a self-protective code of silence surrounding sexual histories, ingenious hiding places, covert escapes, and fugitive anxieties. That the accumulation of slave testimony might work toward the creation of a collective slave identity seems understood in Harriet's reference to the discrepancies between master and slave perspectives: "*We* could have told them a different story!" (146–47).[7]

The close sibling bond that Harriet and John forged out of the shared traumas of their early childhood—parental loss and soon afterwards the harmful psychological, physical, and sexual conditions of their mutual enslavement—is pivotal to their sense of family relations and, consequently, to each of their identities. Orphaned, they create an emotional unit to substitute for their loss. My first line of argument explores the ways in which their master's sexual harassment of Harriet had a profound impact upon this sibling relation, as well as on each slave individually. For, despite Brent / Jacobs's explicit argument that the nature of the oppression of slave men and women differs not only in degree but in kind, their fates are completely entwined. As mulattoes in a family exhibiting varying degrees of independence (besides their self-supporting father, they had free relations, and their grandmother lived in her own house), Harriet and John S. Jacobs, as slaves within the Norcom household, must have troubled the master's sense of a self-evident boundary between his master class and theirs. The twisted and tireless nature of his sexual pursuit of Harriet, ending only in his defeat, suggests this anxiety of power: he clearly wanted the illusion of her consent to be his mistress. Nevertheless, the structure of their relations originated with him. Orlando Patterson uses the terms slavery's "relation of domination" or "relation of parasitism" to describe the relation of master to slave. "[P]ower ... [in slavery] rests overwhelmingly on influence: it is essentially psychological in nature and rests solely on the character of one person, the master" (335, 307).[8]

My second line of argument concerns the origin and nature of Harriet's and John's mutual and separate resistances to slavery. In this connection, I claim that their overlapping memories of their father, Elijah, are key; for it is Elijah's furious feelings of revulsion against being a slave, his "having more the feelings of a freeman than is common among slaves," that instill in his children the intense hatred of slavery and desire for freedom (*Incidents,* 9). My rereading of *Incidents* in the final sections of this chapter, therefore, begins with an exploration of the ways in which the image of the dead father, Elijah, looms large in his daughter's internal world and how John reinforces the rebelliousness their father symbolized.

Born a slave in Edenton, North Carolina, around 1813, Brent / Jacobs recalls that until she was six, when her mother died, she did not know she was a slave. At that time, she was sent to live with her mother's mistress who, upon her death (betraying a promise to Brent / Jacobs's mother), willed the twelve-year-old slave girl to her sister's five-year-old daughter, the child of Dr. Flint / Norcom. Flint / Norcom began harassing Brent / Jacobs for sex when she turned fifteen, just over two years after her father died. Tormented by the harassment, and mistreated brutally by Flint / Norcom's jealous wife, Brent / Jacobs agreed to become the mistress of Mr. Sands / Sawyer, a neighboring lawyer, who expressed concern for her suffering. Confessing her "sin" to her grandmother, and begging forgiveness, Brent / Jacobs met with stern disapproval; nevertheless, her grandmother took her in after the birth of her two children (the grandmother lived in her own house, earning money by selling her baked goods; her presence and home were stabilizing forces for her family and others in the community).

After Flint / Norcom arranged to send Brent / Jacobs away to his son's plantation and threatened to sell her children, she decided, against her grandmother's advice, to run away, in the hopes that Flint / Norcom would sell her children and relent in his obsession with her. Taking flight, first she hid in the house of a neighboring white woman, who had always been friendly toward her grandmother. But in revenge, Flint / Norcom imprisoned her aunt (her mother's sister), her brother, and her children. After one month, he released the aunt (Mrs. Flint / Norcom needed her at home); after two months, he agreed to sell William / John and the children to Mr. Sands / Sawyer. Brent / Jacobs's family and friends then secured another hiding place—her "loophole of retreat"—a cramped, airless garret in her grandmother's house, where she hid for nearly seven years, while Flint / Norcom's pursuit of her and threats against her family continued. Finally, she was helped to escape North by an old apprentice of her father; reaching New York, she found work with the Bruce family (the family of Nathaniel Parker Willis). After being reunited with her children, who had been sent North separately, Mrs. Bruce / Willis, without her prior knowledge, bought Brent / Jacobs her freedom.

For readers of *Incidents,* "A True Tale" confirms Brent / Jacobs's impressions of people and many of the events she recounts, and supplies details about John's experiences beyond the sister's knowledge or focus—for instance, the private conversations John had with Dr. N—— (Brent / Jacobs's master and tormentor, Dr. Flint / Norcom), whom he assisted; his experiences in jail after Harriet went into hiding; his relation to his new master and his medical practice among the slaves, his plans for escape, and his feelings about running away. In form and theme, John's narrative follows the conventional contours of the male slave narrative, although its striking rigor and blunt style reflect John's own experience and suggest his effectiveness as an abolitionist writer. Less than twelve pages long, "A True Tale" appeared in four installments in February 1861 in a serial called *The Leisure Hour: A Family Journal of Instruction and Recreation.* Following the by-then familiar trajectory of the male slave narrator's progress, John S. Jacobs plots his life from his early years as a slave to his solitary escape as a young man, fitting his identity to an image of manhood that evolved out of eighteenth-century American Revolutionary values, such as individualism, equality, and liberty, and nineteenth-century ideals of self-reliance and economic self-sufficiency. He uses a familiar mix of rhetorical set pieces (for instance, one begins: "To be a man, and not to be a man"), dramatic dialogue and narrative, summary, and overview;

also common to the genre (understandably so) are the narrator's intense hatred for slavery and expressively bitter irony about the hypocrisy of slave owning in a country that proclaims itself to be Christian and democratic. Finally, John's overriding theme, that slavery keeps the male slave from fulfilling his fundamental masculine role as protector of his family, is in keeping with the form's predominately political purposes (as propaganda for abolitionism) and with nineteenth-century cultural ideas about masculine and feminine identity.

But the narrative is not altogether typical. For whereas John seems to position himself in the standard slave narrator role as narrator/protagonist, in some basic sense he seems to have trouble in placing himself as protagonist in relation to his sister. A peculiar tension runs through John's narrative, expressed as an ambiguity as to who the narrative's central protagonist is, or should be. On the one hand, as I have mentioned, the narrative follows John's life from slavery to freedom. On the other, it seems to string the moments in John's life like beads along the thread of his sister's story. So, at one point, John uses the transitional "But to return to my subject" to signal his turning to a description of Harriet's troubles with their master (86). However, this is no "return" at all, but rather the introduction of a new "subject" entirely. With its ever so slight reference to the problem of power between them (who is "subject" to whom), this is one of several disjunctive moments in John's account of his relationship to Harriet—moments that seem to correspond to Harriet's narrative ambiguities surrounding their complicated attachment.[9]

Sexual Exploitation and the Slave Family

The sexual persecution of Harriet Jacobs was not only her own personal torture (it was certainly that), but it also became the central fact in John's (and the rest of their family's) enslavement.

John's fate as a slave was tied to his sister's sexual oppression; his narrative theme, that slavery frustrates the male slave in his desire to fulfill the masculine ideal of family protector, is interwoven with Harriet's narrative theme of slavery's sexual exploitation of enslaved women. Nevertheless, the trauma of sexual abuse, though it might weave their recollections into a fabric of related suffering, is the cause of breaks in memory, both individual and collective.

The master's manipulation of his slave girl's sexual feelings (one of the complicated expressions of sexual power) plays upon the affective and sexual feelings of everyone in their intertwined families (hence, for instance, the figure of the "jealous mistress" in slave narratives). These narratives give a clear view of how sexual exploitation interferes externally with the slave narrators' individual sexual lives, while they can only hint at the presence of internal disruptions, the psychological consequences of sexual abuse. Brent / Jacobs acknowledges the toll that Flint / Norcom's pathological tormenting has on her choice of lover: she rejects the free black man she loves (who resembles her father), and acquiesces to the blandishments of a "master" who appears in a relatively benign guise. John's romantic and sexual attachments are all but absent, and both narratives witness Flint / Norcom's destructive impact on their aunt's and uncle's marriage. At least in these narratives, the master's sexuality dominates the slave's; in defense and resistance, brother and sister circulate through one another's textual dramas in various substitutive roles.

Flint / Norcom's ownership of both brother and sister allows him to wield power over the way they feel about themselves in relation to themselves and one another. Several episodes in *Incidents* show this. Brent / Jacobs presents a scene, just after the birth of her son (by Sands / Sawyer), and when Flint / Norcom's rage and frustration are at a pitch, in which Dr. Flint / Norcom orders William / John to relay a note to Brent / Jacobs to come to his office. She appears before him (her brother is present), and Flint / Norcom asks her where she was when he sent for her. When she tells him she was home, she says, "he flew into a passion, and said he knew better" (61). Flint / Norcom then verbally abuses Brent / Jacobs in front of William / John, pressing her anew to become his mistress. Thus, according to Brent / Jacobs, Flint / Norcom humiliates both Brent / Jacobs, with the obscene verbal assault, and her brother, who stands by "in tears," "powerless" to defend his sister (61).

For Flint / Norcom, lust and the love of power are entwined; there is an erotic lure in owning slaves, or, in Emerson's words, slavery "shows the existence, besides the covetousness, of a bitterer element . . . the voluptuousness of holding a human being in his absolute control" (17). As Brent / Jacobs intimates, behind Flint / Norcom's staging of these mortifying encounters lies jealousy of her relationship with her brother: "I was proud of my brother; and the old doctor suspected as much" she writes; then explains, "[t]his manifestation of feeling [when William / John fights back his tears during the confrontation in the office] irritated the doctor" (61). As if he were William / John's rival, Flint / Norcom deploys his power over these adolescents by causing them to feel shamed by the other in order to poison their intimacy: " 'Don't you hate me, Linda, for bringing you these things?' " William / John asks, fearfully, as he hands her the note; she tells him she "could not blame him" in sorrowful response (61).

Flint / Norcom's power to dominate is further expressed in his compulsively relentless pursuit of Brent / Jacobs and his displaced punishment of William / John whenever she evades his grasp.[10] Frustrated by Brent / Jacobs's successful resistance, Dr. Flint / Norcom acts out his rageful humiliation against William / John, whose job as shop-boy for Flint / Norcom puts him in a position of daily vulnerability. As Brent / Jacobs writes, her brother "could do nothing to please [their master]"; and Flint / Norcom, who will eventually propose to confine Brent / Jacobs in her own cabin, so that he might have unlimited sexual access to her, here seeks a measure of gratification by confining her brother instead. He jails William / John for the first of two times (61).

John's memories of their mutually humiliating encounters as young teenagers with Dr. N—— and Harriet's strategy of resistance, to make herself mistress to a different white man, are strikingly elided. These memories begin with his curiously ambiguous remark about his rhetorical position within his text in relation to Harriet: "But to return to my subject. I left my sister in the doctor's family. Some six or eight years have passed since I was sold [to Norcom], and she has become the mother of two children" (86). So, too, his memories of being jailed—he turns at this point to his second jailing, when he was imprisoned with their aunt and Harriet's two children—suggest a discrepancy in narrative motivation between his own narrative and Harriet's. John paints his time in jail as a respite from Dr. N—— ("Now that the old doctor was gone [to New York] I had a good time"). He also reveals a past that is neither parallel nor "subject" to Harriet's:

Mr. L——, the gaoler, was an old acquaintance of mine. Though he was a white man, and I a slave, we had spent many hours together in Mr. J——'s family. . . . Mr. J—— had a very fine daughter, and we were very fond of each other. . . . Mr. L—— allowed me every indulgence. My friends, such as could come, could call and see me whenever they pleased. (87)

These passages reveal relevant differences between the narratives: there is a gap in their depictions of and elaborations on Harriet Jacobs's sexual history; likewise, the focus of John's account of his experience in jail—his own "good" fortune—asserts not merely a differing subjectivity from Brent / Jacobs's view of the same sequence of events, but a differing subjectivity altogether. This becomes clearer when we compare her experience of this time with his. For Brent / Jacobs, who is by now in hiding from Flint / Norcom, this period is one of agonizing torture, as she thinks of her children in the "loathesome jail" and fears that she may be the cause of their death. Desperate to act, she cites a note she receives from William / John, urging her not to try to come to them, at the risk of bringing ruin to "us all." As Brent / Jacobs describes her unfolding feelings, William / John is transformed from being her "poor William!" who suffers merely "for being my brother," to being her children's surrogate parent, doing "all he could for [my children's] comfort" in prison (101). This is one of several times that Brent / Jacobs, hindered by danger or separation, relies upon William / John to stand in for her as parent. However, John's account of his time in prison *barely* mentions the children; instead, he alludes to a romantic interest (not mentioned in Harriet's narrative) and his own "familial" experiences; he then proceeds to describe his various attempts to maneuver for someone to purchase him from Dr. N——.

What begins to emerge in these relatively early textual juxtapositions is a sense of rupture both within and between the narratives that issue from Flint / Norcom's desire for control over Brent / Jacobs. Harriet's and John's mutually debasing enslavement, their master's power over their sexual and affective relations, and his willingness to make the extended Jacobs family hostage to his obsession, exert upon each account the pressure of culturally unspeakable experiences, thoughts, and feelings; each narrator / protagonist seeks to explain these in ways that fit with his or her overall design for self-representation. Brent / Jacobs's portrayals of herself as suffering slave mother and of her brother as loyal companion are both affirmed and contradicted by John's own ambiguously conceived "subject"—the way he presents himself as autonomous yet constrained by his sister's desires and fate.

The Wedding Trip

The ramifications of Harriet's sexual exploitation for the sibling dynamic and the kinds of questions John's narrative raises for a reading of *Incidents* are amplified in John's account of his close relationship with the man, identified as Mr. S——, who in fact buys him out of jail from Dr. N——. Interestingly, John makes no explicit mention of the fact that this Mr. S—— is his sister's pseudonymous Mr. Sands; only readers of Brent / Jacobs's narrative or people acquainted with her life would be able to connect the Mr. S—— who purchases John (along with the two children) with Mr. Sands / Sawyer. But John's wish to obscure "Mr. S——'s" identity and connection with his sister—in keeping with his suppression of the period during which she becomes Mr. S——'s mistress and bears his children—is not exactly absolute. Moreover, John seems to be worrying about the implications of their three-way interconnecting involvements. The defining incident in this triangle occurs when John accompanies the newly elected Congressman (Samuel Tredwell Sawyer was elected to Congress in 1837) on his wedding trip in August 1838 to Chicago, Canada, and parts of New York State, a circumstance unmentioned in *Incidents,* even though Brent / Jacobs discusses its outcome—John's escape. John's account of this trip suggests the interdependence of master and slave within a system of inequality; the cross-purposes, compromises, deceits, and self-deceptions that characterize their indisputable intimacy; and the bizarre modes of power and force such relations spawn.

John's presence during this bridal journey recalls Patterson's "relation of parasitism." Sawyer, John relates, sees this trip to the free states in the North, especially out to the newly admitted

Illinois, as a "trial" of John's loyalty, of which John has assured him (126). The wedding journey occurs twelve years before the Fugitive Slave Act and nineteen years before the Supreme Court's Dred Scott ruling against Negro citizenship anywhere in the United States. Laws restricted black immigration into Illinois during this period, but were rarely enforced (Litwack, 66–74; Friedman, 220–21). Sawyer recognizes a risk in agreeing to John's wish to go to Chicago (and Canada), but he pushes away his suspicions in favor of the psychologically and politically comforting view of their familial relation, as articulated by proslavery ideologues and nurtured in a fantasy of shared experiences and compatible needs and desires.

However, John dissents from this family romance. In a move of textual aggression, he subverts the polite convention of discreetly using initials to preserve "Mr. S——'s" anonymity.[11] Describing the agreement they make before their trip to Illinois, John tells how Mr. S—— instructs him to pose as his servant and "call me Mr. Sawyer"—the Congressman's real name—if anyone asks who he is. John is true to his word not to escape during their visit to Chicago, where Sawyer marries Lavinia Peyton. With family and friends in New York City, he waits until their return East to run away. His "farewell" note to Sawyer stakes out John's claim to equality with his master—as a human being and a citizen—in his wry and witty manipulation of the form and language of letters: "Sir—I have left you, not to return; when I have got settled, I will give you further satisfaction. No longer yours, John S. Jacobs" (126). Later, he linguistically marks the limit of equality, concluding this chapter with the statement that Mr. Sawyer is a man he would be "pleased to meet . . . as a countryman and a *brother,* but not as a master" (italics mine). John's invocation of the commonplace rhetoric of "brotherhood," with its conflation of the familial and the national, becomes more pointed a trope with its subtle allusion to the hidden nature of their relationship through Harriet. As this suggests, there is something perverse about a rhetoric of brotherhood as ideology when it is deployed within the context of taboos against interracial social and sexual intimacy.[12]

In similar fashion, Brent / Jacobs linguistically discharges aggression against the master class through irony and indirect allusion: "If the secret memoirs of many members of Congress should be published," she remarks dryly, "curious details would be unfolded" (143). When tracing her relationship with Mr. Sands / Sawyer, Brent / Jacobs does identify him as her brother's new master, but she does not note the fact of the wedding trip. Thus, her narrative mutes the complexities of this emotionally fraught triangle (the fact that her brother is the intimate, trusted slave of the man whose mistress she became out of the mixed parts of despair, fear, anger, revenge, hope, gratitude, and affection). As readers, we are left with the question of her reticence.

As with John's silence about the details of his sister's sexual history (suggesting an attitude toward the propriety of or need for telling the other's story), we can speculate that what lies behind Brent / Jacobs's declining to mention the occasion of John's escape is a complex cluster of feelings about her brother's position vis-à-vis herself and Sands / Sawyer. That Brent / Jacobs's feelings *would* be engaged at all is possibly a question, but it seems likely they would be: she carefully explains that her decision to become Sands / Sawyer's mistress occurs in part because Sands / Sawyer deliberately "courted" her (he "expressed a great deal of sympathy, and a wish to aid me" and "by degrees, a more tender feeling [than gratitude] crept into my heart"); and their subsequent sexual relationship lasted several years (54). Brent / Jacobs's sorrowful admission that "the poor slave girl" was no proof against the "too eloquent" manipulations of this "educated and eloquent gentlemen" would complicate further her feelings about Sands / Sawyer and about her brother's role (54). Sands / Sawyer's only advantage over her, as Brent / Jacobs suggests, are those that the privileges of class have put in his way; but his real power is a power to seduce, and exists in his desire and ability to win her gratitude and affection, which happens, in a sense, against her will ("a more tender feeling crept into my heart"). Perhaps, then, Brent / Jacobs's occlusion of the purpose of the two men's journey North, by its very silence, is further evidence of Flint / Norcom's power to frustrate her desire to choose her own lover—"to give one's self, [rather] than submit to compulsion"—a desire that finds painful expression in her decision to enter into the secret liaison with Mr. Sands / Sawyer (55).

In this way, the two narratives enact the piecing together of the life fragments that slavery created—the self-division, disruptions, and silences that the traumas of slavery forced upon sister and brother.

Imprisonment and Escape

These narrative discrepancies, ruptures, masks, and suppressions bear the mark of unavoidable conflict between Brent / Jacobs's and her brother's actual and narrative interests. This conflict seems taken up in *Incidents* as a potential theme when Brent / Jacobs, still "imprisoned" herself in her "loophole of retreat," hears word of William / John's escape. Whatever joy and defiance she might feel at his daring are mixed with less jubilant feelings, and her response to his flight—in her depictions of her grandmother's reaction and of her own—conveys elements of her ambivalence.

While her grandmother wept so hard "you would have thought the messenger had brought tidings of death instead of freedom. . . . I was selfish," she writes, for "I thought more of what I had lost, than what my brother had gained. A new anxiety began to trouble me," she continues, that "this might injure the prospects [for freedom] of my children" (134). In her present narrative persona as suffering slave mother, Brent / Jacobs organizes her narrative around her sustained efforts to protect her children; but, as suggested before, she more often than not must rely on others, and frequently on her brother, to watch out for them during her prolonged absences. In John's narrative, the children drop out as figures after their purchase by Mr. S——; but in *Incidents,* William / John continues to be, in some ways (along with their grandmother), their most consistent caretaker. Just as he had looked after them in the South when Brent / Jacobs was in hiding, he does so when she is a fugitive in the North: she "place[s]" her son in her brother's "care" while she works as a live-in servant at the home of the Bruce / Willises; and she relies on William / John for news about her children during her ten-month stay in England with Mr. Bruce / Willis. He also helps her pay for her daughter's schooling, and, following the enactment of the Fugitive Slave Act, he looks after her son, who follows him to California to look for work. Necessity dictates Brent / Jacobs's movements in the North: she is a fugitive whom the Flint / Norcom family continues to hound, and she needs employment. Luckily, William / John, who is no one's obsession and who remains nearby between stints as a sailor, can aid his sister often.

My point is not that John should not have been called upon to play the role of surrogate father, but that, because of the circumstances of Harriet's oppression, he *had* to be. Thus, the curious agitation surrounding the tale's "subject" seems in part to be an expression of the ways in which the complex sibling relation that arose out of Norcom's obsession with Harriet are in conflict with John's development of his own self. So, John's remark about the unfair effects of Harriet's struggle against Norcom on the marriage of their aunt and uncle is haunted by an unspoken comment upon his own unjust fate. "It was most cruel that they should be separated, not for their own, but for another's acts," John writes, referring to the doctor's retaliation against the couple he separates for Harriet's persistent refusal to acquiesce (108). His belief that the narrative somehow demands that his "subject" ought to be Harriet recalls the limitations placed on the young boy and man; and they both seem to be saying, your life is tied to your sister's. In John's remark, then, there lurks an invitation to consider his confusion as an effort to suppress prohibited feelings and desires.

This possibility also seems to shadow John's account of his decision to escape, when his perception of his special obligations to Harriet, who remains in hiding in North Carolina, emerges. John describes how, when trying to choose between "leav[ing]" his master during their stay up North, or returning South, where "there was my sister and a friend of mine" (is this the daughter of "Mr. J——"?), he consults "some of my old friends," asking them, " 'Now tell me my duty'. . . . The answer was a very natural one. 'Look out for yourself first' " (126). John follows their advice, reasoning: "If I returned along with my master, I could do my sister no good, and could see no further chance of my own escape" (126).

John's dilemma—self-interest versus duty to others—is quickly resolved (at least in his narrative). So, too, does the narrative quickly close over the slight window into John's personal life that, perhaps, is opened with the passing reference to his "friend"; for this "friend" disappears from the text entirely, without a trace. Conventions of genre and gender, discouraging intimate self-revelation, may explain the vanishing. Nevertheless, this minor eruption in the textual surface calls into question the narrative identity that John ostensibly constructs, one that is defined primarily by his connection to his slave sister.

Loss and Love in Incidents

The intensity of the relationship between brother and sister implied by some of these scenes is rooted, arguably, in the shared tragedies of their early childhood—the loss of their parents, their mutual enslavement, their mental and physical exploitation and domination by the same man (or men). Brent / Jacobs's earliest memories of her brother confirm this, as they evoke a nexus of feelings associated with her father and her anxieties about loss and attachment (their removal to Flint / Norcom's house and their father's death soon after are important triggering events). After each loss, the narrator expresses her fundamental need to have "something left to love"; this is a phrase that, in her usage, traces her affective and cognitive linking of father and brother as primary objects of love and attachment. A child's identity depends upon having "something . . . to love," which affirms that she is loved. This phrase, however, as it first appears in *Incidents,* is used ironically, to highlight Brent / Jacobs's false sense of security as a young girl: she has just witnessed the burial of a "dear little friend" and the mother's inconsolable grief, and found herself "feeling thankful that I still had something to love" when, the next moment, her grandmother gives her the news of her father's death (9–10).

Brent / Jacobs next uses the phrase in connection with her brother, as she struggles against despair at having felt forced to abandon her dream of marrying the man she loved, a neighboring free-born "colored carpenter." This man's resemblances to her father are affirmed when Brent / Jacobs laments that, to give this man children who would be slaves because of her, would prove "a terrible blight . . . on the heart of a free, intelligent father" (42). Thus, their separation ruffles the layers in the palimpsest of affective memories that make up their lives. Seeking consolation for this thick loss, then, Brent / Jacobs, like other

79

mourners, finds compensation among the present and the living in "my good grandmother and my affectionate brother. When he put his arms round my neck, and looked into my eyes, as if to read the troubles I dared not tell, I felt that I still had something to love" (42). Indeed, while her epithet for her grandmother is "good" and, accordingly, "my good grandmother" is associated throughout the narrative with a certain take on moral courage and sustenance (with her baking, she is the reason the children have enough food), so William / John is "my affectionate brother," linked to the kind of familial attachments that are critical to a child's development and survival. In this way, William / John is functionally and symbolically Brent / Jacobs's father, mother, sibling, and "husband"—a role narratively reinforced by his care for her children.

Under the sexual pressure of the master, the sibling bond that serves as parental substitute, stemming feelings of loss and frustrated rage, thereby may also become enmeshed with other familial, sexual feelings. The triangular involvements the two are enslaved into, first with Norcom / Flint and then with Sands / Sawyer, throw brother and sister into a confusing relation, in which distress and desire become intimately related. These triangles, signs of white disruption and distortion of black familial relations, appear across the historical expanse of African American literature: think of Gustavus Vassa and his sister clasping hands all night across the body of their sleeping master who lies in the middle; of Du Bois's two Johns and sister Jennie in the furious "Of the Coming of John."

The Reunion

Questions of memory and representation arise in the wake of any autobiographical account; when two autobiographies converge upon one another such questions become, in some ways, the point. The two Jacobses' narratives come face to face in an electrifying pair of passages in which the narrators describe their reunion in New York in 1843. Both Brent / Jacobs and William / John are fugitives in the North, and they have not seen one another for five years. She is the live-in nursemaid to the infant daughter of the Bruce / Willises, still separated from her own children (Benny / Joseph is still in the South, while Ellen / Louisa lives in Brooklyn, with first cousins of her father's). William / John, who after his escape had shipped out of New Bedford on a whaling voyage, is just returned after three-and-a-half years. These are the two mirroring passages:

One bright morning, as I stood at the window, tossing baby in my arms, my attention was attracted by a young man in sailor's dress, who was closely observing every house as he passed. I looked at him earnestly. Could it be my brother William? It *must* be he—and yet, how changed! . . . How much we had to tell each other! How we laughed, and how we cried, over each other's adventures! (170)

I found my sister living with a family as nurse at the Astor House. At first she did not look natural to me; but how should she look natural, after having been shut out from the light of heaven for six years and eleven months? I did not wish to know what her sufferings were, while living in her place of concealment. The change it had made in her was enough to make one's soul cry out against this curse of curses, that has so long trampled humanity in the dust. (127)

At first glance, this convergence actually seems to point toward the narrators' alienation, in the radically opposed tones of the passages (hers, sentimental; his, dryly realistic) and in the way the narrators seem to have had totally different experiences ("How we laughed, and how we cried, over each other's adventures!" in contrast to "I did not wish to know what her sufferings were, while living in her place of concealment"): she suggests their meeting was all openness, a rush of words, empathy, and relief; while he recalls reserve and pain. Moreover, the responses are ambiguous. Is the change in William / John in Brent / Jacobs's eyes merely one of age? Or is it the uniform that effects the change? Does he look better, worse, or simply strange? Why does Brent / Jacobs resort to generalized sentiments ("How we laughed," and so forth) to describe what must have been an emotionally complex meeting? On the other hand, why does John not wish to know, and are we to read his response as protective or hostile? These questions are not posed in order to negate the intense familial love between them, nor to dispute that, as Brent / Jacobs ends the chapter, "There are no bonds so strong as those which are formed by suffering together" (170). But they are meant to extend consideration of the ways in which the two narratives show that "suffering together" complicates feelings.

Yet, despite the presence of hints of alienation and aggression, the differing registers within and between their responses, each narrator's own self-representation finds confirmation in the gaze of the other.[13] To be represented in another's text—interior and exterior, in their mind or book—is in itself existential confirmation, regardless of the nature of the correspondence between object and representation. And although identity, some have argued, is violated by representation, it is inconceivable without it.[14]

Their recollected identities—of each other, of their family, of their enslaved culture—are created in the dialectic of these intensely visually rendered counterimpressions of their reunion. To Brent / Jacobs, William / John's appearance embodies the story of masculine freedom: mobile, aggressive, self-supporting, displaying the material gains of his profession. By contrast, she is still confined, tending someone else's baby in someone else's home. For John, his sister's appearance translates into an icon of suffering. When he remarks, "she did not look natural . . . having been shut out from the light of heaven," he notes the connection between physical sign and moral history, and yokes together the physical and spiritual worlds, turning Harriet's pallor (her physical suffering) into an illuminated symbol of spiritual deprivation and oppression. Thus, weaving together the popular American themes of masculine competitiveness, activity, and independence, and feminine selflessness and moral suffering with the theme of the African American experience of bondage and emancipation, these narratives together participate in the task of revising the memory of those living in the antebellum United States.

The Dead Father

> [A] father who is dead may be carried within the child's mind as a very alive figure.
> —Joyce McDougall, "The Dead Father"

It is Elijah's presence in the two accounts—as remembered figure and significant imago in the minds of his children—that creates a bridge between the narratives.[15] He is the key symbolic link between brother and sister, and the starting point in Brent / Jacobs's narrative associative chain, connecting father-uncle-son-daughter-escape. In the rest of the chapter, I take up the rereading of Brent / Jacobs's narrative that the counterpoint with John's narrative suggests, focusing on the presence of the father in the daughter's narrative.

Condemning slavery for its destruction of the slave family, Frederick Douglass argues in his 1845 *Narrative* that slavery killed his "natural" feelings for his mother by forcing their separation when he was an infant (as was the custom, she was hired out to a distant farm). However, his return to (and the return of) his mother in the later revised autobiographies, where she figures more prominently in his childhood memories and functions as an important imago in his internal sense of himself, suggests that a slave child's bonds to his or her parents, like other children's, was made of a synergistic mixture of memories and fantasy, which early loss and deprivation shaped but did not eradicate.

A staple of the critical discussion of *Incidents* is to make a claim for the centrality of the impact of Brent / Jacobs's mother's death on her life and fate as a slave girl—to see it, as she sees it, as the time when she discovered she was a slave. But the death of Elijah six years later, when Brent / Jacobs was around twelve (and John, ten), should be read as an equally clarifying moment in her life story, setting off lifelong reverberations. Moreover, Brent / Jacobs's use of a paternal imago is suggestive of her narrative orientation toward her brother John. Indeed, Brent / Jacobs's narration of the way their relationship gets played out, given the contingencies of slavery and fugitive life, is in part a memorial to their father.

Indeed, the most emphatic overlap between the two narratives is in the characterization of Elijah. Each portrays a man who was independent-minded, sensitive to attacks upon his dignity, and forceful ("he had more the feelings of a freeman than is common among slaves," Brent / Jacobs notes); both stress that it was their father who taught them "to feel that they were human beings" (Brent / Jacobs's phrase) by "bestow[ing] upon both of us" (as John puts it) "some rays of intellectual light, which the tyrant could not rob us of" (*Incidents*, 9, 10; "A True Tale," 86). In his identification with his father, John dwells upon Elijah's anger, frustration, and hatred for slavery, writing that "My father taught me to hate slavery, but forgot to teach me how to conceal my hatred," and he ascribes his father's death to a "mental dejection" caused by slavery, "combined with bodily illness" (86).[16] Both claim to have vivid memories of Elijah: as John writes, "my father made impressions on my mind in childhood that can never be forgotten" (85). And Brent / Jacobs explicitly links her flight to her father's legacy when, in reverie over her parents' graves, she seems "to hear [her] father's voice come from it, bidding [her] not to tarry till [she] reached freedom or the grave" (91). In many ways, these narratives of resistance are textual monuments to a slave father who had the spirit of a freedman, but who, because a slave, would in the usual course of things be destined to oblivion.

This point is made in *Incidents* in several ways: in Brent / Jacobs's comment after his death that "There were those who knew my father's worth, and respected his memory"; in her remark that the "letters" on her father's grave marker were "nearly obliterated"; and in her later observation that, when her Uncle Phillip / Mark died and an obituary notice appeared in a Southern paper, "it was the only case I ever knew of such an honor conferred upon a colored person" (10, 90, 201). In all this, Brent / Jacobs seems clearly to have in mind the significance of her narrative as commemorating the "colored" dead.

Accordingly, it is the death of the father that signals the introduction into Brent / Jacobs's narrative consciousness of the necessity of resistance as a mode of survival and a way out of slavery. She records experiencing her first jolt of rage against absolute authority (her grandmother's idealized, divine Master) when she is told about her father's death: "My heart rebelled against God, who had taken from me mother, father, mistress, and friend" (10). Her grandmother tries "to comfort her," telling her to trust in Him; and as the scene unfolds, Brent / Jacobs recoils from her own anger, and assumes her grandmother's less terrifying attitudes of meekness and self-denial. Religious faith may make slavery bearable (and as history will prove may inspire community, cultural resistance, and political action), but it leaves the stricken child feeling isolated, vulnerable, and guilt-ridden: "My home now seemed more dreary than ever. The laugh of the little slave-children sounded harsh and cruel. It was selfish to feel so about the joy of others" (10). She describes William / John as despairing and bitter, and tells of her attempts to offer him the solace of the powerless.

My brother moved about with a very grave face. I tried to comfort him, by saying, "Take courage, Willie; brighter days will come by and by."

"You don't know anything about it, Linda" he replied. "We shall have to stay here all the days of our lives. We shall never be free." (10)

Their difference at this point, which remains a typical strain throughout, is evidence of John's less conflicted identification with their angry father, an identification both psychologically motivated and culturally endorsed. Brent / Jacobs seems to be using these early scenes to negotiate her desire to follow both mother (embodied in the maternal grandmother) and father— to be like both parental imagos. In her "daily controversies" with her brother, through which she enacts both sides of her embattled feelings, Brent / Jacobs counsels faith and patience, while William / John advocates revolutionary defiance: "he did not intend to *buy* his freedom" (10). (Interestingly, this is the troubling position in which Brent / Jacobs finds herself at the end of the narrative, when the well-intentioned Mrs. Bruce / Willis—whose self-conception as patroness has some maternal aspects—buys Brent / Jacobs her freedom.)

In the next chapter in which the thread of her personal narrative of growing resistance is again taken up (chapter 4, "The Slave Who Dared to Feel Like a Man"), Brent / Jacobs becomes more radicalized, adopting the rebellious attitude of her brother and teenaged uncle. Grandmother's faith in providential deliverance is "a beautiful faith," but no longer persuasive to a girl who has endured two years in Dr. Flint / Norcom's family. This chapter, in establishing the prototype for the slave's resistance, associates Benjamin / Joseph and William / John in their "bold[ness] and daring" and "aversion to the word master," and in so doing makes them textual surrogates for the deceased Elijah, whose hatred for slavery was what he truly willed to his children (17). Building upon these hints of coming into consciousness in the ensuing episodes, Brent / Jacobs interlaces the thoughts and feelings of her teenaged uncle, her brother, and herself as they try to cope with the growing cruelty and perversions of their enslavement. Their wishes are communal: "We reasoned . . . We longed" she writes of her shared secrets with her young uncle (17). "He came to me with all his troubles," she says of her brother (18). Being orphaned is a defining component of their prospectless enslavement: "But we, who were slave-children, without father or mother, could not expect to be happy" (18). To start toward freedom (literally and figuratively) entails the internal reconstitution of family—an inner world symbolically inhabited by parental imagos to love, to be loved by, and identify with. For Brent / Jacobs, this means the internalization of what is perceived to be the father's spirit of rebellion and revulsion against absolute authority, as well as of the maternally associated capacities for self-sacrifice, holding, and remembering. To start for freedom, for Brent / Jacobs, means to have with her her remnant family—her children and herself in her children—in a home of her own. This means to be both mother and father to them and to herself.

Not surprisingly, then, Brent / Jacobs records in this chapter her first forceful act of resistance to Flint / Norcom, marking the moment with her declaration of a new credo which incorporates both maternal faith and paternal aggression, or rather, maternal faith *in* paternal aggression: "The war of my life had begun; and though one of God's most powerless creatures, I resolved never to be conquered" (19). Consequently, her identification with "some sparks of my brother's God-given nature" symbolically conflates father and God (19).

Throughout, Brent / Jacobs's narrative exhibits her careful negotiation of contrary identifications with alternative parental imagos: on the one hand, her idealized, virtuous mother (with her narrative connections to her sympathetic audience); on the other hand, her idealized, rebellious father (with his narrative associations to the heroic Nat Turner). This is given intensified expression in the moving scene at her parents' grave. The shame Brent / Jacobs speaks of feeling throughout her narrative is tied up with her grandmother's resurrection of the idealized maternal imago, whose memory she says is disgraced by Brent / Jacobs's "fall." Still, in order to reach this point, at her parents' graveside, wrangling with her conscience over her decision to leave her children behind, Brent / Jacobs has had to begin to deflect being condemned according to culturally dominant views of female virtue: something she has done by politicizing her decision to become Sands / Sawyer's mistress, arguing that slave women should be exonerated, since they are slavery's and the master's victims. Nonetheless, she comes to the "burying ground of the slaves" in need of further justification in order to transform dreams of flight into action (90).

Brent / Jacobs makes this pilgrimage to the gravesite in anticipation of a double break—from her childhood (that is, from her parents) and from her children; thus, her visit serves both to allay her anxieties over loss, a central theme in her life, and to square her precipitation of further loss (the loss of herself to her children) with motherhood. This occurs during a visionary experience at her parents' graveside, in which she affirms an identification with her father's spirit, an identification that is conveyed in unmistakably revolutionary terms.

Functionally and figuratively, this is the slave's ritual enactment of a scene familiar in the literature of romanticism, a culturally validated rite. The graveyard in the woods is a spot she had "frequented . . . but never had it seemed to me so sacred as now" (90). Coded in the terms of nineteenth-century romanticism, this secluded, solemn site makes provision for a deeply personal and emotional experience. More importantly, it naturalizes and sanctifies the slave's desire to be free. In this scene, the father figures as the principal agent of desire to alter the cultural landscape: "A black stump" is all that is left of a tree he had planted at her mother's grave, and the "letters" on his grave marker are "nearly obliterated" (90). Thus, he points the way, authorizing motive and justification for writing anew—first in action, then in recollection—the story of the slave's desire for agency and autonomy.

The necessity of receiving paternal—and by textual association, ideological—authorization to flee delineates the limitations of Brent / Jacobs's feminism, if we insist on measuring her against twentieth-century standards. But, we might also say that in choosing to follow her father she is following her own heart, and that associating her desire to act with the "masculine" does not constitute an argument for these wishes being essentially "male." In fact, quite the opposite, since the father is as much "inside" the daughter as "inside" the son.

Thus, at this site, in which continuity and loss, the sacred and the worldly are intermingled, the narrative proposes the radical ideas that a slave's revolt is sacred and that running from slavery is a transcendent act: Brent / Jacobs moves associatively from the "wreck of the old meeting house," which she passes, to a recollection of "Nat Turner's time," to her father's voice issuing "God-like" from the house of worship, urging her to get gone: "I seemed to hear my father's voice come from it, bidding me not to tarry till I reached freedom or the grave" (91).[17]

At this point, it might be useful to reaffirm that recognizing Brent / Jacobs's identification with her father, and the degree to which this identification is mobilized through her relationship to her brother, does not of course negate the important role Brent / Jacobs's maternal identification plays in her narrative sense of self, nor the degree to which her grandmother's presence is a crucial, saving one. But the two identifications do seem to be in narrative tension, and Brent / Jacobs subtly suppresses the paternal presence in her own narrative.

The significance of this may be observed in a nexus of memories, beginning with one in which Brent / Jacobs actually seems to insert her brother (as well as her uncle Phillip / Mark) into the narrative as a model for maternal caretaking. Earlier, I emphasized John's paternal care for her children. But it is Brent / Jacobs's description of how he helps to nurse her during her seven-year concealment that hints at the possibility of reconfiguring the narrative's allegedly purely maternal discourse.

During her second grueling winter in the nine-by-seven-by-three-foot garret, her "loophole of retreat," Brent / Jacobs's

limbs were benumbed by inaction, and the cold filled them with cramp. . . . My brother William came and did all he could for me. Uncle Phillip also watched tenderly over me; and poor grandmother crept up and down to inquire whether there were any signs of returning life. I was restored to consciousness by the dashing of cold water in my face, and found myself leaning against my brother's arm, while he bent over me with streaming eyes. (122)

In this tableau, it is the men who "tenderly" (maternally) nurse the invalid, "ben[ding] over [her] with streaming eyes"—a change from their role as protectors—while the concerned grandmother ducks in and out for news. As a "gendered" scene, then, it may be said to run against type; so it is noteworthy that this memory is used to set up two others, in which Brent / Jacobs herself, fearful of detection, is unable to "mother" first her sick grandmother and then, more significantly, her ailing son.

When her grandmother falls sick under the strain of their situation, all Brent / Jacobs can do is pray for her recovery, since she "could not tend upon her, who had so long and tenderly watched over me!" (123). The theme of thwarted "maternal" desire is amplified in Brent / Jacobs's account of her frustration when, during her grandmother's illness, her son is bitten by a dog and stands blood-covered and screaming right outside her peep-hole. It is, she writes, "torture to a mother's heart to listen to this and be unable to go to him!" (123).

Yet it is here that we may return to the question of the suppression of the "male narrative" in the critical literature on *Incidents*. For what happens in this cluster of scenes in Brent / Jacobs's own narrative is a rhetorical move that is mirrored in current criticism of the narrative. Although Brent / Jacobs locates her models for nursing in her brother and this uncle, she immediately situates herself within the discourse of motherhood—"a mother's heart"—thereby rhetorically gendering the concept of caretaking as female, a move reinforced by inversion with examples of granddaughterly love. This gendering (a staple of women's sentimental fiction from which *Incidents* derives) therefore obscures a narrative fact: that the chapter's prominent symbols of caretaking, even in the womblike garret, are two men.

A similar slippage also occurs around the idea of Brent / Jacobs's flight. Again, Brent / Jacobs "learns" how to escape from slavery from the model of various important men in her life— from her father's proud resistant mien, to her uncle Benjamin / Joseph's precedent-setting escape, to William / John's flight from Mr. Sands / Sawyer; indeed, she owes the success of her actual flight North to the planning and guidance of her father's apprentice (in contrast, her various Southern retreats are more fully associated with women). While retreat (as in her "loophole") is symbolic of affiliation to the "feminine," advancing North requires her to become "masculine" in mode: that is, in dress (she wears a sailor's disguise) and in relation to familial encumbrances (she leaves her children in others' hands). But because of the culturally impressed strictures of the genre, as well as the internalized demands of psychology and ideology,

Brent / Jacobs seems to strive to impress upon the reader that the moral and bodily forces behind her flight are to be found in her efforts to live up to Victorian "feminine" ideals of virtue and motherhood.

In so doing, it seems, she was in part following the editorial advice of Lydia Maria Child. We know that in a letter written to Jacobs before the narrative's publication, Child suggested Jacobs significantly revise the ending to emphasize the themes of motherhood and Christian self-sacrifice: "I think the last Chapter, about John Brown, had better be omitted. . . . Nothing can be so appropriate to end with, as the death of your grandmother."[18] Like the ongoing invocations to her female audience that are assertions of difference (I was a slave, you were not), softened by identification (we are all sisters), these narrative deflections of "masculine" aggression by "feminine" suffering seem meant to align Brent / Jacobs as slave girl and woman with the images of slave women popularized by antislavery "women of the North."

That is, by the feminist foremothers of many of us who have taken up our pens on the slave woman's behalf today. The interlocking ideologies of motherhood and sisterhood that structure Harriet Jacobs's narrative are homologous with those undergirding much contemporary feminist writing on women's slave narratives, with its emphasis on communities of women, separate spheres, and maternal object-relations. Because of this, the African American "masculine" counterplot of Jacobs's account—the primacy of her relations to and her identification with slave men—has been obscured from view. But the double resurrection of John Jacobs's narrative and Elijah's memory enables us to paint a more complex portrait of Harriet Jacobs. Such intricacies of identity and family dynamics also should remind us that the structures of opposition that slip readily into hierarchies—of white over black, male over female—and serve to justify enslavement do not, simply in their reversal, ensure emancipation.

CHAPTER 4

Objects of Mourning in Elizabeth Keckley's *Behind the Scenes*

> I considered my clothes and the little things I had when
> in slavery my own but I didn't see it as I do now. I see now
> that every thing I considered my own didn't belong to me,
> but could be taken from me at any time. I didn't set the
> same store by my little things that I do now, for I didn't
> see things then as I do now.
>
> —Mrs. Joseph Wilkinson, ex-slave, 1863

It has been the fate of Elizabeth Keckley's 1868 slave narrative, *Behind the Scenes; or, Thirty Years a Slave and Four Years in the White House,* to be overshadowed by Harriet Jacobs's *Incidents in the Life of a Slave Girl.* One reason for this may be its unsuitability as a representative text. With a title-page describing Mrs. Keckley as "formerly a slave, but more recently modiste, and friend to Mrs. Lincoln," *Behind the Scenes* takes as its subject "the secret history" of Mrs. Lincoln's ill-fated "old-clothes" sale of 1867, not the secret history of slavery. Her purpose in writing is to defend her reputation, in her connection to Mrs. Lincoln. "My own charac-ter, as well as the character of Mrs. Lincoln, is at stake, since I have been intimately associated with that lady in the most eventful periods of her life. . . . To defend myself I must defend the lady I have served" (xiv). Although Keckley's narrative uses many of the *topoi* of the typical antebellum slave narrative—the parting of the parents, the slave auction, the first whipping—it is clearly motivated by different intentions and needs.

Unlike antebellum narratives which elaborate upon the years in slavery in order to underscore its horrors and fuel abolitionism, then wind down quickly after the protagonist / narrator reaches the North, Keckley's postbellum account shifts the emphasis, devoting no more than one-eighth of her book, the first three chapters, to her slavery years.[1] Where the antebellum slave narrative is oppositional, a literature of protest, the postbellum narrative needs to adopt a different posture. "Thirty years a slave" must be, in a sense, narrative prehistory to the main event: Keckley's postslavery identity. Referring to slavery as a "hardy school" which taught her "self-reliance," Keckley seems to stand near the beginning of a line of black autobiographers who treat their years of personal suffering as a process of assimilation into white culture. The trajectory of these lives is (as Booker T. Washington would put it) "up from slavery"; the underlying message to black audiences is inspirational uplift, while the point to be taken by white readers is the non-threatening, "we want to be like you."

Thus, this version of "self-reliance," Darryl Pinckney notes in a 1995 review essay, does not mean "Emerson's aversion to conformity" or "independence of mind"; rather, it takes the form of a "self-satisfaction" about having become—in Keckley's specific case—a successful, Washington businesswoman and model citizen in a colored community which shares and more than exemplifies the values of the dominant white culture (41). With its lessons of hard work, slavery becomes a guarantee of the ex-slave's conformism to Northern social values. In this mode, what William L. Andrews calls Keckley's "materialist and pragmatic mode of self-valuation" replaces the "idealism and essentialism of Jacobs's moral standard" as a means of reshaping the slave narrative genre to meet new historical conditions and ideological and psychological demands ("The Changing Moral Discourse," 237).

But the narrative of success is itself prescriptive, especially in its postbellum forms, shaping as much as reflecting the identity of the culturally marginalized writer. Then, too, it contains traps for the African American, as a history of backlashes against black social, political, and economic advances proves. ("That definition of self-reliance," Pinckney observes of the Emersonian view, "may have been a transcendent goal for the white, but it could end in a lynching for the black" [41].) Not surprisingly, *Behind the Scenes* was targeted for attack. A vicious parody, published in New York by National News, appeared almost immediately, called *Behind the Seams: By a Nigger Woman Who Took in Work from Mrs. Lincoln and Mrs. Davis,* and signed with an *x* (her mark) by "Betsey Kickley." With a class resentment reminiscent of Fielding's parody of Pamela's "vartue" in *Shamela,* the author of this attack clearly sees the mulatta Keckley as an example of a slave girl who has forgotten her place. The *New York Citizen* listed Keckley's book as the latest in a series of scandalous exposés, and called it "grossly and shamelessly indecent . . . an offence of the same grade as the opening of other people's letters, the listening at keyholes, or the mean system of espionage which unearths family secrets with a view to blackmailing the unfortunate victims."[2] Robert Lincoln, the Lincolns's oldest son, had the publisher G. W. Carleton recall the book, and bought up every copy he could.[3] Though variously motivated, the offended all seem to have been antagonized by Keckley's trespass across the racially defined social, class, and behavioral barriers that legalized slavery had reinforced.

Keckley's own relation to her narrative seems highly vexed as well, as indicated by her apparent difficulty in assuming a clearly coherent rhetorical position. Indeed, *Behind the Scenes* seems to enact linguistically the oscillations and fragmentation of Keckley's attitude toward herself and others. These shifts and fissures are perceptible in the narrative transformations of the specific external conditions and events into the significant symbols of Keckley's inner world.

A good example of narrative transformation is in Keckley's response to the vicissitudes of slave motherhood. With her self-identified position as Mrs. Lincoln's "modiste and confidante" (employee and intimate), Keckley refuses identification with an image of Otherness—the suffering, subordinated slave woman who had sustained the antebellum narrative viewpoint. For despite its use as a point of interracial identification between women (a sisterhood of gendered sameness), the emphasis on the passive suffering slave woman highlights her difference from her more privileged, active, white "sisters." More pointedly, in light of Jacobs's precedent, Keckley renounces her claim to the role of suffering slave mother.[4]

Keckley's suppression of her son in the narrative—he even remains unnamed—is one striking feature of her rhetorical position vis-à-vis motherhood, and one to which I will return throughout this chapter. At this juncture, however, it is necessary only to cite the single comment she makes regarding her feelings about his birth—the outcome of an unwanted four-year relationship with a white man whom she also refuses to name. "If my poor boy ever suffered any humiliating pangs on account of his birth, he could not blame his mother, for God knows that she did not wish to give him life; he must blame the edicts of that society which deemed it no crime to undermine the virtue of girls in my then position" (39).[5]

Taken as a piece of social criticism, Keckley's critique of slavery custom and law issues from an analytic position that disavows emotional or cognitive entanglements with the situation itself. As Frances Smith Foster sees it, Keckley unapologetically "assigns to herself the role that Lydia Maria Child played in Jacobs's text"—the white observer whose social and political criticism is not contaminated by involvement in whatever falling off from cultural norms has ensued (*Written By Herself,* 121).[6] Thus, in her apparently guilt-free break from the conflicts intrinsic to surviving the assaults of slavery (conflicts arising out of the need to adapt oneself to a hostile environment), Keckley must suppress at least this one "black" familial attachment. The victim status of the antebellum slave narrator, centered in the assaults against her slave family, underwrites her moral claim to writing a tale of rebellion, redemption, and transcendence; by contrast, Keckley's posture of "self-reliance," which entails some narrative suppression of family, implicates her account as a form of defensive accommodation to suffering as it deflects anger away from white figures of authority. This deflection is hinted at, for instance, in the tone of reproach and blame she takes toward her son (as it would seem) in guilt- and anger-inflected anticipation of his— or her audience's—reproach and blame of *her.*

To read *Behind the Scenes* is to be faced with a range of equally contradictory attitudes and desires, expressive of some of the questions of identity that seem to converge for Keckley as she tries to account for the trajectories of astonishing change, both in the culture at large and in her personal life. Narrative constructions of self take their contours from larger cultural and literary movements in interaction with the historical specificities of individual experience, but the nature of this interaction depends upon the position of the narrating subject in relation to perceived cultural norms.

The Antillean psychiatrist Franz Fanon's psychoanalytic observations on colonial subjects provides a useful framework for understanding Keckley's narrative task, even though the analogy between colonialism and U. S. slavery is not exact. Fanon claims that the white child who moves from the family (the originating focus of psychoanalytic inquiry) to the culture at large experiences a psychological fit.[7] But under colonized conditions, in which the experience of a white self is normalized, the black self "will become abnormal on the slightest contact with the white world" (143). The drama of identity for the black self, Fanon maintains, is always about being "called upon to live constantly with white compatriots" apart from the black family, which has no viable connection with the structure of the nation. Therefore, "the individual who climbs up in [white] society . . . tends to reject his family . . . on the plane of imagination" and push it back into the Freudian "scenes" of early childhood trauma (149).

Writing from within and writing about the tangled relations between enslavement and freedom in her narrative "up from slavery," which entails her ties to "black" family and "white" family and her more generalized relations to white society (the focus of her narrative, though she is clearly also part of a well-defined colored community), Keckley seems to be struggling with the problem of devising a strategy for linguistically orienting herself in relation to an external world of others in a way that is relevant to her inner world of internalized object relations, while using the conventions of a slightly outmoded genre. It is a complicated task, especially during a period when the political status of nonwhite people—and, therefore, of white people—was in a state of upheaval, while at the same time racially structured social and economic hierarchies were still rigidly in place. Fanon's analysis provides for a process of constructing identity in which the black subject's impulse toward a unified sense of self within a white world that has spawned and enforced his or her oppression almost inevitably involves self-suppression and self-fragmentation. *Behind the Scenes* discloses the ways in which Keckley's tale of self-reliance depends upon related strategies of unconscious repression or deliberate suppression, substitutions, splitting, and inversions that seem intended to mask some of the anger and sorrow associated with her experiences of racism and slavery— what lies "behind the scenes" of her success in the white world.

It is my argument, then, that there exists a subtext of unspoken "scenes" more deeply recessed "behind the scenes" than those most obviously referred to in the title. This "behind the scenes" is, indeed, the necessarily suppressed and repressed life of a mulatta woman serving in a White House in the 1860s. So framed, this approach to Keckley's narrative constitutes an attempt to take into account the many tensions between opposing and layered narrative elements: the upward-mobility encoded in her narrative plotting and her high valuation of self-reliance and—"behind" these—the concealed scenes of personal mourning and the displaced expressions of both rage and longing for personal losses.

As linguistic manifestations of their narrators' desire and suffering, slave narratives hinge upon strategies for turning losses into gains. For Keckley, the symbolic nexus of loss and gain is evoked in its most compressed fashion in the belongings and mementoes she gathers and saves over the course of her life— "the most precious mementoes of my existence . . . the old faded letters . . . full of love" (25). Here, she is referring specifically to her father's letters to her mother, written after their permanent separation when Keckley was between four and eight years old, but the way these letters figure in her sense of her own "existence" is true of the many documents and mementoes she places before the reader throughout her narrative. Keckley's father's letters, born of his absence, seem meant to document textually her experiences of her father; when she interpolates one into her own narrative it seems to be presented as proof of her father's existence and love, not only as a "fact" in the past but (more importantly) as a reality in the present—as long as rereading is a possibility.

In her movement from antebellum slave to postbellum businesswoman, Keckley accumulates a narrative identity in the process of accumulating possessions. At the same time, these additions to her narrative self-presentation are entwined functionally and figuratively with her antebellum life's mournings. Keckley's accumulation and valuation of personal possessions is, therefore, a work of psychological significance—one response to the master class's repeated destruction of stable familial ties, coupled with prohibitions against slave mourning: so, for example, when her father was sent away, Keckley tells us, her mistress chided her mother for mourning his loss, saying, "if you want a husband so badly, stop your crying and go find another" (25). Losses mourned live on in many ways; unmourned they remain losses inconsolably longed for. Thus, in this strategy of emotional survival, objects come to replace object relations out of the survivor's urge to recover unmourned losses and to create out of her mementoes an enabling, validating environment for her post-loss existence. In this way, possessions from Keckley's slavery past serve to authorize, and are authorized by, her postbellum conception of self.

As a narrative device for dealing with loss, documentation is associated literally and figuratively with a central change in the postbellum world: the emancipated slave's legally sanctioned power over her own possessions, a right of ownership and use denied her during slavery. Keckley's deployment of the documents in her possession are, therefore, representative of her postbellum status while remaining an oblique reminder of the antebellum fact that, as a slave, she herself was an object of possession, powerless to object to or prevent the losses of people or belongings she might think of as her own.

My view of Keckley, therefore, goes against Andrews's notion of her "materialist and pragmatic mode of self-valuation" and focuses instead on her transposition of value between objects and object relations. Indeed, the items Keckley accumulates are fundamentally unusable objects whose value is mostly sentimental and memorial, rather than pragmatic. Keckley's investment in them is principally emotional: for the ex-slave whose life has been a series of migrations and disruptions, they are signs of attachment, continuity, and accordingly, self-worth. They represent a mode of self-valuation based on powerful affective ties that are at odds with her narrative praise of self-reliance.[8]

The narrative's symbolic association of mourning with possessions is one key feature of Keckley's construction of a rhetorical position to negotiate her relations to herself and others. The origins and nature of this association are the subject of the following five subsections of this chapter. In the chapter's final two subsections, I turn to the ways in which the symbolic linking of mourning and possessions yields a mulatta self at odds with the definition of personhood presumed by her narrative of social and economic advancement. The resultant disjunctures give way to the process of narrative splitting between herself and an Other—her narrative's other subject, Mrs. Lincoln.

To posit the existence of narrative "holes"—areas of deliberate suppression and unconscious repression—suggests, of course, the presence of a figure of oppression. Fanon's further analysis of the plight of the black self in a white world illuminates another important structural aspect of the narrative: the deployment of Mrs. Lincoln as Other. In his discussion of the discrepancy between "black skin" and "white masks," Fanon emphasizes not only the self-divisions that emerge within the black self in confrontation with his or her own "otherness" in the face of the normalized culture of whiteness, but the divisions within the "White House" itself: the anxiety-producing confrontations with Otherness that the presence of the colonized within the dominant culture guarantees. To recall Fanon's formulation of this relation: "the real Other for the white man is . . . the black man. And conversely" (161).

The mistress-slave woman confrontations that characterize women's slave narratives are here imagined as a series of exchanges (dresses for cash; mementoes for service), reinforced narratively by the women's parallel and overlapping tales of loss and mourning. In *Behind the Scenes,* a story of accumulations and debts, the narrator / dressmaker / restrained-mourner Mrs. Keckley and the narrated subject / dressbuyer / unrestrained-mourner Mrs. Lincoln are secret sharers, doubles in mourning and emotional valuation of possessions.[9] In Keckley's narrative confrontation with Mrs. Lincoln, the figure of the First Lady is constituted out of various projected parts of "Otherness" ideologically associated with black people. In these narrative inversions, Mrs. Lincoln "substitutes" for Mrs. Keckley in the imaginary role of social and economic outcast, becoming for her a mechanism of defense on behalf of her self-esteem, in the face of the social and economic reality of her subjugation to the President's widow. From her rhetorical position (a reversal of the positioning of antislavery narrative doublings effected by white women writers—the supplicating slave woman as double), Keckley seems to reject the "Otherness" that has been projected onto the slave woman by projecting it back onto the figure of the mistress, while at the same time, in light of the two women's interdependent relationship, to retain the phantom presence of the Other in her conception of herself.

Manipulating the objects salvaged from a lifetime of losses, a lifetime whose principal condition was being property oneself, the ex-slave narrator sets off psychological and ideological reverberations. Through the repeated displacement of feeling from object relations to objects, and the remarkable narrative role-reversal between mistress and slave, Keckley may be able to give linguistic relief to her conflicted sense of self and achieve a narrative reconciliation with her own traumatic past. In addition, by declaring herself to be at the center of the national trauma—"behind *these* scenes"—she seems able to transcend her own private trauma and her culturally enforced marginality as a mulatta woman and former slave, and to position herself as a public historian of the national tragic ruptures of Civil War and Presidential assassination.

"Worth My Salt"

Elizabeth Keckley was born a slave in Virginia around 1822, her mother's only child. She did not know much of her father: he was owned by another man, and he visited only twice a year (on Christmas and Easter), until his master moved West, taking his slaves with him, sometime when Keckley was between four and eight. When she was around fourteen, Keckley's master, Colonel Burwell, sent her as a slave to his eldest son, thereby separating her from her mother. Not long afterwards, she was forced into a sexual relationship with an unnamed white man and bore a son. After a few years, she returned to her old "white family" and moved with them to St. Louis. Her new master, Mr. Garland, who had married one of the Burwell daughters, did poorly, and Keckley virtually supported the family by becoming a seamstress. Meanwhile, she had married James Keckley, who had falsely represented himself as a free man and who also, to her distress, turned out to be a drunkard. In 1855, with $1200 borrowed from her St. Louis lady patrons, she bought herself and her son out of slavery. She earned enough money to pay back her patrons, and, in 1860, left St. Louis alone—after telling her husband she was leaving him and, apparently, establishing her son at Wilberforce College in Ohio.

Keckley soon arrived in Washington, D.C., where she secured

work sewing for the wives and daughters of officers and politicians. Over time, her business would grow so prosperous that she would employ twenty seamstresses to help her. Obviously talented and ambitious, Mrs. Keckley took as one of her first Washington jobs a position as seamstress for Mr. and Mrs. Jefferson Davis; she worked for them until they returned South, just before the secession. Not long afterwards, another customer, Mrs. General McClean, recommended Keckley to Mrs. Lincoln; of this prospect, Keckley writes: "my long cherished up hope [of working for the "ladies of the White House"] was . . . realized" (83). During Keckley's White House years, Mrs. Lincoln came to depend on her as an intimate friend; it was Keckley whom she asked to sit with her the night the President lay dying. When Mrs. Lincoln tried to set up the sale of her old clothing, she relied on Keckley alone: Keckley came to New York to meet Mrs. Lincoln, who insisted upon traveling incognito, in order to assist her in her dealings with the New York brokers.

In Keckley's narrative, self-ownership is for the ex-slave a symbol of liberty, however enmeshed it might be in the ironies of a system of property in which she was once owned. Ownership and possession pertain to questions of identity in slave narratives, reflecting their centrality in the slave experience. Slaves legally owned nothing; their master's claim was always greater. They did not own their person; they did not own the fruits of their labor; they owned no possessions that were protected by law. The master's power over the slave also comprised ideological and psychological domination, wielded with its most devastating effect against the slave's "right of possession" to a sense of self-worth. In part, Keckley's resistance to the rhetoric of victimization and her embrace of "materialism" are motivated by her wish to disprove her first master's taunt that "I would never be worth my salt" (21). This assault against reality (a denial of the facts of the young slave girl's hard labor) and attack on her self-esteem rankles for years. With its overtones of tears and savors, being "worth my salt" lodges itself in Keckley's memory as the irritant she needs to cleanse from her self-conception, and the means of cleansing. So she notes with some pride and some bitterness that while her last master, Mr. Garland, failed to prosper, and was so poor that he could not pay the postage for a letter, she,

> with my needle . . . kept bread in the mouths of seventeen persons [her master's household] for two years and five months. While I was working so hard that others might live in comparative comfort, and move in the circles of society to which their birth gave them entrance, the thought often occurred to me whether I was worth my salt. (45–46)

Given the racism in nineteenth-century proslavery thought, the slave girl Keckley could never be "worth her salt"—that is, in a sense, refined or white (unrefined salt is dark). As a gesture of defiance, Keckley's reappropriation of the phrase at once takes apart the essentialism of her master's equation of whiteness with worth, birth with entrance into dominions of social and economic power; but, although she undercuts the essentialist structure of relations the master assumes, Keckley retains her master's standards and system of economic value as part of her psychological furniture. Psychologically, her postbellum sense of self is shaped by the memories and habits of enslavement. Her scattered expressions of dashed expectations and diminished hopes hint at the apprehension of failure behind her rhetoric of success. Moreover, her mode of subjectivity, though it may spring from resentment at, and in defiance of, the way proslavery ideology defines her, is constrained by the frustrations of having to function within a predominantly white world and of having to contend with the continual impingement of the dominant culture upon her sense of self.

Behind the scene of her master's mockery, hovering in the image of salt, are traces of tears of rage and grief that, like the child's wail for help, contain an admission of weakness, which she now is determined to disprove. Anger against the master who is responsible for negating one's sense of self-worth may be a driving force behind the wish to prove one's worth (emotionally) by being "worth one's salt" (economically). But external objects, laboriously earned, are inadequate substitutes for internalized loving object relations: they cannot rehabilitate an inner world that has been brutalized by punitive masters and systematized abuse. Nevertheless, the conflation of objects with object relations that underlies this mechanism of defense constitutes an adaptation to the master's objectification of the slave self as a piece of property.

Mourning and Slavery

The constellation of images having to do with possession and loss of possession that organizes Keckley's narrative perception of self and other lends itself to an understanding of emotions as something metaphorically owned or possessed. It is clear that the master class, as an expression of its ultimate ownership, used legal sanctions to regulate slaves' expressions of affective ties by its control over the constitution of slave families: marriages were often forbidden or disregarded; slaves could not receive inheritances or make wills. Accordingly, unofficial reinforcement for legally coded prohibitions is also to be found in individual encounters between masters and slaves.

Proslavery ideologues held that slaves, taking their servile status as natural, accepted slavery's assaults against body and soul as being in the nature of things as well. The belief that slaves did not possess the "natural" feelings whites did for their children or lovers was standard proslavery rhetoric, used to justify forced separations or sexual unions. Open grief was open resistance, often suppressed and sometimes punished. To return to how Keckley, writing over thirty years later, remembers her mistress responding to her mother, grieving for her husband whose different master has taken him away to the West: "There are plenty more men about here," Mrs. Burwell scolds; "and if you want a husband so badly, stop your crying and go find another" (25). Slave family members are as replaceable as inanimate objects, and so grief for a lost husband is a childish pique. Keckley dramatizes this scene in order to expose the injustice and cruelty in her mistress's complaint; but there is also on display her mistress's desire for the "illusion of consent" (Annalucia Accardo and Alessandro Portelli's apt phrase) that her slave's silence would create and foster.[10] Therefore, Keckley's first object lesson against the slave's mourning is filtered through the spectacle of the mistress's dependence upon a fantasy of her slave woman's shallowness and reliance upon *her*. (This point will become relevant in connection with Keckley's relations to Mrs. Lincoln, and her marked silence about her own son's death while elaborating Mrs. Lincoln's mourning for her son, Willie.)

Occasions for grief and mourning were pervasive in the lives of slaves, and rituals for mourning the dead, often a syncretic expression of African and American styles and beliefs, were used to send the dead person's soul along its way.[11] But traumatic separations from loved ones, likely to be permanent, also require mourning. It is precisely these deathlike separations—when hope of recovery must be abandoned—that seem an early preoccupation of Keckley's narrative. After writing about how her mother was rebuked for lamenting her husband's forced march, Keckley records her second experience of a slave woman's mourning, which taught her about the futility of expecting sympathy and expressing grief (a lesson that seems applicable to the case of her white audience's hostile reactions). She recalls what became of the mother of a boy whose sale she witnessed when she was seven years old. This was the first sale of a human being Keckley ever saw, and she says that she remembers it vividly.

[The mother] pleaded piteously that her boy should not be taken from her; but master quieted her by telling her that he was simply going to town with the wagon, and would be back in the morning. Morning came, but little Joe did not return to his mother. Morning after morning passed, and the mother went down to the grave without ever seeing her child again. One day she was whipped for grieving for her lost boy. Colonel Burwell never liked to see one of his slaves wear a sorrowful face, and those who offended in this particular way were always punished. (29)

The linguistic ambiguities in this memory of the slave mother whose child was sold—mournings or mornings? whose grave?—recall one of the most famous African American spirituals, "My Lord, What a Mourning," also often printed as "My Lord, What a Morning." W. E. B. DuBois called these spirituals the "sorrow songs." Frederick Douglass, astonished by the view that "singing among slaves . . . [was] evidence of their contentment and happiness," advised those who wished to be impressed with "the soul-killing effects of slavery" to listen to the bitterest anguish and unhappiness, expressed in their sorrowful songs (*Narrative*, 24). Slave lives were filled with mournings after mournings; and denied direct expression of their grief, they, like other people, would find it in indirect ways.

The matter of slave mourning, however, cannot be understood simply as a response to the master's prohibitions—whether in willful resistance, deliberate "acquiescence," or a less conscious internalized identification with the aggressor's ways. Slave funeral rituals are evidence and affirmation of the resources of community and memory among slaves themselves. Yet even without explicit interdictions against mourning, the conditions of slavery—the family splittings, with their consequent parental neglect and emotional deprivation; the psychological and sexual abuse of young adolescent slaves; the fact of being overworked, undernourished, and facing ever-present threats of punishment; the perpetualness of servitude—would have forced any "survivor" of the slavery experience into a confrontation with highly conflicted feelings upon a loved one's separation or death.[12] Adult responses to loss, psychoanalysis suggests, are modeled upon childhood responses to similar experiences, and Keckley's early education in slave mourning suggests a style of response that may be discerned in the narrative strategies by which she deals with loss. The contradictions in tone and thrust of her narrative—sentimental and ironic, determined to advance and needing to return—and also her mode of detachment seem to bear witness both to the ambivalence that inevitably arises from the complicated emotional attachments slavery fostered and to the dangers to the slave (politically from without and psychologically from within) of uninhibited protest.

Mourning Children

Mourning is a process of both remembering and forgetting—a gradual turning away from desiring and expecting the lost object, carried out over time (as Freud described it) by calling up memories of the object one after another, until the process of detachment, a kind of compromising action between remembering and forgetting, is completed.[13] The tug-of-war waged within Keckley's narrative self, between remembering and forgetting, going home and getting ahead, getting along and getting over, is suggestive of the earlier experiences of having constant reasons to mourn with little opportunity for mourning. If a pattern of managing loss evolves in her early years (out of submissions to losses, including parental separations and an uncle's grisly suicide), this pattern finds narrative expression in her comments about diminished hopes and disappointed expectations. So, she writes in a letter to her mother, when she is around fifteen, speaking of her family "both black and white" from whom she has been separated: "I love you all very dearly, and shall, although I may never see you again, nor do I ever expect to. . . . I have often wished that I had lived where I knew I never could see you, for then I would not have my hopes raised, and to be disappointed in this manner" (40–41).

Keckley's reticence about the losses she suffers in adulthood is another mechanism for handling loss. So, she dismisses discussion of her husband quickly and comments only briefly that she leaves him. We find out that her parents have died only because she refers to their graves. And she treats her son's death as nothing but a footnote to her account of the death of young Willie Lincoln.

We can move closer to understanding the origins and nature of these striking narrative gaps and the ways in which they are generative of the multiple, contradictory selves that characterize Keckley's self-presentation, by returning to the important episode of the mother grieving for her auctioned-away son. Intrinsic to this episode are the narrative concerns with separation, anxiety, rage, and sorrow. These run like a thematic thread through various early scenes, connecting them to this emblematic episode in which slavery breaks the mother-child bond.

For example, there is an even earlier memory, of when Keckley was four, about the time she says she "first began to remember," when she was assigned to look after the master's and mistress's baby, a girl also named Elizabeth (19). Despite her claim of being pleased at thus being "transferred from the rude cabin to the household of my master" (up *in* slavery), the slave girl's treatment of her identically named charge betrays other feelings (20). In this memory, Keckley describes rocking the infant white girl, "when lo! out pitched little pet on the floor" (20). This anecdote functions as a multivalent indirection. The "accident" becomes an angry outburst against her owners, an expression of hatred and rivalry directed at her white double, and a reenactment of her own removal from her family's cabin, experienced by the child as a rejection, like being pitched out from *her* cradle into the danger zone of slavery. This last point is underscored by the way in which this incident serves as Keckley's initiation, prior to her witnessing the slave auction, into the brutalities of slavery: Mrs. Burwell, rushing in to find the slave Elizabeth in the act of trying to scoop-up her Elizabeth with a fire-shovel, gives orders that Keckley be lashed. "This was the first time I was punished in this way, but not the last" (21).

The scene of the auction, another first, is presented as a more displaced memory of initiation: of someone else's mother returning morning after morning to retrieve her forever-lost son. But with its emblematic relation to separations in Keckley's own life, including this early move into the master's house, it functions emotionally as a displaced site of longing, used to reenact symbolically the repeated returns to search for the lost object, rather than a process of mourning. The deaths of her mother and son, particularly, seem to hover in the background. For the scene is an enactment of mirrored images of longing: a mother for a son (or daughter) and, invisible in the text, but implied by it, a son (or daughter) longing for a mother.

In "Screen Memories" (1899) Freud theorizes that powerful childhood memories may be "associatively displaced" onto other, more trivial ones as a screen of defense against the primary memory. In addition, the elements stressed in screen memories pertain to adult anxieties and fantasies that exist at the time the memories emerge as well as to childhood ones. Adapting the concept of screen memories to the use of conventional *topoi*, I would like to consider how slave narrators might filter their individual childhood memories through the screens of conventional *topoi* as a substitute for more intensely powerful, personal memories.[14] In this way, form and convention are the protectors of sanity. Keckley's comment that she remembers this auction scene vividly suggests its symbolic relation to the memories of absolute loss that she does not dramatize—when she is separated from her mother or her son, or learns of their deaths. The unrepresented scenes of separation that exist "behind the scenes" lend support to the idea that the narrative masks inconsolable longing and functions to put to rest feelings of helplessness and vulnerability. She will not—if she can help it—be like that supplicating slave mother, whose cries go unheeded.

The images encoded in the memory of the slave auction—a mother and child, the survivor's search, and an unmarked grave—reappear when Keckley explains why, during her trips back South to Vicksburg as a free woman, she has never visited her own mother's grave. Because her mother is buried in public ground beneath obscure markers she feels she can never be sure where the body actually lies. "To look upon a grave and not feel certain" who is buried there "is painful, and the doubt which mystifies you, weakens the force, if not the purity, of the love-offering from the heart" (240).

The anonymous slave mother, the lost child, and the unmarked grave reverberate across the many layers and many texts of slaves' recollected accounts. In Jacobs's narrative, for example, the "nearly obliterated" inscription on her father's grave is recoverable through the daughter's own writing; but for Keckley, the irrevocableness of loss is embodied in the two kinds of textual substitutions mentioned earlier. First, there are the documentary interventions in the narrative. These treasured texts stand as replacements for obscure markers and missing bodies. Second, there is the "substitution" of Mrs. Lincoln for Mrs. Keckley and the positioning of Mrs. Lincoln as narrative Other.

The two modes of substitution are subtly engaged in the narrative's handling of its most prominent "missing body"—Keckley's son. I argue throughout this book that slave narratives, in addition to their more obvious function as protest narratives, often serve as memorials for lost lives and loves. Through memory, the past is mourned and honored in formal, ritualized ways. But, as I have suggested earlier, this work of mourning, of resolution and of hope, seems not to be what happens with memory and mourning in *Behind the Scenes*. Unlike Jacobs, whose narrative is rhetorically a tribute to her grandmother (and through her, her mother), but more deeply a remembrance of her father, and an almost ceremonial enactment of Jacobs's father's command to reach freedom or the grave, Keckley's narrative seems to take a highly ambivalent attitude toward its place in the chain of familial memory, rhetorically subsuming her black family narrative in her "behind the scenes" account of a white family—the Lincolns.

The complications for black familial relations when embedded within the context of a dominant white family, and their implications for Keckley's self-presentation in view of a white audience, emerge in the moment in which she informs the reader of her only son's death. How she does this hints at a desire to turn narrative attention away from her own familial mourning and suggests a certain estrangement from this form of the familiar. She situates her son's death in the context of two obliquely related losses which would have had a far greater resonance with a postbellum Northern audience—losses that would be more familiar, and strike closer to home, because more akin to losing the (white) family they recognize: the deaths of a "gallant" general and of Willie Lincoln, who was in Keckley's view the Lincolns's favorite son.

Previous to this [Willie's death] I had lost a son. Leaving Wilberforce, he went to the battle-field with the three months troops, and was killed in Missouri—found his grave on the battle-field where the gallant General Lyon fell. It was a sad blow to me, and the kind womanly letter that Mrs. Lincoln wrote to me when she heard of my bereavement was full of golden words of comfort. (105)

This brief mention, in the midst of an extensive account of young Willie Lincoln's death and his parents' grief, particularly

Mrs. Lincoln's famously terrifying mourning, leaves the impression that this "sad blow" is included primarily to highlight an aspect of Mrs. Lincoln's character. Even the point of her son's brave sacrifice is subordinated to the significance of Mrs. Lincoln's "golden words." Moreover, in place, perhaps, of documenting this "sad blow" of the loss of her only son, she documents (instead) the impact of Willie's death by copying from her scrapbook (she says) Nathaniel Parker Willis's tribute to the "bright-eyed boy."[15]

Taken alongside the narrative disavowal of desire or responsibility regarding his birth, this footnote on her son's death disrupts the narrative in various ways, calling attention to what is not said. It evokes the narrative's "self-reliance," while at the same time raising questions about the price (rhetorical and psychological) of its attainment. When Keckley heads to Washington she is, in William L. Andrews's words, already "emotionally baggageless," leaving behind her mother ("I did not know much of my father," she remarks), her unreliable husband, and her son (who by then had gone off to Wilberforce College) (Andrews, "The Changing Moral Discourse," 235; Keckley, 22). Her only explicitly expressed grief at the time she is planning to head North is for what she fears is the loss of trust "by those [six white St. Louis gentlemen] whose respect I esteemed" (53). It is this loss (recalling her first master's attempts to "steal" her sense of self-worth) that commands her grief the night before she has plans to head North to raise the sum for freedom. "There was no morning for me—all was night, dark night" (53). Accordingly, the narrative suppression of mourning for her son within the context of mourning the Other son, entails a form of internalized aggression, a redirecting of anger away from the more powerful external objects of white authority and back against the self.

Belonging

The epigraph with which the chapter begins refers to the sensation of ownership during and after slavery in terms that, in light of slavery's equation of slaves and things, has ontological overtones for the ex-slave after Emancipation. "I considered my clothes and the little things I had when in slavery my own," Mrs. Joseph Wilkinson told her interviewer in 1863. "I see now that every thing I considered my own didn't belong to me, but could be taken from me at any time."[16] This use of "belong" has not only a linguistic association with the word "belonging," in the sense of being connected or a part of, but their relation is deeper: both express a quality of attachment that is falsified (as Mrs. Wilkinson suggests) by slavery. When Keckley speaks proudly of being "raised up" from her rude cabin to the master's house, she reveals a fantasy of belonging *in* the master's house (as opposed to belonging *to* the master). Yet, this fantasy of "belonging" entails a feeling of not belonging in her rude cabin (experienced perhaps as both a sense of superiority and a feeling of rejection); it is contradicted by the reality of "belonging to" her master, a piece of property after all.

What I wish to suggest is the nature of the damage done by slavery to relations defined by "belonging," a fundamental condition for growth, development, and the preservation of self-esteem. Orlando Patterson identifies natal alienation as one constituent element of slavery. The question of belonging is paramount and complicated in the lives of a dislocated people, whose first act after slavery was, for many, to migrate to yet a new and alien place. Keckley comments disdainfully upon the difficulties she notices migrating ex-slaves have with separation. "The colored people are wedded to associations," she explains,

and when you destroy these you destroy half of the happiness of their lives. They make a home, and are so fond of it that they prefer it, squalid though it be, to the comparative ease and luxury of a shifting, roaming life. (140)

Yet for her, rejection of the past is not as easy as she apparently chooses to make it sound in this passage. There is, as I have suggested, a far more compelling, contradictory current that runs throughout the narrative, one that looks backwards, clings to associations, collects memories, returns to a place it definitely calls home and to a family left behind. What emerges between these two modes—the mode of rejecting the past and the mode of retaining the past—is a narrative disjuncture that serves as another signal of the presence of something "behind the scenes" that simply does not conform to the linear progression implied by "up from slavery."

Keckley's tendencies to husband past associations emerge in a medley of comments about the ingrained nature of memories. Calling up these memories, Keckley muses, "I often find myself wondering if I am not living the past over again. The visions are so terribly distinct" (18). Her slavery childhood, she notes, still lives in her mind, dominating her attitudes. "I cannot forget the associations of my early life," she states, referring to her some-times "peculiar notions" about maintaining a hierarchical struc-ture of relations between herself and the "ladies, attached to the Presidential household" for whom she sews (152–53). These are ideological and psychological holdovers, she underlines with her choice of words, of her thirty years under the "peculiar institu-tion."

The complexities of Keckley's bonds to her slavery past, and the degree to which that past remains a site for belonging, are most explicitly exemplified when she returns to St. Louis, the place of her enslavement, after Lincoln's assassination, for a reunion with the Garlands, the family who once owned her. Often, since living in Washington, she says, "I recalled the past, and wondered what had become of those who claimed my first duty and my first love" (241). To Northern friends who think her naive to "have a kind thought for those who inflicted a terrible wrong upon you by keeping you in bondage," Keckley defends her desire to return to the site of slavery and the origins of memory as being consistent with her present liberty, not compromising it:

You forget the past is dear to every one, for to the past belongs that golden period, the days of childhood. . . . To surrender it is to surrender the greatest part of my existence—early impressions, friends, and the graves of my father, my mother, and my son. These people are associated with everything that memory holds dear, and so long as memory proves faithful, it is but natural that I should sigh to see them once more. (241–42)

With their trace of monetary worth, words like "dear" and "golden" recall the price she has had to pay because of slavery and the ongoing emotional cost of slavery memories. For as she sorts out the foundations of her identity, she cannot reject the effects of her oppression without rejecting herself. Personal memory constitutes identity and is precious to the individual, no matter how it is conditioned by larger cultural and political forces of oppression. Her comment is perhaps a corrective to the attitudes of her Northern friends, probably whites for whom demonizing white slaveholders is self-justifying, but for the ex-slave, such splitting between North and South means suppressing both her ties to the South and potential criticism of the North. Acknowledging personal origins is the work of recovering a sense of belonging. Therefore, when she writes, "[t]o surrender the greatest part of my existence," we should take her at her word: the journey into the South is a necessary personal pilgrimage into the self.

As Andrews has recently argued, the charged reunions between former slaves and their ex-masters may serve several purposes. The ex-slave can be seen "demonstrating moral leadership" during an era when the desire for political reunion between North and South and also Southern reconstruction were emerging as postwar priorities: the use of the very word "surrender" recalls the recent Southern defeat and so makes integration both a personal and a national goal. Then, too, these reunions may enable slave narrators to achieve a psychological reconciliation with their slavery past.[17] Returning in triumph to their defeated, often ailing ex-masters, these former slaves perhaps seek a recognition denied them during slavery.[18]

As a mechanism for mourning, seeking reunion with former masters may also help former slaves to come to terms with one of the illusions seemingly necessary to childhood—the illusion of the "golden period," before the fall into reality. As Freud remarks in "Mourning and Melancholia," mourning is also the reaction to the loss of a cherished abstraction, like "My Golden Childhood"; and Keckley's wish for return seems motivated by a need to replot her life, to locate in it an essential point of gold—when self-worth was self-evident—prior to the batterings of experience. Thus, within her narrative of success and self-reliance is a narrative of loss of the valued self and beloved others.

Narrative Attachments

To learn "self-reliance" in a world in which adults are unreliable is an adaptive measure meant to transmute the insecurities and betrayals of dependence into the virtues of independence and hard work.[19] Yet the narrative linguistically maintains its attachments to those upon whom Keckley has depended, with the documents that Keckley uses as stand-ins for the absent objects of love. Consequently, the self is sustained through the retrieved fragments left behind from the breakdown of constant object relations. Time and again, she deploys a strategy of textually documenting attachment to the lost object by giving proof with an object—a letter sent or received—that seems an effort to renegotiate the balance within the narrative emotional economy of loss and gain. Where once a person was, now a letter (or other memento) will be.

Psychoanalysts have observed that young children whose parents leave or die sometimes compensate for their losses by an apparent overvaluation of material objects, and an emotional attachment to belongings when their own much-needed sense of belonging to someone who values them has been shattered.[20] The narrative rearrangement of value by translating emotional loss into objective gain makes its appearance early in Keckley's work, in the way in which textual documentation for the lost parent replaces unmediated expressions of grief or anxiety. Storing up her own or her mother's personal letters over the years, guarding their yellowing pages as if overseeing an accumulation of scars, the narrator interpolates personal letters into her account as a form of symbolic transcendence over separations that—as a child and slave—Keckley would have been powerless to prevent. Yet, in the way in which they expose the inner conflicts they are meant to lay to rest, the contents of these reprinted letters finally seem to emphasize the affective breaks the separations provoked.

A letter from her father to her mother provides one example. Written in 1833, it is presented unedited and uncorrected. The difference between the prose of the letter-writer and that of the narrative persona, indicative of the social and economic gap yawning between them, reminds us that the slave father existed in a world to which Keckley in important ways no longer belongs. Additionally, the letter reveals the father's sense of disconnection eating up his hope for connection, and so underlines the unreliability of objects, as well as object relations, in the slave's world.

I have wrote a greate many letters since Ive beene here and almost been reeady to my selfe that its out of the question to write any more at tall: my dear wife I dont feel no why like giving out writing to you as yet and I hope when you get this letter that you be Inncougege to write me a letter. . . . I want Elizabeth to be a good girl and not to thinke that becasue I am bound so fare that gods not abble to open the way. (26–27)

Evidently one in a series of letters written, yet not answered, or necessarily received, this text contradicts the attachment and stability its presentation seems meant to affirm. Recovering, saving, rereading, and publishing letters may be Keckley's process for suturing the broken relation, but it leaves jagged edges exposed.

A more penetrating example of the inadequacy and yet partial efficacy of these textual objects as objects of attachment is a letter Keckley wrote to her mother in 1838 from her master's son's house, where she had been sent to work. This letter also draws attention to disrupted connections. "I have been intending to write to you for a long time," she begins, "but numerous things have prevented me, and for that reason you must excuse me" (40). The remainder of the letter stresses the writer's feelings of remoteness from her former family, and her tone is one of bewilderment and dejection. I quote at length in order to show the repetitions in the letter.

I thought very hard of you for not writing to me, but hope that you will answer this letter as soon as you receive it . . . I want to hear of the family at home very much, indeed. I really believe you and all the family have forgotten me, if not I certainly should have heard from some of you since you left Boyton, if it was only a line; nevertheless I love you all very dearly, and shall, although I may never see you again, nor do I ever expect to. Miss Anna is going to Petersburgh next winter, but she says that she does not intend to take me; what reason she has for leaving me I cannot tell. I have often wished that I had lived where I knew I never could see you, for then I would not have my hopes raised, and to be disappointed in this manner. . . . Give my love to the family, both white and black. I was very much obliged to you for the present you sent me last summer, though it is quite late in the day to be thanking for them. . . . There have been six weddings since October; . . . I was asked to be the first attendant, but, as usual with all my expectations, I was disappointed. . . . I must now close, although I could fill ten pages with my griefs and misfortunes; no tongue could express them as I feel; don't forget me though; and answer my letters soon. (39–42)

As textual presences, these letters, like ghosts, end up being persistent reminders of the distances and broken connections they are meant to bridge somehow. They interject a melancholic counternarrative to be read against the larger, more public, and continuous narrative of *Behind the Scenes.* They also suggest the life strained by continually unappeased longings.

In the final autobiographical passage (which is surrounded by documentation), the narrative voice exudes depression and resignation as it struggles toward something like acceptance and transcendence. Here, transcendence means acceptance of material loss. After inserting lists of Mrs. Lincoln's unsold old clothing, and the receipt for Mrs. Lincoln's payment of the $820 she owed her New York City brokers, Keckley concludes, "This closed up the business, and with it I close the imperfect story of my somewhat romantic life."

The labor of a lifetime has brought me nothing in a pecuniary way. I have worked hard, but fortune, fickle dame, has not smiled upon me. If poverty did not weigh me down as it does, I would not now be toiling by day with my needle, and writing by night, in the plain little room on the fourth floor of No. 14 Carroll Place. And yet I have learned to love my garret-like room. Here, with Mrs. Amelia Lancaster as my only companion, I have spent many pleasant hours, as well as sad ones, and every chair looks like an old friend. In memory I have travelled through the shadows and the sunshine of the past, and the bare walls are associated with the visions that have come to me from the long-ago. As I love the children of memory, so I love every article in this room, for each has become a part of memory itself. (330)

In this passage, with financial rewards out of reach, material objects metamorphose into human beings, with the mid-paragraph shift from room to person—in the person of Mrs. Amelia Lancaster, her only companion. Afterwards, there continues the fantasies of fluidity in Keckley's imaginative and emotional economies. Chairs look like old friends; bare walls are associated with visions from long-ago, although it is unclear whether this is because, like the "garret-like room," they remind Keckley of the impoverished dwellings of slavery, or because the bare walls act as screens for projection, against whose blank spaces she can cast her mental images. Memories are the furniture of her mind and apartment, and the inner world of memory and the outer world of her belongings intermingle, creating a realm for fantasy and emotional reconciliation.

If articles are the children of memory, then for the orphaned and childless Keckley, the "articles" of her narrative compilation may perhaps be felt as filling familial gaps left by the years. In this description of place resonant with the generic images of slavery (poverty, enclosure, work by day, and work by night), Keckley sees in the objects of her present the memory traces of object-relations of her slavery past.

This transferential habit, which structures the narrative's relation to loss, finds further narrative reinforcement in the collection of Lincoln memorabilia Keckley carefully gathers and saves. These include the right-hand glove Mr. Lincoln wore at his first reception for his second inaugural in 1864, a glove which Keckley asks Mrs. Lincoln to give her in exchange for agreeing to stay on as her seamstress and helper. After the assassination, Mrs. Lincoln gives Keckley the bloodstained velvet cloak, bonnet, and earrings she wore that night, and also the President's overshoes and his comb and brush, with which Keckley often brushed his hair. Unlike Mrs. Lincoln, who cannot bear to save the belongings connected to her dead and who risks her reputation to sell off her clothes, Mrs. Keckley, even when pressed for money, turns down offers to sell these things; she later donates all but the glove as "sacred relics" to Wilberforce College in Ohio, her son's alma mater. The glove she keeps as a "precious souvenir" of the man whom she saw as the Moses to her people (367). My claim is not that Keckley is unaware of the monetary value of her possessions, or unwilling to exploit it, but that her conception of her belongings is invariably conflated with her feelings about the people to whom they once belonged.

Material objects function as part of the chain of recollection that constitutes a great part of individual identity—a process of remembering that links one to generations past and future, and links one across time to one's own childhood. Yet, they are also the means of lateral connections between self and other that are not intergenerational. It is important that when she buys her freedom, Keckley insists on paying back the money her white St. Louis female patrons advance her, a refusal of patronage, that not only underscores her valuation of "self-reliance," but also creates a defining moment in postslavery racial ethics. For this episode resonates with the relations between other African American women's autobiographers and their white women patrons, from Brent / Jacobs and the second Mrs. Bruce / Willis to Zora Neale Hurston and her "Godmother," Mrs. R. Osgood Mason.[21] Moreover, with her account of the repayment, Keckley rhetorically repositions herself in relation to white women (we might recall Foster's interesting equation between the seemingly patronless Mrs. Keckley with Jacobs's editor and literary sponsor, Mrs. Child). Accumulation and debt thus become operative motifs in the narrative strategy of confrontation with a "double" in the figure of Mrs. Lincoln.

Opposing Selves:
Mrs. Lincoln and Mrs. Keckley

When Keckley rhetorically positions herself alongside Mary Todd Lincoln as the subject with whom she shares narrative center stage, she openly alters one of the working assumptions ordering antebellum narratives—the subordinate position, relative to the white woman, of the female slave. From their initial encounter, when they haggle over the matter of Keckley's fee and Mrs. Lincoln's purse (" 'my terms are reasonable' " she assures the poverty-pleading, compulsive-shopping First Lady), the two women relate to one another in a complicated series of crossings and shiftings in the balance of power (85).[22]

I cannot say on what level of consciousness Keckley recognizes herself in her employer. But the doubled focus of *Behind the Scenes* suggests Keckley's awareness of the narrative mirroring and of the subversive ironies implicit in their identification. Still, Keckley admits to being drawn to Mrs. Lincoln in ways that feel like impulsion and cannot be altogether explained. "I had been with her so long, that she had acquired great power over me," she writes when trying to describe why she unwillingly went when summoned to Chicago by the newly widowed Mrs. Lincoln after she was no longer her modiste and Mrs. Lincoln had admitted that she could not pay her (209). In going, Keckley leaves behind her business at a time when she can least afford to—a notable decision, considering her investment (financial and psychological) in her profession and her concern for her reputation.

In Keckley's complicated relationship with Mary Todd Lincoln, gestures toward equality are colored by an overriding context of inequality. Mrs. Lincoln's open expressions of friendship and respect are never entirely liberated from their situation within the framework of Keckley's being a paid servant in the Lincoln household; in turn, this hierarchichal relation is filtered through Keckley's memories of her former enslavement and her entangled relations with her former masters and mistresses. The tension between subordination and equality is conveyed in the preface, in which Keckley equates her own reputation with Mrs. Lincoln's, even suggesting that her own self-interest exceeds her desire to clear Mrs. Lincoln, as she also gives due to her sense of her own inferior position. "My own character, as well as the character of Mrs. Lincoln, is at stake, since I have been intimately associated with that lady in the most eventful periods of her life. . . . To defend myself I must defend the lady I have served" (xiv). Keckley's postbellum rhetorical stance of freedom is not easily maintained, since it is partially structured by the demands of a narrative that had been used to articulate the concerns of the antebellum fugitive, and it must succeed within the context of racist and sexist barriers that stand erected against her claims to freedom.

Work provides Keckley access "behind the scenes," her point of intersection with Mrs. Lincoln, and the key sign of their social and economic inequality. Like women from different class and ethnic backgrounds who have lived before and after them in a culture of consumption, Keckley and Mrs. Lincoln engage in a material exchange: in this case, the more powerful buys what the less powerful produces and cannot afford to buy herself with her wages. Mrs. Lincoln also buys Mrs. Keckley's service and loyalty, which the former slave gives, and gives beyond the period during which Mrs. Lincoln can actually pay, further evidence of their complicated relationship. During this unprecedented period in their connection (in 1867), outside of the hierarchical structure of the White House, Mrs. Lincoln writes to Mrs. Keckley from Chicago, "How much I miss you, tongue cannot tell. Forget my fright and nervousness of the evening before. Of course you were as innocent as a child in all you did. I consider you my best living friend, and I am struggling to be enabled some day to repay you. Write me often as you promised" (301). As this letter reveals, with its scrambled-up expressions of neediness and paternalism, their difficult relationship is one based on interdependence, underwritten by real similarities but strained by hierarchical social and class relations, racial segregation, radically different experiences, and ultimately, conflicting goals.

According to Keckley, Mrs. Lincoln (anticipating Thorstein Veblen) understands her conspicuous consumption as a business—*her* business. Keckley, in keeping with Mrs. Lincoln's self-understanding, structures the First Lady's compulsive consumption, which leads to indebtedness, as being directly related to the white woman's self-worth; this is in complete opposition to Keckley's own association of "self-reliance" with "self-worth." "I must dress in costly materials," Keckley reports Mrs. Lincoln as having said. "The people scrutinize every article that I wear with critical curiousity. The very fact of having grown up in the West, subjects me to more searching observation" (149); in another explanatory mode, Mrs. Lincoln declares, "Mr. Lincoln is so generous . . . I expect that we will leave the White House poorer than when we came into it; . . . and it will be policy to sell [my clothes] off" (270).[23] Narrative splitting is evident in their opposition with respect to consumption: while Mrs. Keckley works to pay off her creditors by making clothing, Mrs. Lincoln piles up unpaid bills for the dozens of pairs of gloves, bonnets, shawls, cloaks, dresses, and bracelets she buys—until at one point, near the end of Lincoln's first term, she owes (as Keckley reports) "twenty-seven thousand dollars; the principal portion at Stewart's, in New York" (149). In all, Mrs. Lincoln's debts are said to run to $70,000 by the time of her husband's assassination.

The First Lady's extravagant consumption is also played off against the far more modest expectations of former slaves. The chapter which lays out the extent and nature of Mrs. Lincoln's debts begins with a discussion of the "extravagant hopes" of the freedmen and freedwomen who flocked into Washington after Emancipation. In delineating these "extravagant hopes," however, Keckley offers the anecdote of the newly freed old woman who, complaining about Mrs. Lincoln's stinginess, compares her unfavorably to her former mistress. This new "missus," she laments, has not given her "one shife" in the eight months she'd been in Washington; "My old missus us't gib me two shifes eber year" (141). As an example of the genre of self-debasing post-slavery tales, this vignette seems to fall into a general pattern of Keckley's desire to separate herself from the old plantation ways and dialect.[24] Where this woman sees a mistress, Keckley sees an employer who pays her cash for her labor. But the "joke," if considered in the context of the chapter, actually seems to draw critical attention to Mrs. Lincoln's unearned and unpaid-for extravagance.

This episode functions further as part of an interwoven pattern of contrasts between Keckley and Mrs. Lincoln in terms of the issue of work. Keckley frequently portrays herself as working in various ways: sewing and fitting dresses, brushing Mr. Lincoln's hair, drumming up business, or taking care of the children. But she expresses surprise when she sees white women working. One scene, which begins like so many, with Mrs. Keckley sewing a dress, describes Mrs. Keckley coming to the White House on business early in President Johnson's term. "I found Mrs. Patterson [one of Johnson's daughters] busily at work with a sewing-machine. The sight was a novel one to me for the White House, for as long as I remained with Mrs. Lincoln, I do not recollect ever having seen her with a needle in her hand" (225). The white "lady's" ineffectualness is a repeated theme. One of the letters Keckley has printed as evidence of the regard in which she is held is an 1867 letter written to her by one of the Garland girls, Nannie, now Mrs. General Meems. In the letter, Mrs. Meems complains about her "very inefficient servants . . . so I have had to be at times diningroom servant, house-maid, and the last and most difficult, dairy-maid" (260). Keckley follows this with another letter, also addressed to her in 1867, from another of her Garland charges, Maggie. Maggie describes the job she has held for two-and-a-half months as a schoolteacher. She then refers to her mother as the former slave Keckley might have, and writes, "None of 'Miss Ann's' children were cut out for 'schoolmarms,' were they . . . ? I am sure I was only made to ride in my carriage, and play on the piano. Don't you think so?" (265–66).

Mourning and Melancholia in the White House

An overriding theme in Mrs. Lincoln's life, as in Mrs. Keckley's, is the relentless call to mourning; and one important function of Keckley's narrative is to be an inside witness to Mrs. Lincoln's devastation after the deaths of her son and, then, husband. (Mary Todd Lincoln also lost two half-brothers who fought for the Confederacy during her White House years; but she felt personally and politically distanced from them.) [25] As with materialism, narrative splitting occurs around the issue of mourning. Keckley's depiction of the family's mourning, especially Mrs. Lincoln's for her son and husband, is notable for its relation to the narrative's other explorations of modes of grief. Throughout, Keckley associates the Lincolns' open expressions of grief with a child's powerlessness and lack of control. She wonders at President Lincoln's passionate sorrow for his son, Willie: "His grief unnerved him, and made him a weak, passive child" (103). Mrs. Lincoln was "so completely overwhelmed with sorrow" that she did not go to the boy's funeral, and Mr. Lincoln told her that if she were not able to "control her grief . . . it will drive you mad" (104–5).

After the President's assassination, Keckley "pictures" Mrs. Lincoln as being "wild with grief" (187); when she finally arrives by her side, Mrs. Lincoln is "nearly exhausted with grief" (189); "in a new paroxysm of grief" (191); giving vent to the "wails of a broken heart, the unearthly shrieks, the terrible convulsions, the wild, tempestuous outbursts of grief from the soul" (191); "a terrible tornado" whose "terrible outbursts awed" and frightened her son who pleaded with his mother not to cry or it would "break [his] heart" (192).

What the two women share, according to the narrative, is the tendency to use objects and object-relations in symbolic interrelatedness; yet their mode of handling emotional absence through material gain seems to be diametrically opposed. Keckley's depiction of Mrs. Lincoln's mourning, as it is directed toward off-setting loss with gain, makes it the emotional equivalent of her materialism—all-consuming and self-directed. Mrs. Lincoln's impulse to get rid of everything connected to her dead while at the same time adding to her mourning wardrobe suggests that she experiences the death of loved ones as blows against herself, and not against another. When Willie dies, Keckley notes, it is "as if she could not bear the sight of anything he loved . . . She gave all of Willie's toys—everything connected with him—away" (181). She does the same thing with the President's possessions after his assassination.[26]

It may be an element of the narrative strategy of opposition to position the differing emotional economies of the two women in such a way as to show their relation to differing senses of privilege and expectation. For the more culturally powerful white woman, these traumatic deaths are experienced as injuries to the imagined omnipotent self; thus, her mourning emerges out of a sense of unjust injury. She is, as she laments to Keckley in a personal letter, "a creature of *fate*," buffeted about (Mrs. Lincoln's emphasis, 301). But to the former slave—who, as we have seen, once wrote to her mother, "I have often wished that I had lived where I knew I never could see you, for then I would not have my hopes raised, and to be disappointed in this manner," and who, in that same letter, with reference to another dashed hope, continues "as usual with all my expectations, I was disappointed"—for this ex-slave, injury may be felt as constitutive of her culturally denigrated condition. It is true that Keckley's resistance to the degradations of her enslavement even take the form of physical resistance: at eighteen, she struggles to prevent a flogging by a neighboring schoolmaster, whom she calls her mistress's "ready tool." But her comment on her self-defense suggests the overwhelming difficulties of maintaining a sense of identity that is proof against unceasing abuse: "Nobody," she tells her mistress's lackey, "has the right to whip me but my own master" (33).

Keckley's revelations about Mrs. Lincoln's intense grief delineate her own shifting relations to elements of subordination and domination. When she connects the Lincolns' mourning with traits ideologically assigned to African Americans (wild, child-like, passive, weak) in a narrative in which the suppression and displacement of her own mourning is a recurring motif, a narrative inversion takes place, in which the "mistress" comes to be cast in the role of the black slave as Other. In another apparent inversion of convention and ideology, Mrs. Keckley's account of Mrs. Lincoln's trip to New York recalls the image of the fugitive slave, traveling in disguise, fearful of being recognized. But Mrs. Keckley's reactions are a disavowal of this association, as she questions the appropriateness of this behavior for one of Mrs. Lincoln's rank. "I could not understand why Mrs. Lincoln should travel, without protection, under an assumed name" (271). And she seems to revert once more to more presumptive hierarchical expectations when she describes her response to meeting Mrs. Lincoln in her hotel in New York: "I never expected to see the widow of President Lincoln in such dingy, humble quarters" (276).

The major *topos* of the slave's acquisition of literacy is also transformed by Keckley's use of inversion. In this slave narrative's account, the President's young son — not a slave boy — is the illiterate figure; and his inability to comprehend that "A-P-E" does not spell "monkey" is the focus of his reading lesson.

Keckley's comment, that had Tad been a young Negro boy, his ignorance would have been an example of racial inferiority, suggests that the overtones of racial stereotyping in "ape" are surely not accidental.

Keckley's narrative, with its heavy use of textual documentation and its apparent focus on national (as opposed to autobiographical) historical events, seems a limit case for reading the slave narrative as a window into the individual narrator's mind. Yet the narrative oscillations, disjunctures, and suppressions that give rise to a sense of contradictory rhetorical positions do give a view into the ways in which ideological and psychological pressures converge upon the narrator's inner world. The questions of identity, memory, loss, and ownership raised explicitly by the narrative reveal a narrator who is acutely aware of the social, political, and psychological boundaries her text crosses. Composed at the very beginnings of post-Emancipation history, Keckley's account lays bare the drama of identity facing a newly freed black woman who attempts to reposition herself at the center (behind the scenes) of the nation's cultural and political life.

The fragmenting effects on the narrator of this drama are suggested in the many names Keckley is called by the white people whom she has served, all of them names she responds to (and proudly records): Elizabeth, Lizabeth, Lizzie, Madam Elizabeth, Mrs. Keckley, Yib. Keckley's acquiescence to the multiple namings, like her shaping of her self-perception to the prescriptions for selfhood of the American narrative of success, is both compromise and adaptation: the necessary maneuverings of a marginalized black self engaging the codes and symbols of a dominant white culture.

Behind the scenes of Keckley's narrative present run the conflicting currents of her relation to her slavery past. They reveal the ways in which the complex memory of slavery inhabits the postbellum slave narrator's mind, functioning as a filter through which present desires and frustrations are experienced. Though written from this side of freedom, the postslavery narrative makes it clear that working over the slavery past in memory is one form of labor from which there is no ready release.

Obtuse

$$90° - 180°$$

CHAPTER 5

Enduring Memory: Kate Drumgoold and Julia A. J. Foote

The end of African American enslavement in the United States, as we have seen with Elizabeth Keckley's *Behind the Scenes,* did not end the production of slave narratives, but rather changed the premises and motivations behind their composition, publication, and reception. Slave narratives continued to appear, in print and in oral histories, as long as there were slaves to remember—and to be remembered—well into the twentieth century.

In this chapter, I want to explore the enduring presence of slavery in memory in two post-Reconstruction narratives that seem fraught with the tensions of remembering enslavement. This is so despite the fact that one, *A Slave Girl's Story: Being an Autobiography of Kate Drumgoold* (1898), is the autobiography of a woman who had spent only the first few years of her life as a slave, and the other, *A Brand Plucked from the Fire: An Autobiographical Sketch* (1879, 1886), the spiritual narrative of Julia A. J. Foote, tells the life of the child of former slaves, who had bought their freedom during the antebellum period. Written years after slavery's end, these two narratives nevertheless reveal their authors' conscious and unconscious links to slavery, most clearly in the central tropes with which they locate and organize their conceptions of self.

I bring Foote and Drumgoold together, in part, because of their radically differing strategies for creating lives of integrity and purpose in a dominant culture in which African American women were permitted only to identify with identity fragments— for instance, with a sensual self, or a submissive self, or an ignorant self.[1] Yet, their differing narrative postures—Drumgoold, as invalid narrator, and Foote, as muscular narrator—represent two sides of one coin: they are intrinsically related strategies used to fend off self-negation by taking on elements of the aggressors' identities and transforming them to suit one's own desires and needs.[2]

"A Slave to Sickness": Kate Drumgoold's Story

> I can not help telling some one of it, that they may feel as grateful as I feel . . . and if there is one that should feel grateful it is this feeble-bodied slave girl.
>
> —Kate Drumgoold

Born in Virginia of slave parents in 1858 or 1859, Kate Drumgoold was therefore four or five when, in 1863, President Lincoln issued the Emancipation Proclamation; two years later, what remained of her family (ten daughters and their mother) moved to Brooklyn, where Drumgoold grew up and lived, working as a domestic to raise money for her education (before she was twenty, she would study for almost four years at the Wayland Seminary, in Washington, D.C.). Consequently, by the time Drumgoold began to write her slave narrative, *A Slave Girl's Story*

(1898), her actual life as a slave—which had itself been brief—had been long over. But as her narrative demonstrates, being a slave is not only (as if that were not enough) the organizing fact of her childhood history; being a "feeble-bodied slave girl" (small and weak—like the child she actually was) shapes her view of herself nearly forty years later.

All narratives of traumatic experiences recounted after the events raise questions about liberation and enslavement as they relate to the act of telling. Finding a measure of linguistic relief in telling, narrators sought to liberate themselves from their memories. But the particular form of liberation slave narratives could provide was at least double. Given that the ideology of racism, extending well beyond the slavery years, argued that African Americans were not fully human, to show that one did "suffer . . . from reminiscences" (one of Freud's earliest psycho-analytic formulations) was to make both a political statement, against bigotry and abuse, and a psychological one, against suffering. In recounting the events of her life, Drumgoold, like other narrators, asserts her humanity as a desire and capacity (through writing, which had often been forbidden to slaves) to free herself from bad memories by transforming them into a positive gain. Yet, as a "*slave* narrator"—retaining being a slave as a unifying metaphor in her narrative life—she also enacts another autobiographical rite: the repetition (in the sense of reenacting, not retelling) of memory.

The tensions between liberation and enslavement are implicit in all narratives: narrative conventions emerge out of the need to make sense of the world, then imprint themselves upon our understanding, becoming the master stories which we serve.[3] But liberation and enslavement, which were more than metaphors in the life of a slave, provided the ground upon which those slaves who wrote constructed the symbols and themes to come to terms with their past suffering and to change their worlds. For the autobiographer who was once a slave, and for whom the "constraints of the real" (to recall John Paul Eakin's phrase) have been more profoundly *literal* than they commonly are (in the struggle for narrative and in the slave experience), writing an autobiography is entirely bound up in the tensions between liberation and enslavement (what Eakin calls "a simultaneous acceptance of and refusal of the constraints of the real") (*Touching the World,* 46).[4]

Drumgoold's central trope of identity—that "I was such a slave to sickness"—a trope that, when utilized in the late 1890s, seems to be an acceptance of enslavement, is also a refusal of its terms (16). Drumgoold uses "sickness" to bridge the socially, economically, and legally enforced racial divisions that seem bent on separating into "black" and "white" what, in her inner world, is mixed.

I mean this to indicate a state of interior consciousness, obviously at odds with external conditions—a consciousness and conditions that have their tense encounters in Drumgoold's narrative. Drumgoold wrote in 1897, one year after the landmark Supreme Court ruling in *Plessy v. Ferguson* in favor of the doctrine of "separate but equal." This ruling marked the culmination of the legal backlash against African Americans who had only recently won some civil rights. Meanwhile, three decades of intensifying violence against blacks had made a similar point about the powerful reach of white supremacism.

It is within this context that being sick becomes Drumgoold's strategy for invalidating external conditions of racial segregation and inequality by identifying herself as an invalid—a slave to sickness—who seems to exist in the rupture between the "black" and "white" worlds. For "sickness" in Drumgoold's inner world is the means for reconciling her contradictory psychological positions that rest at the heart of her affective life—her conflicting

attachments to the mistress she calls her "white mother" and to
the black slave mother who actually bore and—except when
their master or mistress separated them—raised her.

"Mothers" Lost and Found

Hortense J. Spillers has commented that, given slavery's disruption of the slave family, the extended "family romance" in African American writing "is a tale of origins that brings together
once again children lost, stolen, or strayed from their mothers."[5]
For many women slave narrators, the loss or threatened loss
of the mother marks an originating moment in their psychic
enslavement, necessitating a lifelong, anxious struggle for self-
definition.

Writing on the symbolic significance of the maternal imago
in the individual's mental life, psychoanalyst Helene Deutsch
observes, "There is only one mother relation from birth until
death, though it undergoes various changes in accordance with
the childhood development."[6] If the mother, as psychoanalytic
theory tells us, plays a central role in the child's psychological
development, early traumatic separation, deprivation, or abuse
will shape the child's character—and the child's maternal
ideal—in multiple ways.[7] Issues of maternal identification for
slave girls under the conditions of slavery were far more complicated. As the slave narratives in this book show, it was common
for slave girls who had lost their own mothers to find surrogate
mothers in the adult women on the plantation. Thus, slave girls,
who, like other girls, sought to develop identities in part through
identification with older women—the slave women and their
mistresses who seemed to offer maternal care—were bound to a
struggle against a damaging self-division: a contradictory psychological position of identification with maternal figures who were
culturally, socially, and politically opposed.

Drumgoold's narrative struggle for self-definition seems to spring from the loss of her own mother and the finding of a surrogate mother in her mistress: thus, her mistress is her "white mother"; she has had, she tells us, "two darling mothers" (56). Indeed, one underlying motive that emerges for her writing would seem to be her need to turn this losing of one mother into the winning of another. One consequence is that Drumgoold's rhetorical position seems fixed at the point of being an *emotionally* dependent daughter. Another is that the former mistress (the "second" mother) comes to embody Drumgoold's maternal ideal. Mrs. House, the "white mother," is associated for Drumgoold with the core of Christian beliefs that shape her life: so Drumgoold prays for God to "help my feeble life to be formed like hers [the mistress's]" (408).

With its touches of bodily language ("feeble" and "formed"), Drumgoold's prayer is suggestive of the intimate connection in her life between linguistic and physical expression. Accordingly, Drumgoold's relationship to this complicated "motherhood" is symbolically manifested in both linguistic and physical ways. Her narrative dramatizes her repeated efforts to heal the self-fragmentation, expressed partially in physical ailments, that results from her disrupted and conflicted maternal attachments. Through Drumgoold's eyes we see the arc of a life composed in an attempt to negotiate an identity out of the contradictions inherent in trying to connect mistress and slave, both intra- and interpsychically. In the process, she engages some of the themes that were prominent in earlier published women's slave accounts: the themes of memory, loss, longing, self-denial, and forbidden aggression.

The "White Mother"

Although for children born into slavery there is no "before" when they were not slaves, slave narrators conventionally construct in memory a time before they knew or felt like slaves. Such a scene is generally an opening vignette, and works to set up the chiasmic structure (from "freedom" to slavery to freedom) so common to the narratives. This is true, as we have seen, for Harriet Jacobs, who writes, "When I was six years old, my mother died; and then, for the first time, I learned, by the talk around me, that I was a slave" (6).

Such scenes of recognition are important in the women's narratives because they help to generate the cluster of images that will become associated in the narrator's mind with slavery's negation: home, love, safety, freedom, and (in this culture) whiteness. As Jacobs tells us, on the death of her mother, she finds her "home . . . with her mistress. . . . I would sit by her side for hours, sewing diligently, with a heart as free from care as that of any free-born white child" (7).

Ironically, for Drumgoold, her "before" occurs during a time when slavery's impact upon her life was most keenly evident—at the beginning of the Civil War, in 1861, when Drumgoold's mother was sold South to raise money so that "the rich man," her master, could pay a "poor white man" to take his place in battle. Meanwhile, her father, assuming (not unrealistically) that his wife would never return, seems to have remarried and dropped out of the family picture.

"I was not troubled then about wars," Drumgoold writes, describing this period, "as I was feeling as free as any one could feel, for I was sought by all the rich whites . . . as they all loved me" (4). To be "rich" is, in Drumgoold's narrative, a recurring sign of white people's love, exhibited in the "presents" they give to the slave girl. She, for her part, would "stand and talk and preach for some time for them" (4).

The figures contained in this recollection are the absent mother (more significant than the father in Drumgoold's narrated life; hence, my focus on her), the present "rich" whites, and the narrating girl, and they are assigned particular meanings—"not troubled" by mother's absence, and feeling free because feeling loved by and at the center of attention of white people. On one level, this may be read as an elaborate instance of "signifying": "the rich man" is exposed as impoverished, both spiritually and materially (he sells Drumgoold's mother to raise cash, after all); on top of that, the white adults are depicted as extravagant dupes, since the narrating and preaching girl gets them to pay for something they already own—her performance. Consequently, "feeling free as any one could feel," under the circumstances, depends on an ironic reversal of the meaning of "free." For "any one" (her master, a "rich white" person) must buy his way out of serving in the war, and "any one" (her audience, the reader included) is readily manipulated.[8]

These same passages, however, may also be interpreted as suggesting a pattern of defense and adaptation meant to obscure alternative *emotional* revelations—for instance, that Drumgoold might feel anguish at her mother's disappearance (I am all alone); that not all white people loved her (my master cruelly sold "dear mother"); and that she was admired in the manner of a performing animal (I am a slave).

In this second reading, the adult's more complex intellectual troping emphasized in the first reading is submerged in the child's emotional strategies. Accordingly, to understand how Drumgoold's narrative functions as a strategy for psychological transformation we need to examine an earlier, analogous episode, for which this opening vignette about the Civil War's impact serves as context.

Just before Drumgoold's mother was sold South during the Civil War to finance her master's replacement, her mistress died of an illness that Drumgoold says her mistress caught from her. It is this death—not the war—that is the context for her mother's absence which appears to have remained uppermost in the slave girl's mind. Indeed, when Drumgoold was three, Mrs. House (her mistress) took her to live in the main house, away from her mother's house. Before that, as Drumgoold tells us, her mistress "was always at my mother's house to see me" (29). Then, within the space of about a year or so Drumgoold became sick; Mrs. House nursed her, fell ill with jaundice, and died; Drumgoold's mother was sold.[9] Accordingly, Drumgoold, who saw her absent mother as a "clear space in the sky," which she watched for three-and-a-half years until her return just after the war, considered her mother's disappearance to be the consequence of her mistress' death which, in turn, she caused by her own illness (5).[10]

Such a line of thinking points to the presence of feelings of aggression toward the mother(s), while repeated declarations of gratitude suggest a reaction founded in fear and guilt. This experience as prototype is reinforced throughout the narrative, as separation, sickness, and the nexus of ideas and feelings Drumgoold associates with them find expression in the entangled strategies of self-representation that structure her story, especially as they are energized in her relationships with white women.

As Drumgoold writes of the period before the Civil War began, Mrs. House, her "white mother," had

her heart so fixed that she could not leave me at my mother's any longer, so she took me to be her own dear, loving child, to eat, drink, sleep and to go wherever she went, if it was for months or even years; I had to be there as her own and not a servant, for she did not like that, but I was there as her loving child for her to care for me, and everything that I wanted. (7)

Drumgoold compensates for the initial separation from her mother (when she went to the main house to live) by transferring her desire to be loved to the white mother, idealizing the white mother's power to fulfill her wishes and needs endlessly ("for months or even years"), and, finally, identifying herself with this mother by imagining herself as the white woman's "own dear, loving child."[11] This position in relation to the white mother is the one she maintains for the rest of her life, praying to God to "help my feeble life to be formed like her's" (16), idealizing her own "feebleness" as it serves to return her to the state of childhood, when her white mother's attentions seem to have made Drumgoold feel lovable and special.

This blissful vision of early childhood with Mrs. House (whose significance for the young Kate is contained in her name) conjures up a wealth of pleasures, and contrasts starkly with Drumgoold's version of her childhood in the two houses of her own mother, before and after emancipation—a contrast that serves Drumgoold's need to offset her initial "abandonment" by turning it into an advantage. The contrast also helps to deflect forbidden feelings of aggression by transforming anger against the objects of authority (both mothers, as we shall see) into gratitude.

The only memory Drumgoold records of her slave home is of a fire that destroyed it during the night. This happened when she was two, she tells us: her father had gone to a dance and her mother, "alone . . . got the children and threw them out" the door. Drumgoold, however, too frightened to call out, hid under the bed, and was left behind—rescued only after her mother, remembering her "lost" child, returned and "found" her. Following this fire, "I had not to stay there then, for the time is near at hand when I shall go to my white mother's to live" (12). Identification with her own mother (both mother and daughter are left "alone," the mother by her husband and Kate by her mother) is obscured by Drumgoold's fear at being left behind. Then, too, fear is couched in anger, in the image of the raging fire and Drumgoold's phrase, "I had not to stay there then," intimating a wish to get away from "my own slave mother's house" (12). And though this story of a lost child is resolved when she is found by her own mother, Drumgoold seems to locate the greater resolution in the white mother's superceding "rescue" of her from the "slave . . . house."

Contrasted wealth is also important in Drumgoold's symbolic system. As a freed child in Brooklyn, she recalls, she had to work to help support the family's minimal existence, forfeiting, for a time, what she dearly desired—her education; but as a child in slavery with Mrs. House, nothing was forfeited. When her "white mother" wanted to buy her a pair of shoes and a "fine hat," but was told they were twenty dollars and "too much for to spend on a hat for me," Mrs. House admonished the white shopkeeper, and "told him nothing would cost too much for her to get me" (13).

As these examples indicate, Drumgoold seems to organize her life in terms of a narrative of loss and recovery. So, "a mother returning back to her own once more" as her mother returned to her after the fire, or as her mother returned after the Civil War, is the dynamic that Drumgoold apparently seeks to generate. Yet, the ways in which the maternal splitting between her (worse) "own slave mother" and her (better) "white mother" functions within the dynamic of these "recoveries" will become clearer when we explore how "sickness" and "slavery" perform as the operative metaphors in Drumgoold's slavery recollections and reenactments.

Becoming a "Slave to Sickness"

A Slave Girl's Story unfolds mostly, but not entirely, chronologically, since Drumgoold stops and restarts several times, going over early material about her "two mothers" with differing emphases and details, as if she were reorganizing history by reorganizing her memory. The persistent return to the sites of loss, however, suggests that Drumgoold's sense of guilt over the double loss of black mother and white mother imprints itself upon her self-image in the shape of masochistic relationships to those she would love and be loved by. What she derives from this position, expressed rhetorically in such self-descriptions as "my feeble life," is what she found as a child—the care of a (white) maternal figure—who has taken up residence in her inner world as an ideal maternal imago. This is emphasized in the catalogue of benevolent maternal figures, presented as a series of feminine ideals who follow the footsteps of Mrs. House, who, like their prototype, are said to take care of Drumgoold during her recurring bouts of illness. They are the white mothers—Miss L. A. Pousland, "who is one of the loveliest ladies that ever lived, for she loves me to-day as a daughter" (21); Mrs. Potter, Mrs. Purdy, Mrs. Haseltine, and the list of other white female employers.

The cycle of "loss / illness and recovery" repeats itself in numerous guises, while Drumgoold's rhetorical position throughout the narrative is that of dutiful, beholden daughter. For instance, even "fathers" figure in maternal, caretaking roles, as Drumgoold remains accepting and grateful: medical doctors, all named and given tribute; religious doctors, who preside over her being "born again" in the North; and above all, "Doctor Jesus," who comes to her aid in everything. In fact, repeatedly, Drumgoold's sufferings and sicknesses are rhetorically deployed to reinforce the sense of her neediness, and hence goodness, in God's eyes. Positioning herself as helpless before Him, Drumgoold utilizes her feebleness as a key element in her faith. In light of this self-conception, God as a Father is unlike her earthly parents, for He is *always* there to protect her: "For God loves those that are oppressed, and will save them when they cry unto him, and when they put their trust in Him" (3).

Drumgoold's position as grateful daughter is also underlined by her use of the rhetoric of filial piety with reference to the men she calls the emancipators of her race. She honors "Father Abraham" Lincoln, "Father John Brown," and "Father Charles Sumner"; she calls Frederick Douglass, "the greatest of men among the negro race of this country or of any land on the globe" (34–36). The language of family, certainly a convention of African American liberationist rhetoric, nonetheless also serves as a perceptual filter through which Drumgoold's engagement with social, political, and religious movements becomes enmeshed with the specifics of her childhood past. Thus, good occurrences (becoming well, becoming free) are understood as proof of parental love. As this implies, however, it is sickness and slavery that trigger the show of that love.

Indeed, sickness and slavery become inextricably entwined notions, informing Drumgoold's bond to her two mothers. In recounting her feelings about her own mother's death—the final departure when her mother, in Drumgoold's religious imagery, goes to a better "home"—Drumgoold reveals the meaning her sicknesses have for her; that is, she reveals both her need for compensatory love and the degree of internalized (self-directed) aggression underlying her subservience. Even though, she writes, her mother "was not a Christian, and the heaviest burden that I have carried was praying for one that was the head of the great family where she should have been a leader of her dear ones to the Lamb of God," Drumgoold praises God for making her able to take her mother's place. Moreover,

God has told us to honor our fathers and our mothers that their days may be long upon the land . . . ; and we can not do them enough honor for the love and the all night watching that we have when we are babies, and if all of the love and care that I had, I am sure that a mother has her hands full; and when now that I think of the care and the worry that it was to take care of my sick body, I can not help telling someone of it, that they may feel as grateful as I feel, for God did give them love for me, and if there is one that should feel grateful it is this feeble-bodied slave girl, for I was such *a slave to sickness*. (15–16, emphasis mine)

Falling short of God's injunction "to honor our fathers and our mothers"—for "we can not do them enough honor"—Drumgoold sets up the guilt-ridden, yet self-affirming cycle of sickness, recovery, and gratitude which shapes her relationships to self and others. As a "slave to sickness," Drumgoold psychologically can remain the beloved child to her beloved mistress the whole of her life. Then, too, she can also maintain a connection to her slave mother. Thus, by returning again and again to the position of being a slave through sickness, Drumgoold enacts her sense of a doubled, mixed identity. For she goes back repeatedly to the period of her slave childhood before her mother was sold, when she was not only her mother's daughter, but also the idealized white mistress's "own dear, loving child."

Inevitably, though, within a culture of racism, Drumgoold's sense of identity in its dual notions in connection to "two mothers" is fraught with conflict for the girl and woman. To maintain her self-esteem, Drumgoold must identify strongly with the idealized white mother, whom she strives to be like in all things, but especially in her Christian faith: "I would to God she could see me to-day; it would do you good, Lord, lead me on day by day, and help my feeble life to be formed like her's" (16). But this turning toward the "white mother," which involves a turning against her un-Christian and culturally denigrated black mother, amounts to a violation of her own primary identity, her original bond to and identification with her own mother. Indeed, to turn toward the black mother is a turning against what she perceives to be the potential of motherhood, as well as the cultural ideal embodied in the white woman; but to turn toward the white mother is to turn against herself. Hence, a kind of self-fragmentation is her fate.[12] She can never wholly become the internalized white maternal imago. She can never *wholly* want to become the white maternal imago whose culturally normalized "whiteness" causes her to reject part of herself. Equally, she can never wholly *want* to become the internalized black maternal imago. Nor can she ever completely become her, on account of her early childhood trespass into (or, conversely, trespass by) a world in which there is *for her* a "white mother."[13]

It also appears that Drumgoold's lifelong struggle to break away from the bonds of motherhood gets played out around the issue of education. For late nineteenth-century African Americans, self-help and uplift through education was the logical extension of Frederick Douglass's antebellum assertion that literacy was the "pathway to freedom." During the post-Reconstruction era, to educate black children was to participate in the further liberation of the race. It is striking, therefore, that Drumgoold suffered a breakdown—"when the nerves were all overworked"—while she was teaching at a school in Virginia, during the winter of 1885–86 (47). This may recall Drumgoold's earlier account of how her "anxious" wish to attend school was obstructed by illness: first by her mother's "poor health" and the fact that "no one" but Drumgoold was around to "help her take care of the younger children, and I had to work and do the best I could with my books"; and then by her own protracted bout with small pox, which "laid [me] aside for three or four years . . . and [I] thought that my plans were all broken" (21).

Such passages expose how entangled the problem of Drumgoold's illnesses was for her—and is for the reader. Drumgoold's emotional breakdown was at least partially a response to the material conditions of poverty and oppression; certainly poverty and oppression would have made her vulnerable to catching so contagious a viral disease as small pox. In trying to assess the meaning of Drumgoold's lifelong pattern of illness, we must make distinctions, since suffering from small pox is not the interpretive equivalent of having "overworked" nerves. In any case, it would be wrong to regard Drumgoold's illnesses as not real in the sense of saying that they were without objective existence apart from whatever psychological need she may have had to return to the mother of early childhood. My claim is that Drumgoold's narrative is at once a memory of the real and of fantasy. Thus, Drumgoold's plans to study and then to teach might well become infected by her sense of herself as a "slave to sickness," thereby adding narrative reinforcement for her own self-construction as being "feeble" by comparison with her long-dead mistress. It is how, retrospectively, she construes her life's story.

Furthermore, by locating that story within the tradition of the slave narrative, in which education and slavery are repeatedly opposed, Drumgoold herself directs us to the problem of her ambivalence. Education is incompatible with slavery, Douglass had famously asserted in the scene in his 1845 *Narrative* when he discovered his master's fear that he might become educated. Drumgoold, driven to attain the empowering promises of education, is pushed down by the history of enslavement, poverty, and oppression, and hobbled further by a legacy of illness that is both the literal result and symbolic expression of that history. Mostly powerless in life, Drumgoold finds power in narrative, and it is understandable that in her retelling of her history, she should transform poor health into an emotional and spiritual strength.

Narrative Aggression

It would be imprecise, I think, to seek to account for Drumgoold's attitude toward the dominant culture intertextually by simply identifying her work as part of an apologist tradition of African American letters at the end of the century (exemplified for some by Booker T. Washington's 1901 autobiography, *Up from Slavery*). Drumgoold's ostensibly apologist mode seems to express a highly particularized conjunction of early emotional deprivations, engendered and compounded in slavery, and persistent racism.[14]

For to be always a child—to be always that sick child—is Drumgoold's own individually constructed strategy for being. This is not just in relation to her mothers "white and black"; to God, who is a loving parent; to her employers, colleagues, or emancipators; but in relation to her sisters as well. For Drumgoold describes herself at Christmas 1886 among her married sisters "like a child looking for something. Everybody was good to me" (46). Seeing herself "like a child looking for something" suggests this: that the "something" she is looking for is what at some level she feels she never had, a mother who in fact was "good to me." Slavery produced distortions in both maternal relations: she could not have her "own slave mother" because of their enslavement, and she knows she had a "white mother" *only* because of her enslavement.

Indeed, it is that very enslavement that finally taints Drumgoold's conception of her "white mother" and mars her relation to her. Idealizing and identifying with the "white mother" are not just Drumgoold's defenses against the loss of her mother; they are also meant to defend against her feelings of aggression against Mrs. House who, despite Drumgoold's fantasy that "she never liked the idea of holding us as slaves," did keep her a slave. There is, in Drumgoold's description of her mistress's actions, a hint of her recognition of this last fact, in her conflation of love and domination: "So she *took* me to be her own dear, loving child," Drumgoold writes. "I *had* to be her *own*" (italics mine). Thus, her mistress's love is betrayed by ownership and force; and behind the expressed pleasure at going to her "white mother's" lies the trauma of seizure and captivity, a recapitulation of the origins of the slave trade, reenacted in each individual slave's "awakening" into slavery.

Indeed, Drumgoold's identification with the "white mother" is in some ways her identification with the aggressor that is meant to defend against her mistress's hostility. For to be like the "white mother" is to be transformed from the one who is threatened into the one who creates the threat.[15] Elsewhere, she inverts their relation in a telling revelation of her acquisition of power through illness: "It was her delight *to wait on me* and to have her cousin, the doctor, *to be always ready to come*" (29, my emphases).

Idealization and identification in this case are therefore based at least partially in anger and fear: anger at the oppression that kept thwarting the slave girl's desire to be special and to have control over her fate; fear at the possibility of more punishments—that is, more losses, more "sellings South" of her mother. In this way, constituting her life as a "slave to sickness" is also a strategy of atonement for guilt-ridden wishes against this powerful mother—wishes that, in a child's eyes, have the power to kill. Thus, Mrs. House's death, seeming confirmation of the child's imagined omnipotence, may be an overdetermining factor in Drumgoold's fixation with the memory of her "white mother."

Living Memories

The cost of Drumgoold's internal conflicts is evident in the linguistic self-devaluation and self-erasure she enforces by overvaluing whiteness. Drumgoold's frequent linguistically asymmetrical pairing of her "white mother" with her mother is suggestive of how her mistress possessed a crucial element that her slave mother lacked—whiteness—which made all the difference in their lives. Near the end of her narrative, while longing to look into her "two mothers' faces" now lodged in "those bright mansions above," Drumgoold has a vision of heavenly "glory" where all is cleansed "white": "and I know that two darling mothers have washed their robes and made them white" in the blood of the Lamb (56). A conventional image, to be sure; but seemingly resonant in the context of white supremacism, in which "white-ness" is reified as a sign of superiority. Such a state of purification is unattainable in this life for Drumgoold, though its promise in an afterlife may be consoling.

That Drumgoold's self-representation seems to founder on questions of self-esteem is reinforced with each insistence that she is lovable to whites. To this end, even the reader (whom she constructs as white) is solicited as yet another possible mother who will respond with love to the suffering slave girl. To become a narrator of pain is a characteristic pleasure of masochism, according to psychoanalyst Theodor Reik.[16] Thus, there is a kind of masochism in Drumgoold's narrative construction of herself as "feeble" in relation to other powerful "white mother(s)." That is, she uses the reader to help to fulfill her craving to be admired and loved. At one point she writes,

No subject can surely be a more delightful study of a slave girl, and the many things that are linked to this life that man may search and research in the ages to come, and I do not think there ever can be found any that should fill the mind as this book. (24)

As she *is* her book, so her public is like a mother who will "search and research," search and search again for the left-behind slave girl, and take her *in*. "Dear public," she writes,

hoping that this little life will be read with the greatest love for humanity, and I am sure that if you have any love for God of heaven you can not fail to find a love for this book, and I hope you will find a fullness of joy in reading this life, for if your heart was like a stone you would like to read this life. (14)

If in some respects these apostrophes are narcissistic and grandi-ose, they also reveal underlying feelings of unworthiness. Though Drumgoold seems to associate herself with God (if you love God you will love me), it is rather in the way of her submission to an ideal that is necessary to justify her own desire for love and acceptance.

A further tension between her absolute assurance in the effect of her own authority and her total submission to a higher authority emerges in the ways in which her own life is validated by her being a conduit for her "white mother" through her book, which enacts the resuscitation of the expired ideal: "I had many a hard spell of sickness since the death of this lady and the doctors said that I could not live . . . but every time they said so Doctor Jesus said she shall live, for because I live she also shall live" (14).

In this Biblical reference, the "I" is Jesus, and the "she" is Drumgoold. But the sentence is in fact linguistically ambiguous and allows for construing the "I" as Drumgoold and the "she" as Mrs. House; so, through Drumgoold her mistress shall live. This ambiguous semantic doubling underscores the ways in which Drumgoold strives to construct a chain of remembrance through narrative to connect her to those who are invisible—to Jesus, to her dead "white mother," to her lost mother, and to her audience: "For remember," she reminds her reader, speaking about the time her mother was "taken from the whole family . . . , one of the saddest times of life for children . . . ; we have the same feelings for our mothers as any race of people . . . as the richest ones on this earth" (31).

With text and self as memorial link to her mistress (and to her mistress's "race of people" in her audience), memory is both emancipator and enslaver. Writing helps Drumgoold to master loss and fulfill her intense desire to make visible her mistress: "It does seem to me as if I could almost see her by thinking of her so much" (17). But it then becomes another form of service: "She said to all of the friends around that if I should live to remember her that would be all that she would ask" (29).

About midway through her narrative, having already told the story of how she was taken, as a three-year-old, to her mistress's house, Drumgoold returns to retell this significant memory. "I was three years old when I was leaving my own dear mother's home to go to my new mother's home, or should I say to my white mother's home, to live with her, and I left my mother's as happy as any child could leave her own home" (29). With the repetition of "mother's home" (intensified twice with the possessive "own"), and the repeated redirections ("I was leaving . . . to go to . . . or should I say to . . . to live with her, and I left"), the ambiguities in Drumgoold's summation of her feelings come into focus. The reiteration of the phrase, "mother's home," suggests the presence of an originary site of memory, one that is energized with each of her life's successive dislocations. Constituted equally of her "own mother's home" and her "white mother's home," this site of remembrance is, perhaps, a resonant symbol of the possibilities of transcending the bitterness of racial experience in late nineteenth-century America. At the same time, it is evocative of the cruelties of slavery that lay not far behind—and were being reconstructed in—end-of-the-century interracial relations.

The Transmission of Memory: One Legacy of Slavery

Unlike the other narratives examined in this study, Julia A. J. Foote's spiritual narrative, *A Brand Plucked from the Fire: An Autobiographical Sketch* (1879 and 1886), is not a slave narrative—that is, the autobiography of an ex-slave. For Julia Foote was never a slave. Yet her autobiographical account may deepen our understanding of the way slavery persists in a family's collective memory, and how it may impinge on the lives of slaves' descendants. Interpreted in this context, *A Brand Plucked from the Fire* opens up for discussion the notion of the transmission of memory from one generation to the next—from once-slave parents to free-born children. Foote's reliance upon the logic of punishment as redemptive—a way to make a good servant to God (her title is taken from the book of *Zechariah*, known as the Apocalypse of the *Old Testament*)—and her deployment of a key slave narrative *topos*, the master's (or mistress's) "whipping" of the slave, are suggestive of the presence of slavery as an ordering symbol in her inner world. When she imagines salvation as eternal enslavement to a divine Master, she reconfigures the idea of slavery as a perpetual condition (as it had been legally construed in the United States, in contrast to other slave-owning societies), by transforming perpetual enslavement into something desired. Why she does this seems related to her identification with her mother, with whose death her narrative proper draws to a close, and with whose whipping, at the hands of a cruel master, her autobiography begins. Like Drumgoold's, Foote's "attachment" to the memory of slavery is at least in part a function of her attachment to her mother, enacted in her narrative. Yet, also, like Drumgoold, her narrative is the linguistic manifestation of her desire to liberate herself from that maternal legacy and to relocate herself beyond the reach of history: a brand plucked from the fire.

Julia Foote, the child of former slaves, was born in Schenectady, New York, in 1823, four years before New York state abolished slavery (her father had bought himself, his wife, and their first child out of slavery; Foote was, as she interestingly puts it, her "mother's fourth child" [9]). Thus, her spiritual journey, begun in childhood, evolved during the antebellum years. When she was ten, she was sent to live "in the country" with a family called the Primes, apparently as an indentured servant.[17] Foote recollects how she felt like the Primes' surrogate daughter. The "Primes had no children, and soon became quite fond of me. I really think Mrs. Prime loved me" (18). Being well-treated is a focal point of Foote's remembrances of her initial experiences under the protection of the Primes. A prominent family, they sent her to a local school where, as Foote notes, "I was treated well by both teacher and scholars" (19).[18] Yet, as Foote observes, her happiness underwent a radical change, when Mrs. Prime, deciding that the girl had been stealing food, bought a rawhide and whipped her as punishment. She fled to her parents, but was sent back. Two years later, Foote had had enough. This time, she went home and remained.

Soon afterwards, Foote's parents moved the family to Albany, where they joined an African Methodist Church. In her late teens, Foote married another free black; not long afterwards, she began to have the powerful visions that would call her to her vocation as a spiritual leader. Her husband, George Foote, was away for long periods of time on sea voyages, and the couple had no children. This left Foote with "a good deal of leisure" to visit "the poor and forsaken ones, reading and talking to them of Jesus, the Savior" (62). After receiving a visitation from God, in which she was called upon to preach, she began holding meetings, but was excommunicated by the efforts of her church's minister, who could not abide a woman preacher. Following George's death, she went on to become known as a traveling evangelical preacher, affiliated with the African Methodist Episcopal Church in Ohio, the mid-Atlantic states, and southern New England.

Foote's autobiography traces chronologically the series of religious experiences that brought her to her work as an evangelist; in the process, she reveals the friction that her ambitions created with others to whom she was close, most pointedly, her mother and her husband. She writes that she "deliberately disobeyed" her mother when, at fifteen, she decided to seek sanctification.[19] Moreover, her beliefs, she says, put her at odds with her husband, who was not sanctified; she describes how early in their marriage there arose "an indescribable something between us—something dark and high . . . a dark shadow being ever present" (42, 60).

From childhood, according to Foote, the intensity of her inward "religious impressions" was manifested in extreme—and to outside observers, bizarre—modes of behavior: falling down at a dance, the first time she "ever attempted it," while at a quilting, "where the boys came" (29); or passing nights in the presence of her husband in delirium and trembling. When she wishes to visit an elderly couple whom she believes might help her find sanctification, her mother forbids her. " 'No, you can't go; you are half crazy now, and these people don't know what they are talking about,' " Foote remembers her mother saying (41). Foote reaffirms this view when she recalls her husband saying that "I was getting more crazy every day," seemingly in reaction to her efforts to convert him (59).

Conflict is intrinsic to Foote's confrontations with the external world—as a nineteenth-century African American woman asserting unconventional desires. Foote's family's reactions operated within a commonplace network of prohibitions, both within the A.M.E. Church and the culture at large, against women preachers, a view that Foote herself initially supports. Then, too, she faced racist restrictions against free black expression, mobility, and social and economic success.

Foote explicitly associates her resistance to such cultural restrictions with her rejection of her parents' legacies of enslavement. As she notes, her mother's acquiescence to discrimination in the white church they attend when she is a child, where "they were not treated as Christian believers, but as poor lepers . . . was one of the fruits of slavery"; thus, Foote's ambitions to rise in the black A.M.E. Church have roots in her being witness to the persistence of the memory of slavery in her mother's attitudes and behavior (11). In addition, Foote recalls her urgent desire to read, so that she might read the Bible, in terms of her connection to, as it implies her surpassing of, her father, who teaches her the alphabet when she is nine. Like many former slaves, he could not read much more. "There were none of our family," she writes, "able to read except my father, who had picked up a little here and there, and who could, by carefully spelling out the words, read a little in the New Testament, which was a great pleasure to him" (15).

Throughout Foote's narrative, prohibitions seem to energize her personal spiritual quest, at once frustrating and intensifying her desire for self-assertion. Above all, prohibitions, and the authorizing agents they presume, make up the enduring psychological links between her childhood memories of her parents' memories of slavery, her own encounters with punitive authorities, her visionary encounters with divine authority, and her adult confrontations with the dominant culture.

In the spiritual world of being that Foote constructs through language, slavery and slave narratives hover not far in the background, providing the enduring images and tropes for her spiritual self-understanding. Most pointedly, her sense of her relation to God, her Master, seems to take as its prototype the transmitted memory of her mother's relation to her master who whipped her brutally.

It is this that forms the basis of Foote's identification with enslavement and constitutes the terms by which she transforms that state of enslavement into sanctification. "Disobeying" her mother by becoming sanctified, therefore, is associated with the desire not to be a slave *in the way her mother had been*—that is, physically, sexually, and psychologically vulnerable to a punitive and abusive master. Through sanctification Foote can transfigure the slavery master as a divine Master, who "persecut[es] . . . his chosen people for various purposes," and transform herself from a daughter of slaves into a "daughter of Zion" (109).

The master's sexual domination seems particularly crucial in

Foote's ways of remembering her mother's memory of abuse. For the narrative's key transmitted memory of slavery, compressed by Foote into a frightening opening scene of her mother's whipping when she was a slave, seems to emphasize her mother's sexual vulnerability in the face of her master's actual power to enact abuse, at the same time it suggests the dangers, and futility, of directly telling the truth to her mistress. For in this scene, Foote's mother is brutally whipped by her master for refusing to comply with his demands for sexual relations, and for exposing his plans to her mistress (his wife). As with Harriet Jacobs, refusal and retelling are inextricably linked, making remembering itself a form of resistance.

But the message of Foote's narration with reference to her mother's refusal ultimately is ambiguous. As an incident remembered and retold (passed down from mother to daughter, and from daughter to us), it seems that Foote's mother successfully resists sexual, if not physical, abuse. But the sexual content of her relation to her master is simultaneously encoded in the motif of whipping (think of Frederick Douglass's account of witnessing his aunt's sexually charged whipping). Moreover, we might return to Foote's remark that she was her "mother's fourth daughter"—a phrase that, in its ambiguity, raises the problem of identifying the father, thereby alluding to the sexual abuse encrypted in the master's physical domination through whipping.[20]

As a founding scene, therefore, the mother's whipping reverberates across the narrative in a number of ways. Most directly, it anticipates the daughter's own experience of being whipped, in her case by Mrs. Prime, when Foote is under her authority. Reinforcing the narrative kinship with slave narratives established by Foote in the opening scene, this second whipping episode recalls numerous slave narrative motifs and tensions: in Foote's dependence upon Mrs. Prime as a maternal surrogate in the absence of her mother (we might recall Drumgoold); in her account of how, after the beating, she runs away from the Primes and heads for home, like a fugitive from slavery, "through the woods; [where] every sound frightened me, and made me run for fear some one was after me" (24, 26). Then, too, indentured servitude becomes a form of enslavement in the way in which Foote has no say in her fate: her mother speaks "sharply" to the Primes, yet she sends Foote back, "very much against my will."[21]

However, Foote's less direct returns to the site of her mother's punishment express the wish for mastery of the feelings of vulnerability, sexual anxiety, and rage that her identification with her mother seemingly evokes. These include, as I have mentioned, her visitation from God. For in this vision, her *choice* of absolute obedience is rewarded by an encounter with a loving Christ. This encounter, in its inversion of her mother's experience, suggests itself symbolically as a mechanism for mastering the anguish of being hated and abused by punitive objects of authority. In addition, Foote seems to incorporate "whipping" as a trope and mode of oratory and rhetoric, thereby linguistically internalizing the brutality of slavery as a means to persuade others to obey.

Thus, the opening transmitted memory of her mother's abuse, reinforced by Foote's own remembered experience of a similar punishment, generates the associative chain of "enslavement," "mastering," "whipping," and "obedience / disobedience" that comes to structure her spiritual narrative and, inextricably, her sense of self. In this way, Foote's spiritual autobiography participates in a repetition of slavery that, since she was not herself a slave, has its source in the enduring psychological burden of slavery that her family continued to bear.

The Whippings

Foote's gruesome and extended rendering of her mother's punishment for disobedience highlights both the sadism of her mother's master and mistress and the protracted nature of her mother's suffering as a slave. In its intensity and vividness, this scene is suggestive of the impact of this transmitted memory on the freeborn daughter's inner world:

[My mother] had one very cruel master and mistress. This man, whom she was obliged to call master, tied her up and whipped her because she refused to submit herself to him, and reported his conduct to her mistress. After the whipping, he himself washed her quivering back with strong salt water. At the expiration of a week she was sent to change her clothing, which stuck fast to her back. Her mistress, seeing that she could not remove it, took hold of the rough tow-linen under-garment and pulled it off over her head with a jerk, which took the skin with it, leaving her back all raw and sore. (9–10)

Foote's portrayal of her mother's resistance, with its linguistic emphasis on her mother's lack of agency, ultimately sees her mother as a victim, powerless to control her own fate (she was "obliged to call him master"). This view is reinforced when Foote explains, "This cruel master soon sold my mother, and she passed from one person's hands to another's, until she found a comparatively kind master and mistress" (10).[22] Foote's perception of her mother's vulnerability, perhaps, highlighted by her resistance, is significant for Foote's internally held image of her mother: for it traces the tensions entailed for Foote in making an identification with this once-enslaved mother.

The dangers of this identification (an identification that is unavoidable because she *is* her mother), seem to bear upon Foote's management of her own violent encounter with her "mistress," Mrs. Prime. In this episode, Foote struggles with issues of identification and aggression, as she seeks to preserve a sense of control in a situation which, recalling her mother's whipping, denies its victim agency and underlines her dependence. For Foote's record of her own whipping (following soon after her account of the assault on her mother) is entwined with fantasies of revenge, which she attempts to act out, before circumstances "save" her from the "sin" of enactment (25). Thus, Foote seems to alternate in her self-presentation between being the enslaved victim (like her mother) — powerless, but virtuous — and being a hostile aggressor (like her mistress) — powerful, but guilty of sin. The fluctuations of mood in this episode seem to arise from Foote's efforts to suppress her culturally forbidden rage against abuse, especially under conditions of dependency that make it dangerous to attack her attacker directly. But they may also reflect Foote's struggle with conflicted identifications: with her mother, whose vulnerability is frightening and must be warded off by disidentification; and with her maternal surrogate, Mrs. Prime, whose aggression is terrifying, and must be warded off by identification (so Foote can feel like an aggressor, not a victim). Accordingly, Foote, like Drumgoold, seeks to construct an identity within the tangle of contradictions that inhere in such cross-purposed attachments.

The chapter of Foote's whipping, called "The Undeserved Whipping," begins with her overarching observation that "All this time the Primes had treated me as though I were their own child. Now my feelings underwent a great change toward them; my dislike for them was greater than my love had been" (24). "This was the reason," she explains: one day Mrs. Prime accuses her of stealing some cakes, a charge Foote flatly denies, but to no avail.

Thus, the social protection she seems to receive from her association with the Primes when she attends a local school and is "treated well" by her classmates and schoolteacher, is undercut by the privatized abuse she begins to suffer in their home. What emerges in Foote's retelling is the ways in which her direct confrontation with Mrs. Prime unsettles her sense of emotional order, as she must somehow come to terms with what seems to be Mrs. Prime's sudden transformation from a loving surrogate maternal object — "who had always been so kind and motherly"—into a terrifying witch—who "frightened me so . . . that I trembled so violently I could not speak" (24).[23] Provoked, it seems, by the girl's shock and denial (a "refusal" to acquiesce, not unlike her mother's), Mrs. Prime apparently endeavors to justify her error by asserting her power to dominate (as her mother's master had). The next day, Mrs. Prime, along with her husband, returns from town with a rawhide (again, recalling the opening scene in which husband and wife are allied against the servant). But it is the "mistress" who uses it on the ten-year-old girl: "Mrs. Prime applied to my back until she was tired, all the time insisting that I should confess that I took the cakes. This, of course, I could not do" (24).

As noted above, Foote's whipping echoes the opening memory of her mother's punishment, and as that primal scene's descendant, emphasizes the victim's innocence and passive resistance to authority. But it also "rewrites" that founding memory. For Foote's refusal to "confess" to her mistress positions Foote outside of her mistress's domain, in a way that her mother's "confession" to her own mistress fails to do. The mother's confession (of what is, after all, her *master's* lust) seems merely to fuel her mistress's sense of aggrievement against *her,* and is used to buttress what may be her mistress's jealous fantasies about seductive slave women. In contrast, Foote's silence is a refusal to comply with Mrs. Prime's need to see the black girl as an ungrateful thief.

Foote's desire to rewrite her mother's experience in her own history is exhibited in her violent reactions to Mrs. Prime's abuse. She counters Mrs. Prime's torment of her victim, which is the nominal focus of this chapter, with a cluster of fantasies and startling outbursts, unleashing her own tremendous, pent-up fury. In this astonishing way, Foote figures herself as an aggressor, and in so doing recasts the overwhelming threat posed by Mrs. Prime's punishment as one incident in a series of displaced sadomasochistic encounters that culminate in her mutilation of Mrs. Prime's whip. Thus, she assumes some control over her own fate, although her expressions of rage against abuse are locked into a cycle of sadistic and masochistic actions.

Between the threat and the enactment of punishment, Foote fantasizes about committing suicide, a fantasy that gives expression to both the despair she feels over Mrs. Prime's malevolent accusations, against which her denial is no defense, and the anger she cannot vent directly against her mistress (the statement, "I trembled so violently I could not speak," can indicate both anger and fear). Tellingly, Foote's suicide fantasy symbolically is conflated with capital punishment: "That night I wished over and over again that I could be hung as John Van Paten had been"—her association to her memory of witnessing the public hanging of her school teacher, who was convicted of killing a mother of five (25). Van Paten's hanging haunts her dreams as a child: she would "see his head tumbling about the room as fast as it could go" (22). Thus, hanging herself seems to be, unconsciously, her punishment for her own murderous wishes against a mother, however fleeting those wishes might have been permitted to be. Indeed, the association between this mother and Mrs. Prime is underscored in Foote's noting that Van Paten murders in revenge for the disparaging comments his victim made about him.

But Foote, obviously, does not hang. Indeed, when she enters the barn, intent on killing herself (in her first displacement of her aggressive wishes), she finds, instead, an external target for her anger (a second object for displaced rage). In the barn, Foote comes across the boy who works for Mr. Prime, and is the one whom she believes to be, in fact, guilty of stealing the cakes. His sadistic pleasure at her suffering in his stead is infuriating, and her suicidal masochism gives way to an uninhibited impulse to kill *him:* "he laughed at me as hard as he could. All at once my weak feelings left me, and I sprang at him in a great rage, such as I had never known before; but he eluded my grasp, and ran away, laughing. Thus was I a second time saved from a dreadful sin" (25).

The two "sins" Foote refers to are, of course, those "sins" of aggression against herself and the other child. Interestingly, in looking back as an adult at her attack against the boy, Foote does not see any connection between herself and the boy, in whose apparent hunger and servitude she might—in retrospect—see reflected her own condition. She does not identity at all with this other child, reaffirming her affiliation with Mrs. Prime—in spite of the hostility—under whose domestic jurisdiction the cakes (and other food) fall. "I had no need to steal anything," she explains to the reader; "for I had plenty of everything there was" (24).

Thus, Foote's self-conception of her servitude (not unlike Drumgoold's) highlights underlying maternal dynamics. Reading her aggressive wishes as Foote locates them—against the background of the transmitted memory of her mother's abject victimization—we can see the degree to which they provide a form of relief for a culturally forbidden desire for revenge. Yet, when Foote destroys Mrs. Prime's whip after the beating, we get a deepening insight into the buried and displaced rage that links her memories of cruelty to her mother's, in a chain of familial recollection. She says: "That afternoon Mrs. Prime went away. . . . I carried the rawhide out to the wood pile, took the axe, and cut it up into small pieces, which I threw away" (26). Further, these memories create the additional link between the exploitation and abuse of free black Americans and the exploitation and abuse of African Americans under slavery.

Foote's enactment of murder by metonymy is also an image for sexualized rage, impotence, and trauma. The victim's revenge against physical abuse, with its sexual implications, is expressed in the bare aggression of Foote's chopping to bits that whip. Moreover, the whip, bought expressly for the purpose of beating Foote, associates the mistress's and master's dominion over the servant / slave's body with their sheer ability to purchase people and things. Yet, when Foote borrows the Primes' axe to demolish the Primes' whip, she borrows an identity from the aggressor that may be necessary to save her from the additional pain of feeling "objectified" and "abandoned" by her own mother.

For though her servitude and whipping may emotionally connect her to her mother, they are related to her mother's economic connection to Mrs. Prime and Julia's physical separation from her mother. Foote explicitly states her "dislike" of Mrs. Prime as hateful "mother," but Mrs. Prime is her "mistress" by virtue of what seems to be some contractual arrangement (formal or informal) between the Primes and Foote's parents, overriding questions of her personal preference (24). This, too, is framed as a matter of maternal dynamics: after Foote flees Mrs. Prime, returning to her parents' home, her mother sends her back, "very much against my will" (26).

Saved by Sin

A ten-year-old girl returned by her mother to an abusive mistress—"very much against my will"—may need to find a way to understand her own failure to be good enough to protect. Foote seemingly does this, by viewing herself as riddled with sin, and so deserving of punishment, not worthy of earthly love. Repeatedly, she transfers her conflicting fear of and fury against overpowering external figures of authorities into an inner drama of crime and punishment, a fight with what she calls an "inbeing monster" that besets her by tempting her to rage or forbidden forms of desire. Out of internalized prohibitions against libidinal and aggressive instincts arise the inner battle between her spiritual potential and her "carnal mind"—those dark fantasies of hate and longing that she considers to be Satan-sent. So her conclusion to her chapter on the "undeserved whipping" gives rueful expression to her sense of her own failure to please, while simultaneously her statements regarding the central point—how she *was* treated by the Primes—are ambiguous: "They [the Primes] were as kind to me as ever, after my return, though I did not think so at the time. I was not contented to stay there, and left when I was about twelve years old. The experience of that last year made me quite a hardened sinner. I did not pray very often, and, when I did, something seemed to say to me, 'That good man, with the white hair, don't like you anymore' " (26–27).

Earlier in her narrative, Foote had taken her parents' white minister—a man with "long gray hair and beard"—for the Lord; curiously, when he prayed for her, she thought, "I must die" (14). Although it may be that the "good man, with the white hair" is Mr. Prime, the echo of her earlier confusion seems present here, reinforced by the perception of the white man's hostile intentions. There is also some confusion surrounding her relations with those figures of authority, intimated in her revision of the past ("I did not think so at the time") and in the way her being a "hardened sinner" may be understood as either the cause or the effect of "that good man['s]" dislike. This doubled resonance and ambiguity reveal the permeability between the boundaries of the internal and external worlds and the past and the present in Foote's perceptions; they also link her need for spiritual attachment to her conflict over her personal, affective attachments on earth. Moreover, they bind her experience as an individual to her position as an African American in nineteenth-century America: "We were a despised and oppressed people; we had no refuge but God" (39).

Accordingly, Foote envisions her symbolic encounter with a

figure of authority whose Being is validated by, and validates, her suffering by making it not merely a test, but the very condition of being chosen for special care. Self-esteem and emotional security, undermined by an "undeserved whipping," are thus salvaged by partially conflating punishment with love. That the conflation is only partial—and only partially successful as a mechanism of defense—is hinted at by Foote's uncertainty about how the Primes actually treated her. Lurking in the background of every statement about her "sins" is the message that her punishments are "undeserved."

Nonetheless, identifying herself as a sinner, Foote can modulate feelings of unworthiness (I am nothing, therefore I suffer) into the authority of the deserving (I am bad, which is something, therefore I suffer, and thereby prove my worth). Thus, her classic consolation (similar to Drumgoold's): "God permits afflictions and persecutions to come upon his chosen people for various purposes" (109).

Given the logic of Foote's narrative, it practically follows that the scene of her spiritual selection, her "heavenly visitation" when she is chosen by God, will be the functional and figurative equivalent of a slave market. As she describes it, beneath a large tree, the powerful sit—God the Father, the Son, and the Holy Ghost—in the company of others who appear to be angels.

I was led before them: they looked me over from head to foot, but said nothing. Finally, the Father said to me: "Before these people make your choice, whether you will obey me or go from this place to eternal misery and pain." I answered not a word. He then took me by the hand to lead me, as I thought, to hell, when I cried out, "I will obey thee, Lord."

In this fantasy of utter vulnerability, Foote affirms her own powerlessness, yet at the same time deflects feelings of helplessness by emphasizing the potency of the threat and the necessity of obedience. More deeply, such extreme self-suppression before so absolute a Master suggests the underlying presence of a rage so explosive as to require these amassed prohibitions to contain it.

Foote's narrative struggle to subdue her culturally and politically forbidden aggression against phallic authorities—men and women—seems to lead to her own erection of an omnipotent Master who, if one is all His, can gratify one's fantasies of revenge: I may be meek, but "Bless the Lord that he is a 'man of war' " Foote writes, invoking the Old Testament warrior, who also figures in the slave lyric, "The God I serve is a man of war."[24]

As the mode of her enacted rage against Mrs. Prime suggests, as well as her striking shift at the end of the chapter, where she refers to "that good man" who does not "like me," turning to a stronger "father" may be a way to allay anxieties caused by harboring aggressive wishes against a destructive maternal object. As I have suggested earlier, Foote's whipping seems to be associated in her mind with her own murderous wishes against maternal figures. Then, too, we might recall that Foote's pursuit of sanctification is in "disobedience" of her mother (36, 41, 42). Indeed, so strong is her mother's initial aversion to Foote's chosen path, that Foote quotes her as saying, " 'Well, Julia . . . when I first heard [that you were a preacher] . . . I said I would rather hear you were dead' " (84). Though her mother hastens to assure her, " 'It is all past now. I have heard from those who have attended your meetings what the Lord has done for you, and I am satisfied,' " we have Foote's painful memory of her mother's rejection as evidence that it is not all past, especially now (84–85).

Thus, the identification Foote makes between her mother's suffering and her own is one she hopes to sever precisely through sanctification. Accordingly, in her vision, she recreates her "masters" as surrogate nurturing, maternal figures of love. For what follows Foote's declaration of obedience to her domineering Lord is her visionary fantasy of a ceremonial marriage to a gentle, affectionate figure who, referring back to the narrative's

168

opening scene of abuse—the washing and stripping—undoes what was done to her mother and, by substitution and inversion, undoes what her mother associatively did to her in returning her into the hands of the Primes: "My hand was given to Christ, who led me into the water and stripped me of my clothing. . . . Christ then appeared to wash me, the water feeling quite warm" (70). Thus, acts of cruelty (salt water to wash open wounds, being at the mercy of Mrs. Prime's threatening hand) are figuratively transposed into acts of great love. Importantly, this love is depleted of its sexual threat, in its replacement of the sexually predatory master with a soothing figure of "maternal" protection whose washing, despite its erotic overtones, is symbolically related to innocence and baptism.

Indeed, the images of impregnation at the end of this visitation scene are rendered as images of maternal sustenance and nurturance. The Holy Ghost appears and plucks fruit from a tree, and Foote and the angels all sit down to eat. It "had a taste like nothing I had ever tasted before"—and nourishes her as stolen cakes (not actually taken) never could (even if she had taken them) (70).[25] The proof Christ gives her of their encounter to show others intermingles images of paternal and maternal benevolence: he "appeared to write something with a golden pen, and golden ink, upon golden paper"; he then rolled it up and presented it to her to place in her "bosom" (70). Here the whip, transformed into a golden pen, transmits its "message" by displacement onto the paper, which is then rolled up (fetal-like / phallic-like) and nourished within her own bosom. Whatever dangers lurk in forbidden fruits and cracking whips are idealized away and made into tokens of purity and maternal love.

Not surprisingly, anxiety haunts Foote's sexual feelings for her husband, and she seems to deflect these feelings with images of Divine substitution. So Foote can exclaim in triumph over her feelings of desire for George, "Bless God! My desires are satisfied in him [the Lord]" (50). And when Foote quotes from the Bible, "For thy Maker is thine husband" (*Isaiah,* 54.5), she does so to contain her desire for and resentment against her husband when, for the second time early in their marriage, he ships out on an extended sea voyage.

Whipped into Faith

Finally, "whipping" reemerges as the dominant metaphor for Foote's oratorical and rhetorical modes. She elaborates upon her role as a preacher through an exegesis of the Biblical passage "Arise and thresh, O daughter of Zion" (*Micah,* 4.13). Asked to explain the passage, she begins, "Corn is not threshed in this manner by us, but by means of flails," instruments that are "quick and powerful and sharper than any two-edged sword. 'For this purpose,' " she continues, indicating that she is citing *Isaiah,*

"the Son of God was manifested, that he might destroy the works of the devil," and this is one of the weapons he employs ... together with the promise that they shall beat in pieces many people.

There are many instances of the successful application of the Gospel flail, by which means the devil is threshed out of sinners. With the help of God, I am resolved, O sinner, to try what effect the smart strokes of this threshing instrument will produce on thy unhumbled soul. (104–5)

Just as she had accepted her "castigation," so will the sinner whom she addresses. Thus, when she becomes a preacher, Foote, the beaten victim, becomes the "master" (in the sense of "teacher") who beats. Analogously, Christ, the embodiment of Christian suffering, is imaged as punisher, wielder of flails.[26] As martyr and avenger through her transformations of "whipping" as a trope, Foote linguistically tries to achieve some measure of internal integration of her aggressive impulses with the culturally sanctioned and individually internalized ideals of Christian self-denial. From this springs her activist rhetorical posture: "Why not yield, believe, and be sanctified now—now, while reading?" she asks her reader (122). And in a less gentle mode: "If any one arise from the perusal of this book, scoffing at the word of truth which he has read, I charge him to prepare to answer for the profanation at the peril of his soul" (111).

Yet it is not only the instruments of torture that link Foote's self-conception as a preacher to her efforts to overcome the internalized anxieties of being overwhelmed by whipping. Behind the physical abuse of the slave there lies what Julia Stern has called the "motif of the food chain," in which the African American slave is moved down the chain from person, to beast, to meat, to waste.[27] In Foote's narrative, the decline is reversed. When her mother's clothing sticks to her raw flesh, her mistress rips off her undergarment with a jerk, "which took the skin with it" (10). To take the skin from the body of a person is (in Stern's words) "to imagine . . . [her] . . . as an article of clothing or as potential food" (454). Against the background of this motif, the accusation of "stealing cakes" becomes a code for stealing oneself from being erased as a person. Indeed, turning the tables on her mistress, Foote transforms Mrs. Prime, metonymically, into meat, then garbage: "I cut [the whip] into small pieces, which I threw away" (26). When the Holy Ghost offers Foote some fruit to eat, she ascends higher in the food chain, and also inverts the self-debasing "fruits of slavery" that had been internalized by her mother, in her acceptance (as noted earlier) of the discrimination of her church (11). Finally, to be a thresher of human souls for the Lord, separating the human wheat from the chaff, is to have climbed to the top of this chain after all. It is true that, when viewed in this light, Foote's hard-won position of authority seems tainted by its clear references to force and power; but given the cultural prohibitions arrayed against her, it would not have been possible for Foote—a nineteenth-century black woman—to have attained a public voice without utilizing the aggressor's tools—as she had used the Primes' axe—in some fashion.

Before ending, it seems important to state explicitly that I do not think that Foote *must* have had slavery on—or in—her mind, simply because she was an African American author writing during slavery. I reject any notion that the only authorial identity available to nineteenth-century African American writers was, literally or figuratively, that of slave narrator. Such an expectation ignores Ralph Ellison's eloquent and powerful response to Irving Howe's prescriptive view of the "Negro" novel as being of necessity a painful protest against one's experience in American society: that "Negro" experience and, thus, "Negro" expression are varied and variable, the second not confined to being a cry of rage against the oppression presumed to be thoroughly constitutive of the first. As Ellison writes, "Negro life . . . is, for the Negro who must live it, not only a burden (and not always that) but also a *discipline*."[28] Indeed, it can be said that Foote's submissiveness and resistance seem to spring from the same source. That is, her complete self-denial (as eternal servant) and astonishing self-assertion (as an African American woman preacher) are both by-products of the disciplines of learning to "rejoice in persecution" and aspiring to a state of "Christian perfection—an extinction of every temper contrary to love" (120). Still, Foote's repeated narrative return to "whipping" as fact and metaphor does reveal the indirect ways in which her mother's transmitted memory of enslavement constitutes an originary memory in the daughter's sense of self, just as Drumgoold's returns to sickness mark her "mothers' " slavery homes as sites of memory for her. Then, too, the burdens of private, many-layered memory are surely what drive these women to recreate themselves as public figures, where private pain may find amelioration through collective thought and action.

The masochism in Drumgoold's and Foote's narrative strategies of liberation are linguistic manifestations of the persistence of the memory of slavery within the dominant culture's ideas about race and sex. Finally their narratives invite us to consider the ways in which a belief in spiritual transcendence over historical conditions can be not merely a mode of personal defense or adaptation, but also a model for cultural transformation with radical cultural implications. So, we might read Drumgoold's anticipation of her reunion with her "two mothers" in heaven, where their differences will be erased, or Foote's goal of a "colorless" and "sexless" state of being before a God "who is no respecter of persons," as alternatives to the polarizing ways in which bodies were racially and sexually marked in the post-Reconstruction North. Finally, slavery had meant the body in pain: from overwork, undernourishment, disease, and torture. Thus, in translating bodily sickness and punishment into symbols of spiritual endurance, Drumgoold and Foote seek to recover their bodies for their souls through their minds. The need to endure is the mother of strategies of endurance.

In her study of nineteenth- and twentieth-century novels and autobiographies about racial experience in the Old South, Minrose C. Gwin shows how "the peculiar sisterhood in American literature" between black and white women is bound up in the tensions between "interconnection and rejection," tensions which "become not only the external construct of the dynamics of racism, but are as powerfully realized as an internal psychological tension within the female psyche" (4, 171). One of my goals has been to contribute to our understanding of the origins, nature, and effects of that difficult sisterhood as represented in the antislavery and autobiographical narratives of various nineteenth-century women. As Gwin demonstrates, the slave woman's depictions of her relations with her mistress do reveal a "peculiar sisterhood." Yet, as all of the narratives under consideration disclose, the *topos* of the African American slave narrator's first encounter with a white woman is actually represented as an engagement between a child and an adult. The interplay within an interracial "sisterhood," therefore, seems a later expression of a more primary relation—that between a daughter and a mother.

Thus, as we have seen dramatically with Kate Drumgoold, for instance, that primary relation takes shape within a matrix of multiple, ambivalent confrontations: between the narrator / protagonist and her own mother, between the narrator / protagonist and her surrogate "white mother," and between the narrator / protagonist and herself. One effect of these confounding encounters, a consequence of slavery's rupturing of the mother-

ıd, is the narrator / protagonist's ambivalent attitude
er own self as mother. Think of Keckley's suppression
f as mother. Or of the absence, in Drumgoold's account, of any history of her own relation to motherhood, other
than her characterizing herself as an eternally dutiful slave
daughter.

The complications of "motherhood" caused by slavery surface
in Harriet Jacobs's *Incidents in the Life of a Slave Girl,* as well; and
it is to her important text that I would now like to return, in light
of the problematics of motherhood raised throughout my book.
I would draw particularly upon Drumgoold's account (written,
coincidentally, the year Jacobs died), despite the obvious differences between the two narratives. For, like Drumgoold's (as,
indeed, like Keckley's and Foote's), Jacobs's experience of going
to her mistress's house to live as a very young girl is linked in
memory to her separation from her own mother. Moreover, like
Drumgoold, Jacobs responds to the loss of her mother when she
was six, by turning to her mother's (and her own) mistress for
maternal recognition—that is, a sense of herself as this mother's
child: "I was told that my home was now to be with her mistress;
and I found it to be a happy one. . . . I would sit by her side for
hours, sewing diligently, with a heart as free from care as that of
any free-born white child" (7). Reading back across her years of
slavery, Jacobs remarks, "Those were happy days—too happy to
last" (7). Remembering how she wept when her mistress died six
years after her going to live with her, Jacobs explains, "I loved
her for she had been almost like a mother to me" (7).

"Almost like a mother" is the telling phrase Jacobs uses to
describe not only her mistress, but her mother's sister (her Aunt
Nancy) and her maternal grandmother, to whom she also turns.
Telling, because it expresses Jacobs's sense of loss for her own
mother, for whom these other women are always substitutes.
"Almost like a mother" also conveys both Jacobs's recognition of

her need for connection to a maternal figure, and her deeper sense that no one is her mother anymore.

The discrepancy between her own mother and her almost mother-like mistress becomes especially significant for Jacobs upon the death of the mistress. For it is this mistress who, having promised Jacobs's dying mother (the mistress's "foster-sister") that she would free her children in her will, breaks her promise, and, in so doing, becomes the agent behind Jacobs's enslavement to the brutal, lascivious Dr. Flint. Thus, Jacobs finds herself, as she looks back, having to reconcile her memories of having been carefree and loved by her maternal white mistress with her recognition of having been, all the time, exactly this woman's slave. As Jacobs writes of her struggle with this fact of maternal betrayal: "I would give much to blot out from my memory that one great wrong. As a child, I loved my mistress; and looking back on the happy days I spent with her, I try to think with less bitterness of this act of injustice" (8).

Thus, the dynamic between the need for connection and the sense of loss darkens into the tension between the need for connection and the sense of betrayal. Attachment and betrayal persist in Jacobs's wished-for alliances with other white women in whose homes she comes to live, including her embittered and sadistic mistress Mrs. Flint. "The mistress who ought to protect the helpless victim," writes Jacobs with reference to her persecution by Dr. Flint, "has no other feelings towards her but those of jealousy and rage" (27–28). Jacobs's appeal here is for a protective mother; Mrs. Flint, instead, regards the slave girl as a rival. In these passages, in which Jacobs recalls her wish to turn toward her mistress, she reinforces her association of "mother" with "protection," when she observes how Dr. Flint violates the sacredness of the mother-daughter bond: "If I knelt by my mother's grave, his dark shadow fell on me even there" (28). Dead,

Jacobs's mother cannot help her, just as she had been unable to help the twelve-year-old Jacobs when her mistress's written-down will rode over her orally expressed will that her children be left free. Soon, Jacobs reinvokes the image of her kneeling before a mother when she explains that what she wants from the hardened Mrs. Flint is gentleness, nothing more: "I never wronged her, or wished to wrong her; and one word of kindness from her would have brought me to her feet" (32).

The image of Jacobs kneeling is intricately woven into a pattern of associations that seem to position her in relation to various maternal figures. Yet, this image also recalls the abolitionist symbol of the kneeling slave woman beseeching the help of her more powerful, white "sister." As such, Jacobs's complicated attitude toward maternal figures becomes related to the narrative posture she adopts in her preface, when she petitions the "women of the North to a realizing sense of the condition of two millions of women at the South, still in bondage" (1).

Of course, vast differences exist between Jacobs's relations to Mrs. Flint and those to her Northern audience—not least of these, that what Jacobs does personally affects Mrs. Flint, and the reverse. But the modality of Jacobs's rhetorical position in relation to her putative audience seems at least partially derived from her earlier necessary attachments to the white women in whose homes she has served—the white mistresses of her childhood and adolescence. Given the historical, material conditions of those connections (from which her relations to the two Mrs. Bruce's also take their hue), Jacobs's representations of these cross-racial "mother-like" bonds are torn between conflicting modes of attachment and rejection, hope and despair, trust and distrust. Truly invested, on the one hand, in her desire for empathetic identification between enslaved black and free white women, Jacobs is well aware, on the other, of the rejection she is bound to meet. She has met with it before.

Another aspect of Jacobs's relation to "motherhood" is enacted in her representation of herself as a mother. In my earlier discussion of *Incidents,* I argued that Jacobs had to distance herself from the Victorian cult of motherhood in order to follow her father's directive to escape. I would like now to qualify that observation by exploring how, for Jacobs, motherhood is, in fact, the other necessary condition of her flight. That is, motherhood provides a way for Jacobs to come to terms with the problematic "motherhood" she experienced as a girl. Paradoxically, by following the cultural dictate to do all for your children, motherhood gives Jacobs her rationale for "disappearing" from her children's sight in order to try to secure her own freedom and theirs. Yet as a complicated *symbolic* action, running away is at once a rejection of the image she has constructed of her beloved mother—as chaste and passive—but also a repetition of her mother's own "disappearance" from her. Indeed, her plans to flee are in violation of what she represents as her grandmother's code and curse: "Nobody respects a mother who forsakes her children; and if you leave them, you will never have a happy moment" (91).

Her "perilous passage" to becoming a mother is suggestive of the dangers for a slave girl that motherhood entails. Having children was understood to be an obstruction to escape and no protection against sexual abuse. To prevent children from following their fate, slave mothers sometimes resorted to costly measures— among them, running away, infanticide, or abortion. The slave Ellen Craft, having been "torn from her mother's embrace in childhood . . . had seen so many other children separated from their parents in this cruel manner, that the mere thought of her ever becoming the mother of a child, to linger out a miserable existence under the wretched system of American slavery, appeared to fill her soul with horror" (*Running a Thousand Miles for Freedom,* 27).

Jacobs, however, after sending her free black lover away, so that his children would not be slaves, makes what is surely an audacious move—to becoming Mr. Sands's mistress and, predictably, the mother of *his* children. Such a decision seems to grow out of a tangle of feelings—of despair and of hope, of longed-for affection and frustrated desire, of a need for protection, and a wish for revenge. In becoming the mistress of her master's white neighbor, she turns passivity into activity by choosing a white lover instead of waiting to be forced (by her master), thereby taking on the sexual role that she has fought to avoid (mistress to a white man). She also moves from the vocabulary of violence and force to the language of option and choice, even though she feels she has no choice. Thus, she begins her protracted flight from Dr. Flint.

But the psychological advantages in this dangerous move seem to lie, above all, in her ability to hurt her tormentor. One of her stated reasons for accepting Mr. Sands, that Dr. Flint will relent in his pursuit of her when he finds out, is undermined somewhat by her anticipatory pleasure at, as she sees it, having struck out first: "I had a feeling of satisfaction and triumph in the thought of telling *him*" (56).

In fact, however, Jacobs becomes more entangled in her relationship with Dr. Flint: infuriated and jealous, he becomes violent and vindictive. Then, too, her own sense of self is wounded. For although she uses the circumstances of her motherhood to provide a critique of the Victorian ideology of womanhood, writing "that a slave woman ought not to be judged by the same standards as others," she nevertheless judges herself by these standards: "The painful and humiliating memory [of her sexual history] will haunt me to my dying day" (55–56).

Yet, as I have already suggested, becoming a mother as she does, in violation of culturally sanctioned codes of conduct, gives her the requisite self-denying justification to break the law and run away: "more for my children's sake than for my own" (10). Motherhood, perhaps, serves Jacobs in other ways as well. By becoming a mother she can try to alleviate the sorrow and pain of her own experiences of maternal betrayal (the death of her own mother and her failure to protect her, both of which a child might experience as betrayal, and the betrayals of her exploitative white mother-figures). Motherhood also allows her to give symbolic form to her fear and anger at having been left, unprotected, with the abusive Dr. Flint. For in her flight from slavery, Jacobs "abandons" her children to the care of others, thereby figuratively repeating her own maternal loss, but in her recovery of them, she recovers herself in her children, the self who had been left motherless at age six.

In *Incidents,* Jacobs confronts what she fears will be the reaction of white Northern readers in her staging of her grandmother's refusal to forgive her. Believing that Jacobs has succumbed to Dr. Flint, her grandmother responds with melodramatic clichés: " 'O Linda! Has it come to this? I had rather see you dead than to see you as you are. You are a disgrace to your dead mother' " (56). Even after she learns the truth about her granddaughter's relationship with Mr. Sands, she does not retreat from her moralistic position, although she expresses pity for Jacobs, and she helps hide her from Dr. Flint. Yet, an alternative model of reception for Jacobs's narrative is depicted in the chapter Jacobs calls "The Confession," in which she describes how she tells her daughter the story of her own sufferings and her daughter's origin. A story of anguish that bears repeating, what Jacobs tells Ellen is a recapitulation of the narrative the reader has already read.

I recounted my early sufferings in slavery, and told her how nearly they had crushed me. I began to tell her how they had driven me into a great sin, when she clasped me in her arms, and exclaimed, "O, don't mother! Please don't tell me anymore."

I said, "But, my child, I want you to know about your father."

"I know all about it, mother," she replied; "I am nothing to my father, and he is nothing to me. All my love is for you." (188–89)

When her daughter transfers all her love to her, Jacobs reconstructs in their relationship the fantasy of the all-encompassing love between mother and child. " 'All my love is for you,' " the daughter promises; and by inversion, this is the promise of the mother to her daughter. Their symbiotic bond is further affirmed in the fact that they both already share the secret of the father's sin, which comes to be seen as the sin of a parent rejecting his own child. As Ellen continues, " 'I used to wish he would take me in his arms and kiss me, as he did Fanny [her white half-sister] . . . I thought if he was my own father, he ought to love me. I was a little girl then, and didn't know any better' " (189). Touching upon the themes of sexual exploitation and emotional deprivation, the mother and daughter exchange their solitary burdens of degradation and rejection for a mutually reinforcing recognition of their similar pasts. For though Jacobs does not herself have a white half-sister who seems to have all her father's love, she did have a mother whose "foster-sister" betrayed *her*, and she does know the bitterness of the enslaved mixed-race child's experience, one that impresses its lessons upon the very young.

It is significant, too, that in telling her story to her daughter, Jacobs also seeks and receives forgiveness and acceptance for her own absence as a mother, for the years she was in hiding, for her years of silence. That the revelation of her secrets to her audience might also yield forgiveness and acceptance seems to be among Jacobs's hopes and desires. Thus, what she seeks through her narrative confession is recognition of herself as a mother who is not after all unlike the image she has retained of her own mother—virtuous, loving, and beloved.

In this rereading, recovery of her mother through becoming a mother is one tortuous strategy for dealing with the conflicts of identity that being a woman, black, and once-enslaved hold for the fugitive slave woman seeking her home in the antebellum North. It is a necessary psychological maneuver, as necessary as negotiating her more suppressed identification with her angry father, who despises the master class, and does not hide it. Indeed, Jacobs must realign her self-image with the imago of her "dead mother" in order to *justify* and *promote* her escape, just as she must embrace her identification with the imago of her "dead father" in order to *effect* her escape.

Perhaps what draws readers to Jacobs's narrative is the relatively comprehensive and complicated picture of family dynamics under slavery that it seems to afford. Keckley, Drumgoold, and Foote emerge no less vividly through their narrated memories; but their stories are far more fragmented, more ruptured by omissions. We can readily see how slavery and racism impinged upon these autobiographers' tasks of remembrance and revelation. Yet, it is the case that even the narratives of Child and Stowe are constructed around the silences created by the cultural and personal prohibitions that racism and slavery fostered. What all of the authors under study could not or would not say, I have tried to elicit from what they did say. What they did say remains a remarkable testimony to their will to come to terms with the pasts they were given and to write something that might make them their own.

NOTES

Notes to Prologue

1. See "Of *Lily*, Linda Brent, and Freud: A Non-Exceptionalist Approach to Race, Class, and Gender in the Slave South."

2. In an introduction to the 1990 reissued edition of *Black Odyssey: The African-American Ordeal in Slavery* (originally published in 1977), Nathan Irvin Huggins writes, "However much black and white, slave and freedom seem to be polar opposites, we must see them not only as interdependent but as having a common story and necessarily sharing the same fate. That is another way of saying 'community,' albeit unilaterally antagonistic, parasitic, and exploitative" (xliv). For Croly, see Werner Sollors, "National Identity and Ethnic Diversity: 'Of Plymouth Rock and Jamestown and Ellis Island'; or, Ethnic Literature and Some Redefinitions of 'America,' " in Fabre and O'Meally, 92–93.

3. This advice was surely heartfelt: Mattie Jackson dictated her autobiography to a Dr. L. S. Thompson, an African American woman, who wrote it down for publication. Presumably, Jackson was unable to read or write well enough to write her own story.

Notes to Chapter 1

1. For examples of the "response" to Elkins, see Lane, ed., *The Debate over Slavery;* Blassingame, *The Slave Community;* Genovese, *Roll, Jordan, Roll* and *In Red and Black: Marxian Explorations in Southern and Afro-American History;* Stampp, *The Imperiled Union: Essays on the Background of the Civil War;* Gutman, *The Black Family in Slavery and Freedom;* Levine, *Black Culture and Black Consciousness;* White, *Ar'n't I a Woman?* Bertram Wyatt-Brown offers a reassessment of the "slave personality" and the variety of responses in "The Mask of Obedience: Male Slave Psychology in the Old South" (1988).

2. By the nineteenth century, slavery was self-reproducing: that is, most slaves were born into slavery, not kidnapped and transported to the South-

ern plantations by force. Thus, antebellum slavery may be seen as an institution built upon the abuse and neglect of children. Moreover, slave children were vulnerable not only to white adults in their "family," whose power to abuse was culturally and politically endorsed; they were vulnerable also to the outbursts and neglect of underfed and overworked black adults, who were themselves raised under the legacy of abuse.

3. See Olney, " 'I Was Born': Slave Narratives, Their Status as Autobiography and as Literature."

4. Among the early rhetoric-based studies in addition to Gates are Stepto, *From behind the Veil;* Andrews, *To Tell a Free Story;* Houston A. Baker, Jr., *The Journey Back* and *Blues, Ideology, and Afro-American Literature.*

5. "Authority, (White) Power and the (Black) Critic," (27). See also Gates, *Figures in Black.*

6. See Foster, *Written by Herself;* Gwin, *Black and White Women of the Old South;* Carby, *Reconstructing Womanhood;* Valerie Smith, *Self-Discovery and Authority in Afro-American Narrative;* Braxton, *Black Women Writing Autobiography;* Yellin, *Women and Sisters.* In 1988, Valerie Smith wrote,

> A gender-specific analysis of black narrative might now consider the source of the male narrator / protagonist's investment in literacy, the relationship between literacy and the assertion of male power, or the specifically masculine legacy that Douglass and other male slave narrators bequeath to future Afro-American writers. Considerations of gender might also foreground the alternative legacy of a woman slave narrator such as Jacobs. . . . would necessarily focus on more indirect, surreptitious assertions of power and suggest differences in the ways in which Afro-American men and women represent their relation to language. ("Gender and Afro-Americanist Theory and Criticism," 61)

7. Significantly, the feminist "gendering" of slave narratives refocused study of men's narratives with reference to questions of manhood: literacy could be redefined as merely the originary movement from passivity to activity, which then manifested itself in other (American) masculine terms—physical aggressiveness, economic competitiveness, and self-reliance.

8. Freud's account of the compulsion to repeat, like his account of everything, evolved over many years. In "Remembering, Repeating and Working-Through" (1914), he discusses repetition as a replacement for

remembering within the context of the psychoanalytic transference. Here, the patient "acts out" what has been forgotten and repressed, in symbolic repetition of early encounters and experiences. In "The 'Uncanny' " (1919) Freud relates the uncanny to the repetition-compulsion, in that uncanny experiences are the sense of the return of an earlier impression that was deemed unacceptable and gradually repressed. In *Beyond the Pleasure Principle* (1920), he elaborates upon his theory of the compulsion to repeat as an instinct for mastery over unpleasant realities, but then goes on to call it a "daemonic" force independent of and prior to the pleasure-principle, an urge "to restore an earlier state of things"—a death-instinct. Finally, in *Moses and Monotheism* (1939), Freud calls the compulsion to repeat an unconscious fixation to early trauma, which creates in the psyche a "State within a State, an inaccessible party, with which co-operation is impossible, but which may succeed in overcoming what is known as the normal party and forcing it into its service" (76). In this paper, written over the course of four years (1934–38), Freud argues that the history of the Jews is structured like a trauma; therefore, the metaphor of warring States resonates with the crisis that was unfolding in Europe, with its devastating consequences for Jews (and personal implications for Freud) as he wrote.

9. This list of motivations is adapted from Phyllis Greenacre's "Influence of Infantile Trauma on Genetic Patterns."

10. In my chapter on *Incidents* (chapter 3), I handle Jacobs's use of psuedonyms by giving both names, as in Brent / Jacobs. In the other chapters, however, I have decided to avoid the rhetorical awkwardness this creates.

11. This view finds interesting reinforcement in a case study by British psychoanalyst D. W. Winnicott, written up in "On the Basis for Self in the Body" (1970). Winnicott describes the case of an eight-year-old girl of African descent who had been adopted at age one by a white family who already had a three-year-old girl. When Mollie was five, a boy was born. The mother brought Mollie for consultation with Winnicott because of her "persecution" of the little boy. In the course of treatment, Mollie announced she was going to draw a picture of her "bottom." When she was seemingly finished, she immediately began to jab it aggressively with the pencil, while saying, "Oh how I wish I were white." As she continued drawing, she said, "Yes, I'm dark, but I like white better." In Winnicott's view, the idealization of whiteness and the self-denigration were a defense

against aggressive wishes against the "white babies and white mother" (in the way the "bottom" was also mother's cheeks and breast). According to Winnicott, Mollie "had only gradually come to find out" about the ways in which her dark skin relates to a sense of early deprivation. That is, "she accepts her condition but feels cramped by having to dwell in a dark skin, not because of what she looks like now, but because of what it would mean in terms of the earliest stages of experience" (282–83; reprinted in *Psychoanalytic Explorations*).

12. After all, a slave would have had little hope of studying medicine in France—that is, of becoming Fanon. And plans to return slaves to Africa, where they would presumably be able to make a nation among their "own race," were equally unrealistic (as well as based on assumptions about inherent racial traits). The colonizationist position taken by Harriet Beecher Stowe at the conclusion of *Uncle Tom's Cabin* provoked Frederick Douglass to retort, "The truth is, dear madam, we are *here,* & here we are likely to remain" (Hedrick 235). The fact that a number of ex-slaves, Douglass and Jacobs among them, considered settling permanently in England, where they experienced far less race prejudice, suggests the psychologically eroding pressures that living among white Americans, Northerners included, would exert on freedmen and women.

13. Thanks to Eric Haralson for reminding me of Du Bois's use of "other."

14. This is also quoted by Accardo and Portelli in "A Spy in the Enemy's Country: Domestic Slaves as Internal Foes," an especially illuminating discussion about the emotional and political confusions that slavery created for the ruler and the ruled.

15. The status of black women has been a vexed issue in both the histories of civil rights and feminism in this country. The exclusion of women from the Fifteenth Amendment guarantees fractured the American Equal Rights Association into those who wanted to seek black male suffrage first, those who wanted to seek women's suffrage first, and those who wanted to keep black male and women's suffrage linked. Frederick Douglass could not abide the derision of black men that seemed to creep into the rhetoric of feminists, such as Susan B. Anthony and Elizabeth Cady Stanton. In the morning session of the Association's meeting in New York City on May 12, 1869, Anthony is reported as saying, "If intelligence, justice, and moralities are to be placed in the government, then let the question of woman be brought first and that of the negro last." Douglass's

opposing argument for a greater urgency in giving the ballot to "the negro" is suggestive (as is Anthony's statement) of the tendency toward rhetorical erasure of black women as women:

> When women, because they are women, are hunted down through the streets of New York and New Orleans; when they are dragged from their homes and hung upon lamp-posts; when their children are torn from their arms and their brains dashed upon the pavement; when they are objects of insult and outrage at every turn; when they are in danger of having their homes burnt down over their heads; when their children are not allowed to enter schools; then they will have an urgency to obtain the ballot equal to our own. (216)

When a voice from the audience asked, "Is that not all true about black women?" Douglass responded, "Yes, yes, yes, it is true of the black woman, but not because she is a woman but because she is black" (Blassingame and McKivigan, eds., *The Frederick Douglass Papers*, 216–17).

16. I was prompted to write this section by Michael Goldman's essay "Eyolf's Eyes: Ibsen and the Cultural Meanings of Child Abuse."

17. Yellin's notes indicate a thirty-five-year difference; in her narrative Jacobs makes him forty years older. With reference to Harriet Jacobs's experience, Painter advocates using Freud's psychoanalytic insights on the sexual dynamics within the bourgeois European household, which consisted of members of different social, economic, and ethnic groups, to understand sexuality in the nineteenth- and twentieth-century South. Her recently anthologized essay, "Of *Lily*, Linda Brent, and Freud: A Non-Exceptionalist Approach to Race, Class, and Gender in the Slave South," offers us one model for a Freudian approach to sexuality in the South, and lays out an agenda of important work to be done in Southern history. In another essay, "Soul Murder and Slavery: Toward a Fully Loaded Cost Accounting," Painter advocates analyzing slavery through the interpretive framework of recent psychological theorizing on child abuse and its consequences.

18. To take one example, slave narrator Mattie J. Jackson's mother married her second husband six years after her first one was sold; the mother was left alone again four years later when her master sold her second husband. After the war, Mattie's father, who himself had remarried and was living in Massachusetts, tracked down his first family and paid for

his two children, Mattie and her younger brother, to come live with him and attend school in the North.

19. See "The Concept of Trauma in Relation to the Development of the Individual within the Family" (1965), reprinted in *Psychoanalytic Explorations,* 148.

Notes to Chapter 2

1. Stowe is thought to have wavered on the issue of colonization. Biographer Joan D. Hedrick believes that she was swayed most by her father, Lyman Beecher, and husband, Calvin Stowe, in her antislavery views before the Fugitive Slave Act of 1850 radicalized her beyond *Uncle Tom's Cabin's* colonizationist ending.

2. Frederickson describes romantic racialism as "The American 'ethnologic' self-image, whether described as Anglican, Anglo-Saxon, Celtic-Anglo-Saxon, or simply Caucasian, [which] was formulated and popularized at the very time when the slavery controversy focused interest on the Negro character" (100).

3. The ironies of this American genealogy have generally been imaged by African American writers in terms of lost paternity (this is a recurring theme in Douglass's slave narratives); in the mythology of the national identity, it is Thomas Jefferson—who may or may not have fathered children by his slave, Sally Hemings—who has most persistently been used to embody the figure of "founding father" of both freedom and slaves. In *Clotel, or the President's Daughter* (1853), the first version of this novel, William Wells Brown begins with a scene of a slave auction "at which the two daughters of Thomas Jefferson, the writer of the Declaration of Independence, and one of the presidents of the great republic, were disposed to the highest bidder" (123). (In the 1864 edition, retitled *Clotelle: A Tale of the Southern States,* Jefferson drops out.) Brown was himself the very fair mulatto son of a slave woman and his master's white half-brother—a condition which earned him the hostility of his mistress and the resentment of other slaves.

The special bias against the mulatto child is also a theme of Harriet E. Wilson's autobiographical novel *Our Nig; or, Sketches from the Life of a Free Black* (1859). In this novel, however, in which the mulatto child is the offspring of a white mother and a black father, the problematic relationship is with the mother, who allows her daughter to be given away as an indentured servant. (A maternal figure is also her primary tormentor in her new home.) Another intriguing use of an image of maternity at the root of freedom and slavery is Theodore Parker's sarcasm, "The most valuable export of Virginia, is her Slaves, enriched by the 'best blood of the old dominion'; the 'Mother of Presidents' is also the great Slave Breeder of America" (Sundquist, 41).

4. In her slave narrative, *From the Darkness Cometh the Light or Struggles for Freedom,* Lucy A. Delaney describes her mother's doubled response to news of another daughter's escape:

> Mother was very thankful [when her mistress told her], and in her heart arose a prayer of thanksgiving, but outwardly she pretended to be angry and vexed. Oh! the impenetrable mask of these poor black creatures! how much of joy, or sorrow, of misery and anguish they have hidden from their tormentors! I was a small girl at that time, but remember how wildly my mother showed her joy at Nancy's [her sister's] escape when we were alone together [out of sight of the mistress]. (18–19)

5. Hammond's own sexual appetites—discussed with astonishing frankness in his diaries and letters—caused him no small amount of trouble. While he was Governor of South Carolina he secretly engaged in some sort of sexual activity with his four teenaged nieces. Their relations—which included "everything short of sexual intercourse," as he writes in his diary— lasted for two years (from 1841 through 1843) (*Secret and Sacred,* 175). When one of the girls told, their father, Wade Hampton II, one of the South's richest plantation owners, publicly denounced Hammond. Meanwhile, Hammond had several children by a slave named Sally, whom he had purchased along with her one-year-old daughter Louisa in 1839. When Louisa turned twelve, Hammond took her as his mistress and had several more children. Hammond's long-suffering wife, Catherine, who bore him eight children, left him for several years when he refused to give up Louisa.

6. Werner Sollors has recently shown how fear of miscegenation was related to later alarms about the consequences of unchecked immigration from non-Anglo-Saxon countries; racial and ethnic mixing would be a driving issue in the late nineteenth-century debates about where to draw the color line in order to divide, as Henry James would put it in *The American Scene* (1907), "aliens" from "Americans." As Sollors points out, David Goodman Croly, writing in 1888, adopted an oracular persona to make this prophecy:

We can absorb the Dominion . . . for the Canadians are of our own race . . . but Mexico, Central America, the Sandwich Islands, and the West India Islands will involve governments which cannot be democratic. We will never confer the right of suffrage upon the blacks, the mongrels of Mexico or Central America, or the Hawaiians. . . . The white race is dominant and will keep their position no matter how numerous the negroes may become (*Glimpses of the Future, Suggestions as to the Drift of Things;* cited in Sollors, "National Identity and Ethnic Diversity: 'Of Plymouth Rock and Jamestown and Ellis Island'; or, Ethnic Literature and Some Redefinitions of 'America,' " in Fabre and O'Meally, 93).

7. For discussions about the connections between nineteenth-century feminism and abolitionism see, for example, Ellen DuBois, "Women's Rights and Abolition: The Nature of the Connection" and Blanche Glassman Hersh, " 'Am I Not a Woman and a Sister?': Abolitionist Beginnings of Nineteenth-Century Feminism," both in Perry and Fellman, eds., *Antislavery Reconsidered: New Perspectives on the Abolitionists.* Also, see Vron Ware, *Beyond the Pale: White Women, Racism, and History.* This book's project is to trace the connections between race and gender in British feminism, but Ware begins with an examination of the social relations of race, class, and gender in Britain and America during slavery.

8. This paragraph was omitted when the story was republished four years later in *Fact and Fiction,* a collection of short stories. Other stories in this collection, like "The Quadroons," deal with themes of interracial romances and prejudice, motherlessness, and the betrayal of women.

9. For a brief discussion of the assumption of "mulatto superiority" and its persistance after slavery see C. W. Harper's "Black Aristocrats: Domestic Servants on the Antebellum Plantation."

10. See Yellin, *Women and Sisters,* for an extensive discussion of this image and its significance.

11. The first comment appears in a letter to Lucy Searle, June 9, 1861 (Meltzer and Holland, *Letters,* 384). The second is from a letter written in 1862 to Sarah Shaw, mother of Col. Robert Gould Shaw, who led the Fifty-Fourth Regiment of black troops and was killed on July 18, 1863 (quoted in Clifford, 260).

12. See Freud, "Family Romances" (1908).

13. The metaphor of family to describe black and white relations was

also used by proslavery ideologues, partially as a way to argue that the paternalistic system of slavery was far more humane than the industrial, capitalistic class relations up North. The most radical statement of this position came from George Fitzhugh, who called Northerners "slaves to capital, 'slaves without masters' " (282). By contrast, slave society,

> a series of subordination, is consistent with christian [sic] morality— for fathers, masters, husbands, wives, children, and slaves, not being equals, rivals, competitors, and antagonists, best promote each others' selfish interests when they do most for those above or beneath them. Within the precincts of the family, including slaves, the golden rule is a practical and wise guide of conduct. (291)

Nonetheless, one of the premises of this book, as noted in chapter 1, is that the idea of "our family, black and white" cannot be dismissed as merely proslavery propaganda, since it describes not only how white slaveholders *wanted* to view master-slave relations (to rationalize their conduct), but also how slave narrators (as well as their masters) of necessity related to the members of the extended households that were the context for the development of their complex senses of identity. Two recent discussions focusing on the implications of the metaphor of family for white slaveholders, one by Elizabeth Fox-Genovese, the other by Eugene Genovese, appear in Bleser, *In Joy and in Sorrow.* See also their earlier works, Fox-Genovese's *Within the Plantation Household* and Genovese's *Roll, Jordan, Roll.*

14. David S. Reynolds uses the phrase the "paradox of immoral didacticism" in his discussion of the subversive and sensational elements that inhered in the reform propaganda of antebellum America. See Reynolds, *Beneath the American Renaissance,* chapter 2.

15. Anna Shannon Elfenbein sees reproduction of the quadroon mother's story in the daughter's tale as being characteristic of their racially overdetermined fate: "Unlike Hester, her fate was often to reproduce her own tragedy. . . . she could not prevent her daughters from suffering as she had suffered," 3.

16. Xarifa, as Christopher Bongie pointed out to me, is the fair marked by an "X."

17. Legal sanctions against incest in the South did not recognize interracial sexual encounters. For a discussion of incest laws in the Victorian South see Bardaglio, " 'An Outrage upon Nature'; Incest and Law in the Nineteenth-Century South" in Bleser, 32–51.

18. In "Infantile Anxiety-Situations Reflected in a Work of Art and in the Creative Impulse," Melanie Klein explains the alteration between destructive impulses and reactive tendencies as arising out of the anxiety produced by the girl's aggressive impulses toward her mother and her fear that her mother, in turn, wishes to destroy her.

19. Despite the evidence of slave narratives that white Southern mistresses often verbally and physically abused their slaves themselves, proslavery ideology insisted on the physical frailty, delicacy, and passivity of white women for its own purposes. According to Fox-Genovese, such a view of white Southern womanhood implicitly distanced her from her dark African slaves and justified her need for servants. It also turned white male aggression and domination into a positive value, necessary to protect the Southern lady against "unruly" men, white or black. See chapter 4, "Gender Conventions," *Within the Plantation Household*.

20. See Freud, "The 'Uncanny'" (1919). This view of the double is consonant with what Fanon, in *Black Skin, White Masks,* claims is the position of the black self in relation to the white world.

21. Thus, sadism is transformed into masochism. In "A Child Is Being Beaten," Freud considers the implications of the ways in which each figure in the beating fantasy in some sense substitutes for the person who has the fantasy. Eric Haralson offers a fascinating reading of this dynamic with reference to issues of masculinity in Henry James's relation to his American, Christopher Newman; see "James's *The American:* A (New)man Is Being Beaten."

22. The first quotation is from *The Oasis,* edited by Child (Boston: Allen and Ticknor, 1834), cited in Clifford, vii.

23. It is important for Toni Morrison's purposes in *Beloved,* her historical novel about slavery's impact on the interior life of a slave woman, that Sethe's flight takes place in 1855, when the Fugitive Slave Act was in force, for the consequences of this law are devastating for Sethe and her children. Thus, Morrison's narrative engages intertexually with the classic antebellum antislavery narratives in order to bring to the surface what these texts suppressed. It also "make[s] visible what has been absent" in Mark Twain's classic narrative of the slavery experience, as Sylvia Mayer shows in her essay, " 'You Like Huckleberries?': Toni Morrison's *Beloved* and Mark Twain's *Adventures of Huckleberry Finn,*" in *The Black Columbiad: Defining Moments in African American Literature and Culture,* edited by Werner Sollors and Maria Diedrich.

24. An editorial note on the autobiography of the Reverend Josiah Henson, on whom Stowe says she based Uncle Tom, points out that the fact that Stowe "kills her hero" is a license of fiction meant to show the horrors of slavery to their utmost (Henson, 8).

25. In an obverse image, Kate Drumgoold, whose anxieties about maternal loss and abandonment contribute to the themes and structure of her narrative, records an early memory of her slave mother rescuing her from their burning house.

26. Hedrick quotes from an 1850 letter, from Stowe to her husband, in which she recoils with horror from the idea that he, and her brothers, might any of them have given way to sexual temptations outside of marriage. Warning him against sexual passion, she denies that she has any: "for I loved you as I now love God—& I can conceive of no higher love—and as I have no passion—I have no jealousy" (164). Perhaps. She apparently had no aversion to reading or hearing about passion, however. She enjoyed racy contemporary novels, and she would write an exposé of Lord Byron's incestuous liaison with his half-sister, Augusta Leigh, in *Lady Byron Vindicated* in 1870.

27. For D. W. Winnicott, illusion belongs to an early stage in development during which the mother, adapting to her infant's needs, fosters the infant's illusion that what the infant creates in thought really exists. Accordingly, disillusionment, effected when the child recognizes the mother as something outside itself, is necessary for development. The intermediary area of illusion, accepted as belonging both to internal and external (shared) perceptions, finds adult expression in, for one thing, art. See "Transitional Objects and Transitional Phenomena" in *Playing and Reality.*

28. I am grateful to my colleague Judith Fetterley, who brought my attention to this passage several years ago.

29. At the end of his poem, Longfellow reunites Evangeline—now a nun and cholera-ward nurse—with her lost beloved Gabriel at his deathbed. Stowe's description of Tom's death echoes Longfellow's verse on Gabriel's, with Evangeline holding him: "All was ended now, the hope, and the fear, and the sorrow, / All the aching heart, the restless, unsatisfied longing, / All the dull, deep pain, and constant anguish of patience!" (in *An American Anthology,* 119). I am grateful to Eric Haralson for these insights on Longfellow's *Evangeline* (Haralson, "Mars in Petticoats: Longfellow and Sentimental Masculinity").

30. Stowe's narrative tendency toward incorporation and its basis in her tendency to patronize African Americans is illustrated in her encounter with Harriet Jacobs. In 1853, Jacobs learned that Mrs. Stowe wanted to use the "extraordinary event" of her seven years of hiding in a crawlspace in her *A Key to Uncle Tom's Cabin,* rather than assist Jacobs in placing her daughter, as requested. In addition, Stowe had revealed Jacobs's history to her employer, without permission. To all this, Jacobs responded with "such a spirit of rivalry" (as she wrote to her confidante, Amy Post) that "I hardly know where to begin. . . . For I wished it [her narrative] to be a history of my life entirely by itself which would do more good and it needed no romance" (Jacobs, 235).

31. Letter to Lucy Osgood qtd. in Clifford, 5. Letter to Wendell Phillips, in Meltzer and Holland, *Lydia Maria Child, Selected Letters,* 356. Child was buried in a cemetery near her home in Wayland, Massachusetts, next to her husband. The graves of two slaves were nearby. This epitaph was not used.

Notes to Chapter 3

1. Critics have been particularly interested in Jacobs's grandmother, a direction set as early as 1867, when Lydia Maria Child published excerpts under the title, "The Good Grandmother," in *The Freedmen's Book.* See Andrews, Carby, Fetterley, Foster, Gwin, and Yellin, whose writings on women's relationships (inter- and intraracial) and identity in Harriet Jacobs have influenced much subsequent literary criticism. Baker's more recent reading of the commercial and economic dimensions of Jacobs's narrative describes a "community of women" in the narrative. Sanchez-Eppler also writes interestingly on women's relations in Jacobs's narrative. For a somewhat different approach to Jacobs's relationship to the women in her Southern household, see Fox-Genovese, who emphasizes Jacobs's individualism rather than her feminism.

2. Throughout this chapter, I try to keep in view the imaginative and literary dimensions of Jacobs's narrative, partially manifested in her use of psuedonyms for herself and others in her narrative; at the same time, I wish to rely upon the historical and autobiographical connections between the text and the lives to which it refers. I could think of no other way to do this with consistency and clarity than to use the hyphenated Brent / Jacobs when referring to the narrative persona and the figure in *Incidents.* Similarly, I hyphenate the other principals' names. I do this reluctantly, aware

of the rhetorical clumsiness. When writing about John's narrative, h
I follow his example and use historical names, or the initials he u
instance, Mr. Sawyer is sometimes called "Mr. S——").

3. In a recent note in *American Literature*, Jean Fagan Yellin corrects an
error of identification in her 1987 Harvard University Press edition of
Jacobs's *Incidents*. Recent research, she writes, reveals that Jacobs's father,
who was owned by Dr. Andrew Knox of Pasquotank County, North Carolina,
was named Elijah, not Daniel Jacobs. Yellin's further comments about
Harriet Jacobs's omission of her father's second marriage to a free woman
after her mother's death, and the existence of her half-brother, lends
reinforcement to my overall argument that critical omission of the father's
and brother's narratives mirrors Jacobs's own narrative suppressions (see
Yellin, "Harriet Jacobs's Family History").

4. This, I understand, will soon change, with the fall / winter 1995
publication of *New Essays on Harriet Jacobs and Incidents in the Life of a Slave
Girl* (Cambridge), edited by Deborah Garfield and Rafia Zafar, in which
two essays dealing with John S. Jacobs's narrative appear. One of these
essays, based on a talk delivered by Jean Fagan Yellin during a seminar at
the Harvard University W. E. B. DuBois Institute for Afro-American Research in the spring of 1994, is the inspiration for my own chapter. In her
presentation on "A True Tale of Slavery," Yellin raised fascinating questions
about John S. Jacobs that should prove critical for future studies of Harriet
Jacobs, her family, and *Incidents*.

5. Brent / Jacobs's narrative alternates between general, discursive
chapters that examine slavery as an institution and extend the motif of the
slave as representative self and the more personal, autobiographical chapters dramatizing unique events in the narrator's and her family's life. As
Gwin writes, the "tension between communal and individual self is apparent in all slave narratives" (58). Buell suggests that the tendency to subsume
the individual life under a representative self is characteristic not only of
slave narratives, but of autobiography in nineteenth-century America in
general.

6. Indeed, Brent / Jacobs's strategic battles with her master, Dr. Flint /
Norcom, generally interpreted as a struggle of wills, seem founded in the
lesson that the family draws from the young uncle's escape—that is, he
who is not willing to be a slave, can escape. Conversely: "He that is *willing*
to be a slave, let him be a slave" (26).

7. It might be interesting to speculate on the ways in which the collec-

tive memory of slaves, built out of a genre in which so much is repeated ritualistically, might create a suggestive bridge between the autobiographical tradition that emerged out of Western individualism and the African traditions of communal identity.

8. For Hegel's discussion of lordship and bondage, which underlies Patterson's analysis, see *Phenomenology of Spirit*, 104–19. This might be usefully set alongside Genovese's seminal discussion of paternalism in slavery in *Roll, Jordan, Roll*.

9. Jean Fagan Yellin understands this passage differently. In her view, it demonstrates John's sense of himself as his sister's protector.

10. Heinz Kohut has argued that the need for revenge, compulsively sought out, is a species of narcissistic rage, a view which would partially explain Flint / Norcom's behavior: why he does not (apparently) "simply" rape Brent / Jacobs, but instead tries to persuade and bully her to accept his sexual overtures (to gratify his narcissism); why her rejection of him is so enraging (it deals a blow to his narcissism); and why he is unrelenting in his pursuit of her (he feels a compulsion to undo this injury to his self-image).

11. John's suppression of Mr. Sawyer's name brings to mind Ralph Ellison's "Hidden Name and Complex Fate," in which Ellison recounts his struggle as a boy with the fact that his father named him Ralph Waldo, after Emerson. Following his namesake's advice in "Self-Reliance," Ellison explains, "I reduced the 'Waldo' to a simple and, I hoped, mysterious 'W' and in my own reading I avoided his works like the plague. I could no more deal with my name—I shall never really master it . . . than I could find a creative use for my [photographic] lens" (153). Naming and unnaming the *self* is an important *topos* in African American literature, beginning with the custom of newly freed slaves to exchange their master's surnames for new names, sometimes adding a middle initial, standing for no name (see Kimberly W. Benson's, "I Yam What I Am: the Topos of Un(naming) in Afro-American Literature"). But Ellison's "I shall never really master it" suggests the ambiguities involved in suppressing the master's name, when it is also one's own. The Negro name, Ellison writes, tells the geneaology of "a familial past" that has itself been suppressed: of "the fusions of blood, the furtive couplings, the business transactions, the violations of faith and loyalty, the assaults; yes, and the unrecognized and recognized loves through which our names were handed down unto us" (148). Of course, John's reduction of "Sawyer" to "S——" does not directly bear upon his

own name; but it is an attempt "to master," and it does resonate within the whole tradition of name-changing in African American literature and culture.

12. Lincoln's speech of June 26, 1857, on the Dred Scott decision is a good example of the operation of this taboo in antislavery thought (as I have suggested earlier, in chapter 2). Lincoln attempts to preserve the idea of a natural inequality that makes miscegenation revolting, while arguing for a natural equality before the law:

> There is a natural disgust in the minds of nearly all white people, to the idea of an indiscriminate amalgamation of the white and black races; and Judge Douglas evidently is basing his chief hope, upon the chances of being able to appropriate the benefit of this disgust to himself. If he can, by much drumming and repeating fasten the odium of that idea upon his adversaries, he thinks he can struggle through the storm. . . . He finds the Republicans insisting that the Declaration of Independence includes ALL men, black as well as white; and forthwith he boldly denies that it includes negroes at all, and proceeds to argue gravely that all who contend it does, do so only because they want to vote, and eat, and sleep, and marry with negroes! He will have it that they cannot be consistent else. Now I protest against that counterfeit logic which concludes that, because I do not want a black woman for a *slave* I must necessarily want her for a *wife*. I need not have her for either, I can just leave her alone. In some respects she certainly is not my equal; but in her natural right to eat the bread she earns with her own hands without asking leave of any one else, she is my equal, and the equal of all others. (119–21)

Douglass, who turned the standard American rhetoric of filial piety against the hypocrisy of a nation that claimed descent from its founding fathers to excuse its own misdeeds and betrayals (see, for instance, his fifth of July address, "What to the Slave is the Fourth of July?" in Blassingame, et al., *The Frederick Douglass Papers*, Vol. 2), astutely returned to the metaphor in his speech at the dedication of the Freedman's Lincoln Monument in 1876: "You are the children of Abraham Lincoln," he told white members of his audience. "We are at best only his step-children; children by adoption, children by forces of circumstance and necessity" (see Blassingame, et al., *The Frederick Douglass Papers*, Vol. 4).

13. In reading these passages, we might think of Lacan's notion of a

mirror-phase, a stage of ego development in which the self identifies with the other (in the mirror), which then becomes the self's ego; consequently, the ground of identity (the self and ego) is in alienation and aggression.

14. In the prologue and in chapter 1, I discuss some of Harriet Jacobs's anxieties about memory. John, in his narrative, concentrates his anxieties about memory in questions of truth and deception. We speak of being true to oneself as never forgetting who one is. John understands his enslavement as being forced to play a *role* which completely goes against what he really thinks and feels. He speaks of the "policy of this appearance of contentment" which makes slaves sing in order to appear happy before the masters who, playing their part, are eager to disavow any knowledge of their slaves' misery and rage (85). Jacobs rejects slavish lying even when it runs counter to his interests; for example, he walks away from the chance to get a seaman's protection papers at an English custom-house because he would have to "swear . . . to a lie, which I did not feel disposed to do" (126). The master, John suggests, cares little about the truth, but depends absolutely upon the acquiescence of the slave in his deception. Fanon alludes to this dynamic of domination in his work, writing, in the voice of the torturer, "Lie or no lie, you must agree to what I tell you" (*Black Skin, White Masks,* 105). Discounted as testimony by law and custom, a slave's word was nothing in the white world; therefore, John's contempt for his masters's lies becomes a principle of resistance. Claiming narrative autonomy, John rests all on his word. His message, in the end, is exceedingly subversive: the story *I* tell ("A True Tale")—gains its truth by virtue of being told by *me.* Thus, he claims a status for the word of a black man that is the equal of anyone else's word.

15. Jung is credited with having developed the concept of the "imago." My use follows Freud's use of the term to refer to unconscious prototypes that the subject creates and then relies upon to orient himself or herself toward others.

16. John's characterization of the grandmother is interesting: "I should do my dear old grandmother injustice did I not mention her too. There was a great difference between her meekness and my father's violent temper, although, in justice to him, I must say that slavery was the cause of it" (85). This is a less sympathetic view of the grandmother than Harriet offers, and a sharper assessment of what, in *Incidents,* comes across as the grandmother's counsel of patience, faith, and family. At any rate, it says more about John and his feelings about his grandmother than it does

about her, just as Harriet's view of her grandmother is tied up with her own relationship to her. Also, in John's remarks, there is the suggestion that his father's "violent temper" may have fallen more heavily on the children than the narratives make evident; though we do read in *Incidents* of how the father verbally reprimands his son for not obeying his word before his mistress's.

17. See part 1 of *To Wake the Nations: Race in the Making of American Literature*, in which Sundquist argues that the authority of the Revolutionary fathers finds its renaissance in the literature of African American writers of the early nineteenth century, including Nat Turner, Frederick Douglass, and Martin Delaney. To this list we might add Harriet Jacobs.

18. Cited by Yellin in *Incidents*, 244. In an essay on this revision, Bruce Mills usefully argues that Child's recommendation, which "brings the narrative full circle, back to the grandmother's role as a model for domestic values," must have been an effort to downplay the narrative's potentially threatening links to John Brown and "the prospect of violence and disunion . . . [and instead] realign central elements of the story with other woman-centered antislavery narratives" (258).

Notes to Chapter 4

1. On the changing motive for postebellum slave narrative, see Olney's introduction to the Schomburg Library edition of Keckley's narrative. See also Andrews's two essays, "Reunion in the Postbellum Slave Narrative: Frederick Douglass and Elizabeth Keckley" and "The Changing Moral Discourse of Nineteenth-Century African American Women's Autobiography: Harriet Jacobs and Elizabeth Keckley."

2. Quoted in Foster, *Written By Herself*, 128–29.

3. Presumably, to protect his mother from the scandal of exposure. The question of Robert Lincoln's motives with regard to his mother is the subject of some debate. In 1875, against his mother's consent, he attained a court ruling to have her institutionalized as insane. A year later, Mary Todd Lincoln brought her own petition to the same court, where a jury declared her "restored to reason and capable to manage and control her own estate" (Jean H. Baker, 348).

4. It is more than likely, as Andrews points out, that Keckley would have known of Jacobs's *Incidents*, published seven years earlier and publicized in the early 1860s. They may even have met, since both lived and

worked in Washington, D.C., from 1862 through 1865, and helped in the relief efforts for the "contrabands," the refugee slaves from the South.

5. Minrose C. Gwin believes we may infer that he is her master's son, the Reverend Robert Burwell, to whom she is on loan as a slave.

6. Mary Todd Lincoln's biographers all state with varying degrees of certainty that Keckley's narrative was "ghostwritten"; and they mention various possible ghostwriters, among them the abolitionist writer Jane Grey Swisshelm, editor and newspaperman Hamilton Busbey, and James Redpath, who helped other Civil War writers. However, all affirm that the book is based entirely on Mrs. Keckley's memories and papers, and all use the work as an accurate account of the Lincoln White House.

Frances Smith Foster suggests a different scenario. She agrees that Keckley's own high standards "no doubt influenced her [like many other slave narrators] to rely heavily upon her publisher and other professionals for advice and editing" (*Written By Herself,* 128). Foster offers evidence to support Keckley's own claim that she spent hours writing every night before giving her text to her advisors.

I agree with Foster that it is inarguable that Keckley, like other narrators, sought and accepted help with her manuscript, and that how much is not an irrelevant question. But in justification for treating Keckley's narrative as I do, I would like to draw upon Robert Stepto's idea of the "authenticating narrative," which he defines as an example of the genre in which the personal narrative is the occasion for the presentation of authenticating documents of more public events. My reading focuses on the dialogical interaction between the various "authentic" documents in which Keckley seems to invest large portions of her narrative identity and the narrative that these documents are meant to authorize.

7. This is obviously disputable, but I take Fanon's claim as a useful starting point.

8. Further, these object attachments suggest the degree to which the invocation of the culturally endorsed value of self-reliance is linked to Keckley's absence of choice. Trust and attachment are interrelated elements: betrayals of one lead to a loosening of the other. This is a recurring theme in the post-flight sections of antebellum narratives, when the fugitive slave arrives North and discovers that racism is not peculiar to the South. Douglass's fugitive motto "Trust no man!" is echoed in numerous slavery accounts. And as Jacobs remarks about her distrust of the first Mrs. Bruce,

"I longed for some one to confide in; but I had been so deceived by white people, that I had lost all confidence in them" (169).

9. According to several biographers, though unmentioned in Keckley's narrative, Mrs. Lincoln's interest in spiritualism and mesmerism was fostered by Mrs. Keckley; thus, their intense relation to mourning their loved ones overlaps in this way as well. Keckley mentions that Mrs. Lincoln visited seances to contact the spirits of her dead. And there is an amazing photograph, taken in 1872 by William Mumler, a spiritualist photographer, showing Mrs. Lincoln seated, looking very puffy and depressed, with the "spirit" of Mr. Lincoln hovering protectively over her, hands on her shoulders. She apparently refused to believe it had been touched up. The photograph is reprinted in Jean H. Baker and Ishbel Ross.

10. Accardo and Portelli write that the "illusion of consent" was "needed both as a prevention of rebellion and as a cure for the masters' guilt, which is a foundation of the masters' 'consent' to themselves" (80).

11. African slaves throughout the New World believed that when they died they would be free to return to their own country. Burial customs reflected this belief; slaves might be buried with the objects they might need in order to return home and be recognized once they got there. The African custom of decorating a grave with the personal belongings of the dead was also common among Southern slaves. One belief was that this was a way to "lay the spirit" so it would not have to bother to return for its belongings. See Raboteau, *Slave Religion,* and Levine, *Black Culture and Black Consciousness.* Toni Morrison, in *Beloved,* seems to draw upon this history of beliefs about the dead as well as the psychological dimensions of traumatic separation and mourning.

12. For Freud's discussions of mourning and ambivalence, see especially *Totem and Taboo* and "Mourning and Melancholia." For a useful overview of early theories of mourning and a general discussion of mourning, including the function of ambivalence and anger, see Bowlby's sequentially written essays, "Processes of Mourning" and "Pathological Mourning and Childhood Mourning." Bowlby's argument diverges from Freud in several ways, but most importantly in his view of the mourner's primary aim: Freud emphasizes libidinal gratification, while Bowlby, whose work deals mainly with the responses of children to separation, stresses the unconscious urge to recover the lost object as the mourner's central goal (see also, Bowlby, *Attachment and Loss*). My work is also informed by Wolfenstein's analyses on mourning.

Psychoanalytic theories on the effects of ambivalence on mourning are given concrete expression in Douglass's famous comment about his emotionless response to news of his mother's death, a rare direct statement about the damaging effects of slavery upon the slave's love relations. By way of comparison, it is interesting to note how hatred against one's own family is a theme in Cynthia Ozick's grueling story "The Shawl," set in a concentration camp, in which a young adolescent girl starvingly eyes her toddler sister, imagining her death so she can eat her (primitive love and hate compressed together in this image of oral incorporation); when the older girl finally steals her sister's life-sustaining "magic shawl," the narrator says she kills her.

There was little to gain for slave narrators by being as blunt as the narrator in Ozick's grim story; one subject understandably buried in slave narratives is open talk about cruelty and violence within slave families themselves and their devastating consequences. But perhaps we may read backwards from the oral history of Grant Smith, a descendent of slaves interviewed in 1980. Smith associates memories of being repeatedly beaten by his grandmother, mother, and aunts ("all those frustrated women") with recollections of his ambivalence toward his grandmother, his reactions to mourning, and his response to her death.

> Death was a kind of part of life, I guess. Someone was always dying or threatening some dependent with their death. I never hated my grandmother when I lived with her. I needed all the adults I lived with too much to really wish they were dead. . . . It was the funerals which made me afraid of the dead, you understand. There was so much noise and it lasted until the last ounce of restraint was wrung from the living victims. . . . When my grandmother died I did not go to her funeral. (Gwaltney, 42)

13. This is the outline for mourning Freud charts in "Mourning and Melancholia."

14. Many variations on this *topos* exist throughout antislavery literature, generally leading from mourning to what seems the self-induced death of the bereaved mother. The typical sequence is in this four-line verse from William and Ellen Craft's narrative: "O, deep was the anguish of that slave mother's heart, / When called from her darlings for ever to part; / The poor mourning mother of reason bereft, / Soon ended her sorrows, and sank cold in death" (19).

15. Nathaniel Parker Willis is Harriet Jacobs's Mr. Bruce. He was Washington correspondent for New York's *Home Journal*.

16. American Freedmen's Inquiry Commission Interviews, 1863 (Blassingame, *Slave Testimony*, 408–9).

17. See Andrews, "Reunion in the Postbellum Slave Narrative: Frederick Douglass and Elizabeth Keckley," 12–14.

18. In Douglass's well-known reunion with his dying ex-master, Thomas Auld, there are mutual expressions of forgiveness. When Douglass asks him how he felt about his escape North, Auld replies, " 'I always knew you were too smart to be a slave, and had I been in your place, I should have done as you did.' " Douglass responds that he is glad to hear this, for " 'I did not run away from *you*, but from *slavery;* it was not that I loved Caesar less, but Rome more' " (*Life and Times*, 877). Josiah Henson, known as Stowe's model for Uncle Tom, uses his reunion scene with his former mistress to make a different kind of point. " 'Why, Si,' his mistress says, 'you are a gentleman!' 'I always was, madam.' 'Yes, but you are rich! . . . What have you brought me?' 'Nothing. I came to see if you had anything to give me!' " (160).

19. Children who have had to fend for themselves often come across as extremely grown-up, and generally will describe themselves as being independent and self-reliant. One woman, interviewed in 1980, whose parents were both slaves, relates being grown-up to having had always to work, which she sees as fundamental to the experience of African Americans. Her comments are similar to Keckley's, and will become especially resonant in the portions of Keckley's narrative that touch upon work and white women.

> Now, as black woman—no, let me say me—I know and always have known that I have had to do for myself just like any grown person out here. I say "grown person," but I was doing the work of grown people since I was a little child because I had to do that. I think more black women know this than white women because poor white people have a little bit more than poor black people, you know, for the most part. (Gwaltney, 37)

20. In "Loss, Rage, and Repetition," Martha Wolfenstein refers to a "tendency" of young children to react to separation with "a shift away from object relations to an exaggerated evaluation of material things" (440). As an aspect of overall narrative strategy, Mrs. Keckley's attachment to certain

mementoes and Mrs. Lincoln's compulsive shopping, including her extravagant purchases of mourning clothes, may be usefully understood in this
light. This theory is related to D. W. Winnicott's concept of "transitional
objects": objects (frequently stuffed animals, a blanket, a toy) that the child
uses symbolically to manage separation and loss.

21. See Nelson on the distinction between "sympathy" and "understanding" and the problem of an interracial sisterhood in *Incidents in the Life of a
Slave Girl.* Nelson argues that as Linda Brent well knows, her relationship
to the second Mrs. Bruce is structured by Mrs. Bruce's social and economic
power over her; and though Mrs. Bruce may feel "sympathy" for the fugitive, she does not "understand" from the inside Linda's plight, nor could
she, since, as Linda puts it, she "has never been a slave . . . [and] . . . cannot
imagine" (Nelson, 137–47).

22. See Jean H. Baker. Mary Todd Lincoln's niece, Katherine Helm,
offered an analysis of Mrs. Lincoln's intimate reliance upon Mrs. Keckley
which, despite its patronizing attitude and sentimentalized view of the
"black mammy," may contain a grain of truth. In her 1928 biography of her
aunt, Helm speculated that after Lincoln's death, Mrs. Lincoln's loneliness
and despair led her back "to the impulse of her childhood, which had been
to seek the love and help she had unfailingly found in her black mammy
who had shielded her from many a deserved scolding" (266).

23. Lydia Maria Child had the following to say about Mrs. Lincoln's
wardrobe (the "Willis" referred to in the opening line is Nathaniel Parker
Willis, author of the tribute to Willie Lincoln):

> Willis is out again with a florid description of Mrs. Lincoln's autumn
> bonnet, called "The Princess." "Rose-colored velvet, with guipine me-
> dallions, trimmed with black thread lace, put on full, and this again
> trimmed on the edge with a deeper fringe of minute black marabout
> and ostrich feathers. &c &c. . . ."
>
> So *this* is what the people are taxed for! to deck out this vulgar doll
> with foreign frippery! (Letter to Lucy Searle, Wayland, October 11,
> 1861. In Meltzer and Holland, eds., *Letters,* 396)

24. Another example of this type of story is the tale about a post-
Emancipation encounter between a former slave, named Amos, and a
Union officer. In this version of the story, Amos is grumbling about his new
freedom; the upshot is that under slavery, "I eats chicen ev-ry Sund'y. . . .

An' whut's mo', Massa allus save me the tenderes' paht. . . . De gravy, uv co'se!" (*The Atlanta Constitution,* June 13, 1867; quoted in Watkins, 31).

A striking example of the effects of generational differences on black women's expectations is in Charles Chesnutt's *The Marrow of Tradition.* Set in 1898, the novel depicts the completely different attitudes of the dialect-speaking old mammy-figure, Auntie Jane, who serves her former master's family as if she were still a slave in the Old South, and the formally educated, young black nurse, symbol of a generation born after slavery.

25. The multiple losses Mrs. Lincoln suffered as a girl, although they do not enter into Keckley's narrative, may go to explain something about the force of their mutual tie, as well as Mrs. Lincoln's devotion to mourning in later years: a brother died when she was fourteen months old; her mother when she was just under seven; her father when she was thirty-one; and her second-born son, Eddie, in 1850, when he was four.

26. Mrs. Lincoln's reactions correspond in some ways to the state Freud describes in "Mourning and Melancholia," in which, among other things, the mourner responds to the death of a love object with a return to an earlier narcissistic form of attachment involving identification, not object-love; the bereaved also seeks to resolve ambivalence toward the dead beloved by idealizing the loved one and designating others, including the self, as all bad and worthless.

Notes to Chapter 5

1. Erik H. Erikson offers a brief analysis of the power of the dominant national imagery to identify ethnic outgroups, of which he says African Americans are only the most flagrant case, with its own unconscious negative identity prototypes—"identity fragments" (*Childhood and Society,* 241–46).

2. In this chapter, I break with chronology to examine Kate Drumgoold's narrative before Julia Foote's. I do this because Foote's relation to slavery, as the child of former slaves, moves the discussion of memory into new territory.

3. See Sidney S. Furst, "Psychic Trauma and Its Reconstruction with Particular Reference to Postchildhood Trauma," in Rothstein, *The Reconstruction of Trauma.* Furst gives a list of mechanisms associated with the attempt to master trauma, among them explanations and rationalizations that he calls "memory imprints" that persist long after their initiation.

These serve on the one hand to bind anxiety and allay guilt-feelings; on the other, they organize one's understanding of subsequent events, which in turn confirms the original reasoning (33).

4. See my chapter 1 for a fuller discussion of Eakin's work.

5. See Spillers, " 'The Permanent Obliquity of an In(pha)llibly Straight' ": In the Time of the Daughters and Fathers," in Wall, *Changing Our Words: Essays on Criticism, Theory, and Writing by Black Woman* (148).

6. See *The Psychology of Women,* 253. Deutsch's comment emphasizes the importance of the child's fantasies about the mother, over whatever the mother may actually be like.

7. Margaret Mahler's work on separation-individuation is behind my thinking about the impact of early maternal neglect or loss on the child. Mahler's theory of the stages of infantile development from symbiosis through separation-individuation integrates object relations theory with ego psychology—that is, she works with a developmental theory of interpsychic relations that is grounded in a Freudian model of intrapsychic relations: structural development (of ego and superego) and instinctual drives. See Mahler, *The Psychological Birth of the Human Infant.* For a helpful overview of the differences among psychoanalytic models, see Schaye in *Psychoanalysis Today.*

8. On "signifying" in the African American tradition, see Gates, *The Signifying Monkey.*

9. White women often nursed sick slave children and adults. Deborah Gray White cites one slave woman's comment as typical: "We ain't had no doctor, our Missus an' one of de slave would tend to the sick (53). See also Clinton, *The Plantation Mistress,* 22–29 and Fox-Genovese, *Within the Plantation Household,* 129–30. On the archetype of the Mammy as surrogate mistress and mother, who nursed white and black alike, see White, *Ar'n't I a Woman?,* 46–61.

10. Drumgoold's reasoning is likely to be accurate here, since she gives ample evidence of Mr. House's maliciousness toward her mother, while insisting on Mrs. House's relative benevolence. It is difficult to tell; but it is not an unlikely scenario that, when strapped for cash, Mr. House would sell a slave whom he might not have been able to sell were his wife alive to intercede on the slave's behalf.

11. This recalls the feelings of pride with which Elizabeth Keckley records her "transferral" from the rude cabin of her slave family into her master's household (*Behind the Scenes,* 20).

12. In *The Alchemy of Race and Rights,* Patricia J. Williams analyzes her own confrontation with divided identity, when she describes her feelings about her mother's comment just before her first day of class in law school, in which she draws upon Williams's descent from Austin Miller, the white lawyer who bought her great-great-grandmother, Sophie, and immediately impregnated her. " 'The Millers were lawyers," her mother told Williams, "so you have it in your blood.' "

> When my mother told me that I had nothing to fear in law school, that law was 'in my blood,' she meant it in a complex sense. First and foremost, she meant it defiantly; no one should make me feel inferior because someone else's father was a judge. She wanted me to reclaim that part of my heritage from which I had been disinherited, and she wanted me to use it as a source of strength and self-confidence. At the same time, she was asking me to claim a part of myself that was the dispossessor of another part of myself; she was asking me to deny that disenfranchised little-black-girl who felt powerless and vulnerable.
>
> In somewhat the same vein, my mother was asking me not to look to her as a role model. (216–17)

13. My emphasis on Drumgoold's ambivalence toward both her "white mother" and own mother differs from earlier readings. For instance, Hazel V. Carby interprets Drumgoold's daughter-mother relation with her slave mother within the context of a "female family unit working to support each other when the mother had finally gathered them all together after separation. These female households were portrayed as complete families. . . . Mothers were constructed as figures to be emulated by their daughters writing the narratives" (37). My reading of these relationships is closer to Minrose C. Gwin's. Gwin stresses that Drumgoold's depiction of her "white mother" is highly sentimentalized, although she finds that the narrative does show "the capacity of maternal love to cross racial lines" (70). My reading emphasizes the aggression that sentimentality in this case might mask.

14. It should also be obvious that I do not think that the structure of Drumgoold's infantilized position can be explained in terms of a political and social argument about the collective infantilization of black slaves in the antebellum South. In other words, my argument about Drumgoold is not a support of Elkins's views about the "slave personality."

15. See Anna Freud, *The Ego and the Mechanisms of Defense.*

16. See Reik, "The Characteristics of Masochism."

17. It is not absolutely clear from Foote's narrative why her parents sent her to the Primes. However, during the antebellum period in the North, it was not uncommon for free blacks to indenture their children to white families. Indeed, indentured servitude for the children of former slaves was actually written into a New York State law of March 31, 1817, which held that children born after July 4, 1799, would be free, but bound as apprentices to their mother's masters until they were twenty-eight, if they were boys, and twenty-five, if they were girls; and that children born after the passing of the law would be bound until they were twenty-one (see facsimile series, *Slavery, Race, and the American Legal System, 1700–1872*, edited by Finkelman). This was one of many laws, including an 1810 law requiring masters to have their slave children taught to read scriptures, that was established as part of a gradual phasing out of slavery in New York. Foote would not have been bound by this law, since her parents had bought their freedom before 1827. (See Mabee, *Soujourner Truth: Slave, Prophet, Legend,* 10–14; Sterling, *We Are Your Sisters,* 88–89.)

18. Foote later describes her excitement when a school for colored children is opened in Albany by the Phileos family, who had been associated with the Quaker Prudence Crandall's boarding school in Canterbury, Connecticut, which opened in 1831 and admitted African American girls. The Canterbury school was abandoned in 1834, because of the unrelenting harrassment of townspeople and the collusion of state legislators, who passed a law prohibiting the establishment of any school for the purposes of instructing "colored persons who are not inhabitants of this state" (cited in Litwack, *North of Slavery,* 129). Foote speaks of having known a student who had attended the Canterbury school and was so "frightened" by the harrassment "that she went into spasms, which resulted in a derangement from which she never recovered" (39). According to Foote, the Albany school closed down only a few weeks after its opening.

19. A.M.E. preacher Jarena Lee describes the "progress of the soul from a state of darkness, or of nature" in three stages: "First, conviction from sin. Second, justification from sin. Third, the entire sanctification of the soul to God" (*Religious Experience and Journal of Mrs. Jarena Lee,* 9).

20. See Spillers, "Mama's Baby, Papa's Maybe: An American Grammar Book," on this issue.

21. This episode recalls not only the powerlessness of the slave child, but the impact of slavery on the role of the parent as protector.

22. She summarizes her father's enslavement in this way: "My father endured many hardships in slavery, the worst of which was his constant exposure to all sorts of weather. There being no railroads at that time, all goods and merchandise were moved from place to place with teams, one of which my father drove" (10). In this description, her father seems to be both the driver and one of the commodities driven.

23. Foote's painful silence will find a later manifestation toward the end of her narrative, when she describes being "afflicted with [a] throat difficulty" that will interrupt her work (108). In this way, a sickness in adulthood has interesting connections to a childhood crisis. Yet, Foote does not, like Drumgoold, utilize the connection to anchor herself to her past.

24. According to Lawrence W. Levine, "Although Jesus was ubiquitous in the [slave] spirituals, it was not invariably the Jesus of the New Testament, but Jesus transformed into an Old Testament warrior whose victories were temporal as well as spiritual: 'Mass Jesus' who engaged in personal combat with the Devil; 'King Jesus' seated on a milk-white horse with sword and shield in hand. 'Ride on Jesus,' 'Ride on, conquering King,' 'The God I serve is a man of war,' the slaves sang" (*Black Culture and Black Consciousness,* 43).

25. Thanks to my colleague Randall Craig for this last observation.

26. Theophus H. Smith takes up this and other issues involving the transformation of the slave and master in African American theology and religion in *Conjuring Culture: Biblical Formations of Black America.*

27. Stern's wonderful essay, "Excavating Genre in *Our Nig*," arrived in my mailbox too late for me to draw upon for the earlier portions of this book. However, her analysis of the "enormously destructive" maternity in *Our Nig* as essentially gothic, not sentimental, in mode, dovetails with some of my own observations about maternalism in women's slave narratives.

28. See Howe, "Black Boys and Native Sons" (1963) (reprinted in *Irving Howe: Selected Writings, 1950–1990,* 119–39) and Ellison, "The World and the Jug" (1963 and 1964) (reprinted in *Shadow and Act,* 107–43).

Accardo, Annalucia, and Alessandro Portelli. "A Spy in the Enemy's Country: Domestic Slaves as Internal Foes." In *The Black Columbiad: Defining Moments in African American Literature and Culture.* Edited by Werner Sollors and Maria Diedrich. Cambridge, Mass.: Harvard University Press. 1994. 77–87.

Andrews, William L. "The Changing Moral Discourse of Nineteenth-Century African American Women's Autobiography: Harriet Jacobs and Elizabeth Keckley" (1991). In *De / Colonizing the Subject: The Politics of Gender in Women's Autobiography.* Edited by Sidonie Smith and Julia Watson. Minneapolis: University of Minnesota Press. 1992. 225–41.

———. "Reunion in the Postbellum Slave Narrative: Frederick Douglass and Elizabeth Keckley." *Black American Literature Forum* 23:1 (Spring 1989): 5–16.

———. *To Tell a Free Story: The First Century of Afro-American Autobiography, 1760–1865.* Urbana: University of Illinois Press. 1988.

Baker, Houston A., Jr. "Archaeology, Ideology, and African American Discourse." In *Redefining American Literary History.* Edited by A. La Vonne Brown Ruoff and Jerry W. Ward, Jr. New York: Modern Language Association of America. 1990. 157–199.

———. *Blues, Ideology, and Afro-American Literature.* Chicago: University of Chicago Press. 1984.

———. *The Journey Back.* Chicago: University of Chicago Press. 1980.

Baker, Jean H. *Mary Todd Lincoln: A Biography.* New York: W. W. Norton. 1987.

Baldwin, James. "Nobody Knows My Name: A Letter from the South" (1959). In *Nobody Knows My Name* (1961). Reprint. New York: Vintage International. 1993.

Bardaglio, Peter. " 'An Outrage upon Nature": Incest and Law in the Nineteenth-Century South." In *In Joy and in Sorrow: Women, Family, and Marriage in the Victorian South, 1830–1900.* Edited by Carol Bleser. New York: Oxford University Press. 1991. 32–51.

Benson, Kimberly W. "I Yam What I Yam: The Topos of (Un)naming in Afro-American Literature." In *Black Literature and Literary Theory*. Edited by Henry Louis Gates, Jr. New York: Routledge. 1984; reprint. 1990. 151–74.

Blassingame, John W. *The Slave Community: Plantation Life in the Antebellum South*. New York: Oxford University Press. 1972.

———, ed. *Slave Testimony: Two Centuries of Letters, Speeches, Interviews, and Autobiographies*. Baton Rouge: Louisiana State University Press. 1977.

Blassingame, John W., and John R. McKivigan, eds. *The Frederick Douglass Papers: Series One: Speeches, Debates, and Interviews*. New Haven, Conn.: Yale University Press. Vol. 2 (1982). Vol. 4 (1991).

Bleser, Carol, ed. *In Joy and in Sorrow: Women, Family, and Marriage in the Victorian South, 1830–1900*. New York: Oxford University Press. 1991.

Bowlby, John. *Attachment and Loss. Vol. I: Attachment* (1969); *Vol. II: Separation: Anxiety and Anger* (1973); *Vol. III: Loss: Sadness and Depression* (1980). New York: Basic Books.

———. "Pathological Mourning and Childhood Mourning." *Journal of the American Psychoanalytic Association* 11:3 (1963): 500–541.

———. "Processes of Mourning." *International Journal of Psycho-Analysis* XLII:4–5 (1961): 317–40.

Braxton, Joanne M. *Black Women Writing Autobiography: A Tradition within a Tradition*. Philadelphia: Temple University Press. 1989.

Brenner, Charles. "The Masochistic Character: Genesis and Treatment," *Psychoanalytic Quarterly* 18 (1959): 197–226.

Brown, William Wells. *Clotel, or, the President's Daughter: A Narrative of Slave Life in the United States* (1853). Reprinted in *Three Classic African American Novels*. Edited by William L. Andrews. New York: Penguin. 1990.

———. *Clotelle: A Tale of the Southern States* (1864). Reprinted in *Violence in the Black Imagination: Essays and Documents*. Edited with critical essays by Ronald T. Takaki. New York: Oxford University Press. 1993.

Buell, Lawrence. "Autobiography in the American Renaissance." In *American Autobiography: Retrospect and Prospect*. Edited by Paul John Eakin. Madison: University of Wisconsin Press. 1990. 47–69.

Burke, Kenneth. *The Philosophy of Literary Form*. Berkeley: University of California Press. 1973.

Carby, Hazel V. *Reconstructing Womanhood: The Emergence of the Afro-American Woman Novelist*. New York: Oxford University Press. 1987.

Chesnutt, Charles. *The Marrow of Tradition* (1901). Edited with an introduction by Eric J. Sundquist. New York: Penguin Books. 1993.

Child, Lydia Maria. *Appeal in Favor of That Class of Americans Called Africans* (1833). New York: Arno Press and The New York Times. 1968.

———. *Fact and Fiction: A Collection of Stories.* New York: C. S. Francis. 1846.

———. "Slavery's Pleasant Homes." In *The Liberty Bell* by Friends of Boston. Boston: Anti-Slavery Fair. 1843.

Chodorow, Nancy J. *Feminism and Psychoanalytic Theory.* New Haven, Conn.: Yale University Press. 1989.

———. *The Reproduction of Mothering: Psychoanalysis and the Sociology of Gender.* Berkeley: University of California Press. 1978.

Clifford, Deborah Pickman. *Crusader for Freedom: A Life of Lydia Maria Child.* Boston: Beacon Press. 1992.

Clinton, Catherine. *The Plantation Mistress: Woman's World in the Old South.* New York: Pantheon Books. 1982.

Cooper, Anna Julia. *A Voice From the South* (1892). Edited with an introduction by Mary Helen Washington. New York: Oxford University Press. 1988.

Craft, William, and Ellen Craft. *Running a Thousand Miles for Freedom* (1860). New York: Arno Press and The New York Times. 1969.

Davis, Allison. *Leadership, Love, and Aggression.* San Diego, Cal.: Harcourt Brace Jovanovich. 1983.

Davis, Charles T., and Henry Louis Gates, Jr., eds. *The Slave's Narrative.* New York: Oxford University Press. 1985.

Delaney, Lucy A. *From the Darkness Cometh the Light or Struggles for Freedom.* St. Louis, Mo.: Publishing House of J. T. Smith, c. 1891. Reprinted in *Six Women's Slave Narratives.* Edited by William L. Andrews. New York: Oxford University Press. 1988.

Deutsch, Helene. *The Psychology of Women.* Volume I. New York: Grune and Stratton. 1944.

Dew, Thomas Roderick. "Abolition of Negro Slavery" (1832). Reprinted in *The Ideology of Slavery: Proslavery Thought in the Antebellum South, 1830–1860.* Edited with an introduction by Drew Gilpin Faust. Baton Rouge: Louisiana State University Press. 1981. 21–77.

Douglas, Ann. *The Feminization of American Culture.* New York: Avon Books. 1977.

———. "Introduction" to *Uncle Tom's Cabin, or, Life among the Lowly.* New York: Penguin. 1986.

Works Cited

Douglass, Frederick. *Narrative of the Life of Frederick Douglass* (1845); *My Bondage and My Freedom* (1855); *Life and Times of Frederick Douglass* (1893). Reprint. New York: Library of America. 1984.

Drumgoold, Kate. *A Slave Girl's Story* (1898). In *Six Women's Slave Narratives*. Edited by William L. Andrews. New York: Oxford University Press. 1988.

DuBois, Ellen. "Women's Rights and Abolition: The Nature of the Connection." In *Antislavery Reconsidered: New Perspectives on the Abolitionists*. Edited by Lewis Perry and Michael Fellman. Baton Rouge: Louisiana State University Press. 1979. 238–51.

DuBois, William E. B. *The Souls of Black Folk* (1903). New York: Avon Books. 1965.

Eakin, John Paul. *Fictions in Autobiography: Studies in the Art of Self-Invention*. Princeton, N.J.: Princeton University Press. 1985.

———. *Touching the World: Reference in Autobiography*. Princeton, N.J.: Princeton University Press.

Elfenbein, Anna Shannon. *Women on the Color Line: Evolving Stereotypes and the Writings of George Washington Cable, Grace King, Kate Chopin*. Charlottesville: University of Virginia Press. 1989.

Elkins, Stanley. *Slavery: A Problem in American Institutional and Intellectual Life* (1959). Third Edition. Chicago: Chicago University Press. 1976.

Ellison, Ralph. "Hidden Name and Complex Fate" (1964). In *Shadow and Act*. New York: Vintage Books. 1972. 144–66.

———. *Invisible Man* (1947). New York: Vintage Books. 1989.

———. "The World and the Jug" (1963, 1964). In *Shadow and Act*. New York: Vintage Books. 1972. 107–43.

Emerson, Ralph Waldo. "An Address . . . on . . . the Emancipation of the Negroes in the British West Indies" (August 1, 1844). In *Emerson's Antislavery Writings*. Edited by Len Gougeon and Joel Myerson. New Haven, Conn.: Yale University Press. 1995.

Equiano, Olaudah. *The Interesting Narrative of the Life of Olaudah Equiano, or Gustavus Vassa, the African* (1789). In *The Classic Slave Narratives*. Edited by Henry Louis Gates, Jr. New York: New American Library. 1987. 1–182.

Erikson, Erik H. *Childhood and Society* (1950). New York: W. W. Norton. 1993.

Fanon, Franz. *Black Skin, White Masks* (1952). New York: Grove Weidenfeld. 1968.

Fetterley, Judith. "Introduction to Harriet Jacobs." In *Provisions: A Reader from 19th-Century American Women*. Bloomington: Indiana University Press. 1985. 279–85.

Finkelman, Paul, ed. *Slavery, Race, and The American Legal System, 1700–1872*. Series VII. Volume 1. New York: Garland Press. 1988.

Fisher, Philip. *Hard Facts: Setting and Form in the American Novel*. New York: Oxford University Press. 1987.

Fitzhugh, George. "Southern Thought" (1857). Reprinted in *The Ideology of Slavery: Proslavery Thought in the Antebellum South, 1830–1860*. Edited with an introduction by Drew Gilpin Faust. Baton Rouge: Louisiana State University Press. 1981. 272–99.

Foote, Julia A. J. *A Brand Plucked from the Fire: An Autobiographical Sketch* (1886). Reprinted in *Spiritual Narratives*. With an introduction by Susan Houchins. New York: Oxford University Press. 1988.

Foster, Frances Smith. *Witnessing Slavery: The Development of Ante-bellum Slave Narratives*. 1979; Second edition. Madison: University of Wisconsin Press. 1994.

———. *Written by Herself: Literary Production by African American Women, 1746–1892*. Bloomington: Indiana University Press. 1993.

Fox-Genovese, Elizabeth. "Family and Female Identity in the Antebellum South: Sarah Gayle and Her Family." In *In Joy and in Sorrow: Women, Family, and Marriage in the Victorian South, 1830–1900*. Edited by Carol Bleser. New York: Oxford University Press. 1991. 15–31.

———. *Within the Plantation Household: Black and White Women of the Old South*. Chapel Hill: University of North Carolina Press. 1988.

Franklin, John Hope, and Alfred A. Moss, Jr. *From Slavery to Freedom: A History of Negro Americans*. Sixth Edition. New York: Mcgraw. 1988.

Fraser, Walter J., Jr., R. Frank Saunders, Jr., and Jon L. Wakelyn, eds. *The Web of Southern Social Relations: Women, Family, and Education*. Athens: University of Georgia Press. 1985.

Frederickson, George M. *The Black Image in the White Mind: The Debate on Afro-American Character and Destiny, 1817–1914*. New York: Harper and Row. 1971.

Freud, Anna. "Comments on Trauma." In *Psychic Trauma*. Edited by Sidney S. Furst. New York: Basic Books. 1967. 235–46.

———. *The Writings of Anna Freud*. Vol. II, *The Ego and the Mechanisms of Defense*. New York: International Universities Press. 1966.

Freud, Sigmund. *Beyond the Pleasure Principle* (1920). In *The Standard Edition of the Complete Works of Sigmund Freud, 18.* Translated and edited by James Strachey. London: Hogarth Press. 1961. 3–66.

―――. "A Child Is Being Beaten" (1919). *S.E. 17.* 175–204.

―――. "The Dynamics of Transference" (1912). *S.E. 12.* 97–108.

―――. "The Economic Problem of Masochism" (1924). *S.E. 19.* 157–72.

―――. "Family Romances" (1908). *S.E. 9.* 235–44.

―――. *Inhibitions, Symptoms, and Anxiety* (1933). *S.E. 20.* 77–178.

―――. "Instincts and their Vicissitudes" (1915). *S.E. 14.* 109–40.

―――. *Moses and Monotheism: Three Essays* (1939). *S.E. 23.* 3–140.

―――. "Mourning and Melancholia" (1917). *S.E. 14.* 237–59.

―――. "Negation" (1925). *S.E. 19.* 235–42.

―――. "Remembering, Repeating, and Working-Through" (1914). *S.E. 12.* 145–56.

―――. "Screen Memories" (1899). *S.E. 3.* 301–23.

―――. *Studies on Hysteria* (1893). *S.E. 2.* 1–335.

―――. *Totem and Taboo* (1913). *S.E. 13.* 1–162.

―――. "The 'Uncanny' " (1919). *S.E. 18.* 219–52.

Friedman, Lawrence M. *A History of American Law.* New York: Simon and Schuster. 1985.

Furst, Sidney S. "Psychic Trauma and Its Reconstruction with Particular Reference to Postchildhood Trauma." In *The Reconstruction of Trauma: Its Significance in Clinical Work.* Edited by Arnold Rothstein. Madison, Conn.: International Universities Press. 1986. 29–40.

Gates, Henry Louis, Jr. "Authority, (White) Power and the (Black) Critic." *Cultural Critique* 7 (Fall 1987): 19–46.

―――. *Figures in Black: Words, Signs, and the "Racial" Self.* New York: Oxford University Press. 1987.

―――. *The Signifying Monkey: A Theory of African-American Literary Criticism.* New York: Oxford University Press. 1988.

Genovese, Eugene D. " 'Our Family, White and Black': Family and Household in the Southern Slaveholders' World View." In *In Joy and in Sorrow: Women, Family, and Marriage in the Victorian South, 1830–1900.* Edited by Carol Bleser. New York: Oxford University Press. 1991. 69–87.

―――. "Rebelliousness and Docility in the Negro Slave: A Critique of Elkins' Thesis" (1966). Reprinted in *In Red and Black: Marxian Explorations in Southern and Afro-American History.* Edited by Genovese. New York: Pantheon. 1971. 73–101.

———. *Roll, Jordan, Roll: The World the Slaves Made.* New York: Vintage Books. 1974.

Gilroy, Paul. *The Black Atlantic: Modernity and Double Consciousness.* Cambridge, Mass.: Harvard University Press. 1993.

Goldman, Michael. "Eyolf's Eyes: Ibsen and the Cultural Meanings of Child Abuse." *American Imago* 51:3 (1994): 279–306.

Greenacre, Phyllis. "The Influence of Infantile Trauma on Genetic Patterns." In *Psychic Trauma.* Edited by Sidney S. Furst. New York: Basic Books. 1967. 108–53.

Gusdorf, Georges. "Conditions and Limits of Autobiography." In *Autobiography: Essays Theoretical and Critical.* Edited by James Olney. Princeton, N.J.: Princeton University Press. 1980. 28–48.

Gutman, Herbert G. *The Black Family in Slavery and Freedom, 1750–1925.* New York: Pantheon. 1976.

Gwaltney, John Langston. *Drylongso: A Self-Portrait of Black America* (1980). Reprint. New York: New Press. 1993.

Gwin, Minrose C. *Black and White Women of the Old South: The Peculiar Sisterhood in American Literature.* Knoxville: University of Tennessee Press. 1985.

Hammond, James Henry. "Letter to an English Abolitionist" (1845). Reprinted in *The Ideology of Slavery: Proslavery Thought in the Antebellum South, 1830–1860.* Edited with an introduction by Drew Gilpin Faust. Baton Rouge: Louisiana State University Press. 1981. 168–205.

———. *Secret and Sacred: The Diaries of James Henry Hammond, a Southern Slaveholder.* Edited by Carol Bleser. New York: Oxford University Press. 1988.

Haralson, Eric. "James's *The American:* A (New)man Is Being Beaten." *American Literature* 64:3 (September 1992): 475–95.

———. "Mars in Petticoats: Longfellow and Sentimental Masculinity." *Nineteenth-Century Literature.* Forthcoming June 1996.

Harper, C. W. "Black Aristocrats: Domestic Servants on the Antebellum Plantation." *Phylon* 46 (1985): 123–35.

Hawthorne, Nathaniel. "Preface." *The House of the Seven Gables* (1951). New York: The Library of America. 1983.

Hedrick, Joan D. *Harriet Beecher Stowe.* New York: Oxford University Press. 1994.

Hegel, G. W. F. *Phenomenology of Spirit* (1807). Translated by A. V. Miller. New York: Oxford University Press. 1977.

Works Cited

Helm, Katherine. *The True Story of Mary, Wife of Lincoln: By Her Niece, Katherine Helm.* New York: Harper and Brothers. 1928.

Henson, Josiah. *An Autobiography of the Reverend Josiah Henson from 1789 to 1881* (1881). Reprint with an introduction by Robin W. Winks. Reading, Mass.: Addison-Wesley. 1969.

Hersh, Blanche Glassman. " 'Am I Not a Woman and a Sister?': Abolitionist Beginnings of Nineteenth-Century Feminism." In *Antislavery Reconsidered: New Perspectives on the Abolitionists.* Edited by Lewis Perry and Michael Fellman. Baton Rouge: Louisiana State University Press. 1979. 252–83.

Howe, Irving. "Black Boys and Native Sons" (1963). Reprinted in *Selected Writings: 1950–1990.* San Diego, Cal.: Harcourt Brace Jovanovich. 1990. 119–39.

Huggins, Nathan Irvin. *Black Odyssey: The African-American Ordeal in Slavery* (1977). Reprinted with a new introduction. New York: Vintage Books. 1990.

Jackson, Mattie. *The Story of Mattie J. Jackson* (1866). Written and arranged by Dr. D. L. S. Thompson. Reprinted in *Six Women's Slave Narratives.* Edited by William L. Andrews. New York: Oxford University Press. 1988.

Jacobs, Harriet. *Incidents in the Life of a Slave Girl: Written by Herself* (1861). Edited by Jean Fagan Yellin. Cambridge, Mass.: Harvard University Press. 1987.

Jacobs, John S. "A True Tale of Slavery." *The Leisure Hour: A Family Journal of Instruction and Recreation.* London. No. 476 (1861): 85–87, 108–10, 125–27, 139–41.

Jacobson, Edith. *The Self and the Object World.* New York: International Universities Press. 1964.

Karcher, Carolyn L. *The First Woman in the Republic. A Cultural Biography of Lydia Maria Child.* Durham, N.C.: Duke University Press. 1994.

Keckley, Elizabeth. *Behind the Scenes; or, Thirty Years a Slave, and Four Years in the White House* (1868). Reprinted with an introduction by James Olney. New York: Oxford University Press. 1988.

Klein, Melanie. *"Envy and Gratitude" and Other Works 1946–1963.* New York: Free Press. 1975.

———. "Infantile Anxiety-Situations Reflected in a Work of Art and in the Creative Impulse" (1929). In *"Love, Guilt, and Reparation" and Other Works, 1921–1945.* New York: Dell. 1975. 210–18.

————. *"Love, Guilt, and Reparation" and Other Works 1921–1945*. New York: Dell. 1975.

Kohut, Heinz. "Thoughts on Narcissism and Rage." *Psychoanalytic Study of the Child* 27 (1972): 360–400.

Lacan, Jacques. *Ecrits: A Selection*. Translated by Alan Sheridan. New York: Norton. 1977.

————. *Speech and Language in Psychoanalysis*. Translated with notes and commentary by Anthony Wilden. Baltimore, Md.: Johns Hopkins University Press. 1989.

Lane, Ann J., ed. *The Debate over Slavery: Stanley Elkins and His Critics*. Urbana: University of Illinois Press. 1971.

Lee, Jarena. *Religious Experience and Journal of Mrs. Jarena Lee* (1849). Reprinted in *Spiritual Narratives*. With an introduction by Susan Houchins. New York: Oxford University Press. 1988.

Levine, Lawrence W. *Black Culture and Black Consciousness: Afro-American Folk Thought from Slavery to Freedom*. New York: Oxford University Press. 1977.

Lincoln, Abraham. *Selected Speeches and Writings*. New York: Library of America. 1992.

Litwack, Leon F. *North of Slavery: The Negro in the Free States, 1790–1860*. Chicago: University of Chicago. 1961.

Longfellow, Henry Wadsworth. "Evangeline" (1847). Reprinted in *An American Anthology, 1787–1900*. Edited by Edmund Clarence Stedman. Cambridge, Mass.: Riverside Press. 1906.

Mabee, Carleton, with Susan Mabee Newhouse. *Sojourner Truth: Slave, Prophet, Legend*. New York: New York University Press. 1993.

Mahler, Margaret, et al. *The Psychological Birth of the Human Infant*. New York: Basic Books. 1975.

Masur, Louis P., ed. *"The Real War Will Never Get in the Books": Selections from Writers during the Civil War*. New York: Oxford University Press. 1993.

Mayer, Sylvia. " 'You Like Huckleberries?': Toni Morrison's *Beloved* and Mark Twain's *Adventures of Huckleberry Finn*." In *The Black Columbiad: Defining Moments in African American Literature and Culture*. Edited by Werner Sollors and Maria Diedrich. Cambridge, Mass.: Harvard University Press. 1994. 337–46.

McCarthy, Mary. *Memories of a Catholic Girlhood* (1957). San Diego, Cal.: Harcourt Brace and Company. 1974.

McDougall, Joyce. "The Dead Father: On Early Psychic Trauma and Its Relation to Disturbance in Sexual Identity and Creativity." In *Psychoana-*

lytic Views on Female Sexuality. Edited by Claudia Zanardi. New York: New York University Press. 1990. 159–83.

Meltzer, Milton, and Patricia Holland, eds. *Lydia Maria Child: Selected Letters, 1817–1880.* Amherst: University of Massachusetts Press. 1982.

Mills, Bruce. "Lydia Maria Child and the Endings to Harriet Jacobs's *Incidents in the Life of a Slave Girl.*" *American Literature* 64:2 (June 1992): 255–72.

Morrison, Toni. *Beloved.* New York: New American Library. 1987.

———. "The Site of Memory." In *Out There: Marginalization and Contemporary Cultures.* Edited by Russel Ferguson, et al. Cambridge, Mass.: MIT Press. 1992.

Nelson, Dana D. *The Word in Black and White: Reading "Race" in American Literature 1638–1867.* New York: Oxford University Press. 1993.

Nott, V. Josiah C. "Two Lectures on the Natural History of the Caucasian and Negro Races" (1844). Reprinted in *The Ideology of Slavery: Proslavery Thought in the Antebellum South, 1830–1860.* Edited with an introduction by Drew Gilpin Faust. Baton Rouge: Louisiana State University Press. 1981. 206–38.

Nudelman, Franny. "Harriet Jacobs and the Sentimental Politics of Female Suffering." *ELH* 59 (1992): 939–64.

Oakes, James. *Slavery and Freedom: An Interpretation of the Old South.* New York: Vintage Books. 1991.

Olney, James. " 'I Was Born': Slave Narratives, Their Status as Autobiography and as Literature." In *The Slave's Narrative.* Edited by Charles T. Davis and Henry Louis Gates, Jr. New York: Oxford University Press. 1985. 148–75.

———. *Tell Me Africa: An Approach to African Literature.* Princeton, N.J.: Princeton University Press. 1973.

Orwell, George. *The Collected Essays, Journalism and Letters of George Orwell: An Age Like This, 1920–1940.* Edited by Sonia Orwell and Ian Angus. New York: Harcourt Brace Jovanovich. 1968.

Painter, Nell Irvin. "Of *Lily,* Linda Brent, and Freud: A Non-Exceptionalist Approach to Race, Class, and Gender in the Slave South." In *Half Sisters of History: Southern Women and the American Past.* Edited by Catherine Clinton. Durham, N.C.: Duke University Press. 1994. 93–109.

———. "Soul Murder and Slavery: Toward a Fully Loaded Cost Accounting." In *U.S. History as Women's History: New Feminist Essays.* Edited by Linda K. Kerber, Alice Kessler-Harris, and Kathryn Kish Sklar. Chapel Hill: University of North Carolina Press. 1995. 125–46.

Parish, Peter. *Slavery: History and Historians.* New York: Harper and Row. 1989.

Patterson, Orlando. *Slavery and Social Death: A Comparative Study.* Cambridge, Mass.: Harvard University Press. 1982.

Picquet, Louisa. *The Octoroon: or Inside Views of Southern Domestic Life* (1861). By H. Matison. Reprinted in *Collected Black Women's Narratives.* With an introduction by Anthony G. Barthelemy. New York: Oxford University Press. 1988.

Pinckney, Darryl. "Promissory Notes." *New York Review of Books* (April 6, 1995): 41–46.

Raboteau, Albert J. *Slave Religion: The "Invisible Institution" in the Antebellum South.* New York: Oxford University Press. 1978.

Randall, Ruth Painter. *Mary Lincoln: Biography of a Marriage.* Boston: Little, Brown. 1953.

Reik, Theodor. "The Characteristics of Masochism" (1939). *American Imago* 46:2–3 (1989): 161–95.

Reynolds, David S. *Beneath the American Renaissance: The Subversive Imagination in the Age of Emerson and Melville.* Cambridge, Mass.: Harvard University Press. 1988.

Ross, Ishbel. *The President's Wife: Mary Todd Lincoln: A Biography.* New York: G. P. Putnam's Sons. 1973.

Sanchez-Eppler, Karen. *Touching Liberty: Abolition, Feminism, and the Politics of the Body.* Berkeley: University of California Press. 1993.

Schaye, Shirley Herscovitch. "A Theoretical Overview." In *Psychoanalysis Today: A Case Book.* Edited by Elizabeth Thorne and Shirley Herscovitch Schaye. Springfield, Ill.: Charles C. Thomas. 1991. 5–20.

Shengold, Leonard. *Soul Murder: The Effects of Childhood Abuse and Deprivation.* New Haven, Conn.: Yale University Press. 1989.

Smedley, Audrey. *Race in North America: Origin and Evolution of a Worldview.* Boulder, Colo.: Westview Press. 1993.

Smith, Valerie. "Gender and Afro-Americanist Theory and Criticism." In *Speaking of Gender.* Edited by Elaine Showalter. New York: Routledge. 1989. 56–72.

———. *Self-Discovery and Authority in Afro-American Narrative.* Cambridge, Mass.: Harvard University Press. 1987.

Smith, Theophus H. *Conjuring Culture: Biblication Formations of Black America.* New York: Oxford University Press. 1994.

Sollors, Werner. "National Identity and Ethnic Diversity: 'Of Plymouth Rock and Jamestown and Ellis Island'; or, Ethnic Literature and Some

Redefinitions of 'America' " (1992). Reprinted in *History and Memory in African-Amerian Culture.* Edited by Genevieve Fabre and Robert O'Meally. New York: Oxford University Press. 1994. 92–121.

Spillers, Hortense J. "Mama's Baby, Papa's Maybe: An American Grammar Book." *Diacritics* 17:2 (1987): 64–81.

———. " 'The Permanent Obliquity of an In(pha)llibly Straight': In the Time of the Daughters and Fathers." In *Changing Our Own Words: Essays on Criticism, Theory, and Writing by Black Women.* Edited by Cheryl A. Wall. New Brunswick, N.J.: Rutgers University Press. 1989.

Stampp, Kenneth. "Rebels and Sambos: The Search for the Negro's Personality in Slavery" (1971). Reprinted in *The Imperiled Union: Essays on the Background of the Civil War.* New York: Oxford University Press. 1980. 39–71.

Stepto, Robert. *From behind the Veil: A Study of Afro-American Narrative.* Urbana: University of Illinois Press. 1979.

———. "I Rose and Found My Voice: Narration, Authentification, and Authorial Control in Four Slave Narratives." In *The Slave's Narrative.* Edited by Charles T. Davis and Henry Louis Gates, Jr. New York: Oxford University Press. 1985. 225–41.

Sterling, Dorothy, ed. *We Are Your Sisters: Black Women in the Nineteenth Century.* New York: W. W. Norton. 1984.

Stern, Julia. "Excavating Genre in *Our Nig.*" *American Literature* 67:3 (1995): 439–66.

Stewart, Maria W. *Productions of Mrs. Maria Stewart.* Reprinted in *Spiritual Narratives.* With an introduction by Sue E. Houchins. New York: Oxford University Press. 1988.

Stowe, Harriet Beecher. *Uncle Tom's Cabin, or, Life among the Lowly.* New York: New American Library. 1981.

Sundquist, Eric J. *To Wake the Nations: Race in the Making of American Literature.* Cambridge, Mass.: Harvard University Press. 1993.

Ware, Vron. *Beyond the Pale: White Women, Racism, and History.* London: Verso. 1992.

Washington, Booker T. *Up from Slavery* (1900). Reprinted in *Three Negro Classics.* With an introduction by John Hope Franklin. New York: Avon Books. 1965.

Watkins, Mel. *On the Real Side; Laughing, Lying, and Signifying: The Underground Tradition of African-American Humor that Transformed American Culture, from Slavery to Richard Pryor.* New York: Touchstone. 1994.

Works Cited

White, Deborah Gray. *Ar'n't I a Woman? Female Slaves in the Plantation South.* New York: W. W. Norton. 1985.

Williams, Patricia J. *The Alchemy of Race and Rights: A Diary of a Law Professor.* Cambridge, Mass.: Harvard University Press. 1991.

Winnicott, D. W. "The Concept of Trauma in Relation to the Development of the Individual within the Family" (1965). In *Psychoanalytic Explorations.* Edited by Clare Winnicott, Ray Shepherd, and Madeleine Davis. Cambridge, Mass.: Harvard University Press. 1989. 130–48.

———. "On the Basis for Self in Body" (1970). In *Psychoanalytic Explorations.* Edited by Clare Winnicott, Ray Shepherd, and Madeleine Davis. Cambridge, Mass.: Harvard University Press. 1989. 261–83.

———. *Playing and Reality.* New York: Routledge. 1991.

———. "The Theory of the Parent-Infant Relationship." In *Essential Papers on Object Relations.* Edited by Peter Buckley. New York: New York University Press. 1986.

Wolfenstein, Martha. "How Is Mourning Possible?" *Psychoanalytic Study of the Child* 21 (1966): 93–123.

———. "Loss, Rage, and Repetition." *Psychoanalytic Study of the Child* 24 (1969): 432–60.

Wright, Richard. *The Man Who Lived Underground* (1944). Reprinted in *Eight Men: Stories by Richard Wright.* New York: Thunder's Mouth Press. 1987.

Wyatt-Brown, Bertram. "The Mask of Obedience: Male Slave Psychology in the Old South." *American Historical Review* 93 (1988): 1228–52.

Yellin, Jean Fagan. "Harriet Jacobs's Family History." *American Literature* 66:4 (December 1994): 765–67.

———. "Texts and Contexts of Harriet Jacobs' Incidents in the Life of a Slave Girl: Written by Herself." In *The Slave's Narrative.* Edited by Charles T. Davis and Henry Louis Gates, Jr. New York: Oxford University Press. 1985. 262–82.

———. *Women and Sisters: The Antislavery Feminists in American Culture.* New Haven, Conn.: Yale University Press. 1989.

Index

Men, in women's slave narratives, 62–63, 83–92

Mesmerism, 203 n. 9

Mills, Bruce, 201 n. 18

Miscegenation, 9, 36, 191 n. 6, 199 n. 12. *See also* Mixed race

Mistress, 66, 102–3, 107; the jealous, 62, 177; as surrogate mother, 8, 24–25, 31, 138–54, 158–64, 175–77, 181, 190 n. 3, 208 n. 9, 209 n. 13

Mixed race, 9, 28, 34, 39–41, 136, 146, 182, 209 n. 12

Morrison, Toni, 14, 194 n. 23

Motherhood: cult of, 3, 43–44, 52–60, 62, 92, 179; and mistress, 25, 30–31; and slavery, 8–9, 18–19, 72, 77, 88, 90–92, 96, 99–100, 107–14, 137–53, 172–3, 175–83

Mourning, 93, 99–123, 128–32, 203 n. 9; 203 nn. 11, 12, 204 nn. 13, 14, 207 nn. 25, 26. *See also* Slave family

Mulatto, 28, 36–37, 51–60, 65, 95, 99, 101, 190 n. 3; 192 n. 9. *See also* Miscegenation; Mixed race; Tragic quadroon

Naming, 74, 131, 198 n. 11

Narrative, and subjectivity, 65–68, 71–83, 91–92. *See also* Slavery, and narrative

Nelson, Dana, 206 n. 21

Nott, V. Josiah, 36

Nudelman, Franny, 39

Object relations, 92, 98, 100–102, 106, 109, 118–23, 129, 142, 159, 168, 205 n. 20, 207 n. 26. *See also* Imago; Maternal dynamics; "Other," the

Orwell, George, 1

"Other," the, 7, 19, 22–26, 44, 48, 59, 96, 98, 101–2, 112, 114, 123–31

Ozick, Cynthia, 203 n. 12

Painter, Nell Irvin, 9, 11, 189 n. 17

Pamela, 38, 95

Parker, Theodore, 190 n. 3

Patterson, Orlando, 27, 65, 73, 115, 198 n. 8

Passing, 35

Picquet, Louisa, 25, 35

Pinckney, Darryl, 94–95

Portelli, Alessandro, 107, 188 n. 14, 203 n. 10

Proslavery ideology, 31, 33, 35–37, 74–75, 105–6, 192 n. 13, 194 n. 19

Psychoanalytic theory, 4–5, 12–13, 20, 29–30, 54, 98, 109, 119. *See also* Abuse; Aggression; Ambivalence; Child abuse; Childhood; Family; Freud, Sigmund; Imago; Idealization; Identification; Maternal dynamics; Masochism; Memory; Mourning; Object relations, Repetition-compulsion; Repression; Sadism; Sadomasochism; Splitting; Trauma; *and names of individual theorists*

Racialism, 15–16, 23–24, 33–44, 46, 59–60, 92, 98, 106, 123, 131, 135, 146–47

Reik, Theodor, 151

Repetition, 4, 15, 21, 111, 120; and memory, 135, 144, 146, 159, 179. *See also* Repetition-compulsion

Repetition-compulsion, 19–22, 24, 32

Repression, 2, 5, 15, 20, 31–32, 45, 48–49, 50, 64, 99–101; return of the repressed, 25–26, 40, 45, 48–50, 183

Reynolds, David S., 193 n. 14

Romance forms, 37–45, 47, 50, 88–89, 91, 211 n. 27

Romantic racialism, 34, 37–38, 59. *See also* Racialism

Sadism, 69–71, 159, 194 n. 21. *See also* Sadomasochism

Sadomasochism, 52–53, 163, 180. *See also* Masochism

Sanchez-Eppler, Karen, 196 n. 1

Schaye, Shirley Herscovitch, 208 n. 7

Scott, Dred. *See* Dred Scott decision.

Scott, Walter, 42

Self-reliance: Emersonian, 94; in John Jacobs, 67, 82–83; in Elizabeth Keckley, 97, 99, 101, 114, 118, 123, 126; and racial experience, 205 n. 19

Sentimental fiction. *See* Romance forms

Sexual abuse, 2, 18–19, 26–29, 45, 47, 49, 61, 64–73, 79–80, 86–87, 96, 103, 108, 157–58, 160–61, 164–65, 169–70, 177, 179–80, 182, 191 n. 5